To Kit

HAPPY BIRTHDAY!

Love Charles & Chrissie xx

Erica Wagner is the author of *Gravity: Stories*; *Ariel's Gift: Ted Hughes, Sylvia Plath and the Story of Birthday Letters* and a novel, *Seizure*. Her stories have been widely anthologized and broadcast on the radio; *Pas de Deux/A Concert of Stories*, a show co-written with storyteller Abbi Patrix and musician and composer Linda Edsjö, tours around the world. Twice a judge of the Man Booker Prize, she was literary editor of *The Times* for seventeen years, and she is now a contributing writer for the *New Statesman* and consulting literary editor for *Harper's Bazaar*. Her biography of Washington Roebling, chief engineer of the Brooklyn Bridge, will be published by Bloomsbury in 2017.

FIRST LIGHT

A CELEBRATION OF THE LIFE
AND WORK OF

ALAN GARNER

EDITED BY

Erica Wagner

unbound

LONDON

This edition first published in 2016

Unbound
6th Floor Mutual House 70 Conduit Street London W1S 2GF
www.unbound.co.uk

All rights reserved

© Erica Wagner, 2016
'Jiffy Bag' © Erica Wagner 2015
'At the Edge' © David Almond 2015
'The Cosmic Lighthouse: Alan Garner and Jodrell Bank' © Teresa Anderson 2015
'The Full Moon Shopping Mall' © Margaret Atwood 2015
'Reading Together, Reading Apart' © John Burnside 2015
'In the Same Room at the Same Time' © Susan Cooper 2015
'Where the Starlight Sings' © Frank Cottrell-Boyce 2015
'The Still Foot of the Compass: Alan Garner's Siblings' © Amanda Craig 2015
'The Gatepost' © Bob Cywinski 2015
'– Go, in the Form of a Bird' © Maura Dooley 2015
'The Owl Service: Crossing the Threshold' © Helen Dunmore 2015
'Possessions' © Mark Edmonds 2015
'Of the Earth, Earthy . . .' © Stephen Fry 2015
'Storytellers, Shapeshifters' © Cornelia Funke 2015
'The World and the Worlds: Some Musings and Two Book Reviews'
© Neil Gaiman 2015
'The Given' © Elizabeth Garner 2015
'The Othering: Down from Oxford, finding my place' © Joseph Garner 2015
'Mr Garner's Reading Lesson' © Ben Haggarty 2015
'The Sleeping King and the Body of the World' © Nick Hennessey 2015
'Pockets' © Dougald Hine 2015
'Alan Garner and Alan Turing: On the Road' © Andrew Hodges 2015
'Alan to an Academic: History and Mythology in Alan Garner's Novels'
© Ronald Hutton 2015
'The Speaking of the Stones: Two Things I Learned from Alan Garner'
© Paul Kingsnorth 2015
'Gripe Griffin' © Olivia Laing 2015
'The Weirdstone of Talybont' © Katherine Langrish 2015
'The Joining of the Song' © Hugh Lupton 2015
'But Still We Walk' © Helen Macdonald 2015
'The Edge: A Name Map' © Robert Macfarlane 2015

'The Bull-roarer' © Gregory Maguire 2015
'It Wasn't Meant to Be Like This' © Bel Mooney 2015
'Unfinished Business' © Richard Morris 2015
'From Calcutta to Cheshire' © Neel Mukherjee 2015
'A Ghost Book: The "Stone Book"' © Richard Ovenden 2015
'Beyond the Singularity' © Neil Philip 2015
'An Oak Shovel … Roughly Used' © John Prag 2015
'Of Things and People' © Francis Pryor 2015
'Alan Garner: Craftsmanship' © Philip Pullman 2015
'Righteous Garner' © Ali Smith 2015
'Feeding the Spark' © Ian Thorpe 2015
'Quiet in Disquiet: The Owl Service' © Salley Vickers 2015
'Here or There or Elsewhere' © Elizabeth Wein 2015
'Alderley: For Alan Garner' © Rowan Williams 2015
'The Caves of Wonder and the People of the West' © Michael Wood 2015

The right of Erica Wagner to be identified as the editor of this work has been asserted in accordance with Section 77 of the Copyright, Designs and Patents Act 1988. No part of this publication may be copied, reproduced, stored in a retrieval system, or transmitted, in any form or by any means without the prior permission of the publisher, nor be otherwise circulated in any form of binding or cover other than that in which it is published and without a similar condition being imposed on the subsequent purchaser.

While every effort has been made to trace the owners of copyright material reproduced herein, the publisher would like to apologise for any omissions and will be pleased to incorporate missing acknowledgments in any further editions.

Text Design by Peter Ward

A CIP record for this book is available from the British Library

ISBN 978-1-78352-252-1 (trade hbk)
ISBN 978-1-78352-253-8 (ebook)
ISBN 978-1-78352-292-7 (limited edition)

Printed in Great Britain by Clays Ltd, St Ives plc

Dear Reader,

The book you are holding came about in a rather different way to most others. It was funded directly by readers through a new website: Unbound. Unbound is the creation of three writers. We started the company because we believed there had to be a better deal for both writers and readers. On the Unbound website, authors share the ideas for the books they want to write directly with readers. If enough of you support the book by pledging for it in advance, we produce a beautifully bound special subscribers' edition and distribute a regular edition and e-book wherever books are sold, in shops and online.

This new way of publishing is actually a very old idea (Samuel Johnson funded his dictionary this way). We're just using the internet to build each writer a network of patrons. Here, at the back of this book, you'll find the names of all the people who made it happen.

Publishing in this way means readers are no longer just passive consumers of the books they buy, and authors are free to write the books they really want. They get a much fairer return too – half the profits their books generate, rather than a tiny percentage of the cover price.

If you're not yet a subscriber, we hope that you'll want to join our publishing revolution and have your name listed in one of our books in the future. To get you started, here is a £5 discount on your first pledge. Just visit unbound.com, make your pledge and type **FIRSTLIGHT** in the promo code box when you check out.

Thank you for your support,

Dan, Justin and John
Founders, Unbound

Contents

Introduction: Jiffy Bag
Erica Wagner
3

At the Edge
David Almond
9

The Cosmic Lighthouse: Alan Garner and Jodrell Bank
Teresa Anderson
15

The Full Moon Shopping Mall
Margaret Atwood
21

Reading Together, Reading Apart
John Burnside
27

In the Same Room at the Same Time
Susan Cooper
33

Where the Starlight Sings
Frank Cottrell-Boyce
37

The Still Foot of the Compass: Alan Garner's Siblings
Amanda Craig
45

The Gatepost
Bob Cywinski
55

– Go, in the Form of a Bird
Maura Dooley
63

The Owl Service: Crossing the Threshold
Helen Dunmore
65

Possessions
Mark Edmonds
71

Of the Earth, Earthy . . .
Stephen Fry
79

Storytellers, Shapeshifters
Cornelia Funke
81

The World and the Worlds:
Some Musings and Two Book Reviews
Neil Gaiman
83

The Given
Elizabeth Garner
93

The Othering: Down from Oxford, Finding My Place
Joseph Garner
99

Mr Garner's Reading Lesson
Ben Haggarty
107

The Sleeping King and the Body of the World
Nick Hennessey
115

Pockets
Dougald Hine
123

Alan Garner and Alan Turing: On the Road
Andrew Hodges
129

Alan to an Academic:
History and Mythology in Alan Garner's Novels
Ronald Hutton
135

The Speaking of the Stones:
Two Things I Learned from Alan Garner
Paul Kingsnorth
141

Gripe Griffin
Olivia Laing
153

The Weirdstone of Talybont
Katherine Langrish
157

The Joining of the Song
Hugh Lupton
163

But Still We Walk
Helen Macdonald
175

The Edge: A Name Map
Robert Macfarlane
177

The Bull-roarer
Gregory Maguire
185

It Wasn't Meant to Be Like This
Bel Mooney
195

Unfinished Business
Richard Morris
201

From Calcutta to Cheshire
Neel Mukherjee
217

A Ghost Book: The 'Stone Book'
Richard Ovenden
223

Beyond the Singularity
Neil Philip
235

'An Oak Shovel . . . Roughly Used'
John Prag
243

Of Things and People
Francis Pryor
253

Alan Garner: Craftsmanship
Philip Pullman
261

Righteous Garner
Ali Smith
267

Feeding the Spark
Ian Thorpe
275

Quiet in Disquiet: The Owl Service
Salley Vickers
283

Here or There or Elsewhere
Elizabeth Wein
287

Alderley: For Alan Garner
Rowan Williams
293

The Cave of Wonders and the People of the West
Michael Wood
295

Alan Garner: A Selected Bibliography
301

ACKNOWLEDGEMENTS
303

SUPPORTERS
305

FIRST LIGHT

INTRODUCTION

JIFFY BAG

Erica Wagner

> A bottle of cold tea; bread and a half an onion. That was Father's baggin. Mary emptied her apron of stones from the field and wrapped the baggin in a cloth.

The books arrived in rough grey sacks. We unloaded them and set them on a table across from my desk; at some point in the day I would open the Jiffy bags in which the books arrived. It was really my assistant's job to open the books, but I liked to do it myself. It meant I got up from my chair, it meant I got to do something with my hands other than type – and it meant I really saw, however briefly, every book that had been sent to the literary editor of *The Times*, which I was, to my own astonishment. Later on, I'd stop being astonished, but just then – in 1999 – I was still surprised by the job I was doing. Because I was a woman, because I was young, but maybe most of all because I was American and my job description seemed about as English as you could get. But then I had always known – somehow – that I would end up in England, although I never understood why I knew that, or really why I felt it. I did know that it wasn't anything to do with being literary editor of *The Times*, but here I was, all the same, opening envelopes stuffed with books one afternoon in the early spring.

The Stone Book Quartet was the title of the book which slid into my hands. It was by an author called Alan Garner, and it was published by an imprint of HarperCollins, Flamingo Modern Classics.

> The hottest part of the day was on. Mother lay in bed under

> the rafters and the thatch, where the sun could send only blue light. She had picked stones in the field until she was too tired and had to rest.

I had never heard of Alan Garner. And however astonished I was to find myself behind the literary editor's desk, I still reckoned that I should know of an author whose work was considered to be classic.

> Old William was weaving in the end room. He had to weave enough cuts of silk for two markets, and his shuttle and loom rattled all the time, in the day and the night. He wasn't old, but he was called Old William because he was deaf and hadn't married. He was Father's brother.

Silk for two markets: perhaps that was me, one market in London and the other in New York, where I had been born, the place I had left. Where did I belong? I didn't know. I was a seeker. And yet the threads were being woven together. The book in my hands was not like any other book I had ever read, but it seemed familiar – more than familiar, for all it spoke of a world from which I could not have been more distant. Here was memory in object and in word, a deep familial, cultural history which was no artefact but a living thing. It was like listening to the tune of a song I had never known was always inside me.

I was mesmerised. I was very curious about this Garner person, too. So I decided I would interview Alan Garner. Surely this was one of the privileges of being the literary editor of *The Times*. Suffice to say, the interview came to pass, but it took some doing to make it happen, and looking back I am amazed that I managed to pull it off. *Suffer fools gladly* and *Alan Garner* are not five words you really want to yoke together. Was I a fool? Perhaps the right kind of fool, curious, ready to follow a river along a new course. I travelled to Cheshire, and was welcomed into the kitchen of the Garners' home, Toad Hall; I walked through the Old Medicine House and sat in its chimney. I found a stone book and saw owls and flowers and flowers and owls. And perhaps I was lucky that I came to Alan's work, and Alan, perfectly fresh; for what was 'classic' over here in Britain had never even made it to the United States. Up until fairly recently, books published for children didn't jump across oceans in the way books published for adults did. Growing up, I read E. B. White, not C. S. Lewis. I saw pictures by Shel Silverstein and none by Judith Kerr. Please note I write 'books published for children', for the way in which an author's books are published is, more often than not, out of the author's hands – and one of the first things Alan ever said to me was this: 'I feel instinctively that children's writing can't be literature. It is ghetto writing. C. S. Lewis said that if a book can only be enjoyed by children then it's not a good book. I never considered myself a writer for children.'

As I kept following the bed of that strengthening stream I'd hear those ideas expressed again, from people such as David Almond (whose words you'll find in the book you hold in your hands) and the late Maurice Sendak too. 'To work "without waste and easily" is to know where and who you are,' as archaeologist Mark Edmonds writes, quoting Alan, in his essay here. The work is what it wants to be. Other people can call it what they like. It is itself.

I had the privilege of learning that first-hand, walking with Alan and his wife Griselda through the ancient landscape of Alan's books and of his life. Our friendship now is old and very dear, but I often think of its beginnings. We walked from Thieves' Hole, by Seven Firs and Goldenstone; to Stormy Point and Saddle Bole. We followed Gawain's trail down into Ludchurch, the words of the poem a map in my ear; and once, a dozen years ago, we went to Thursbitch, and I will tell you truly that I hope never to see that place again. Maybe you think I'm joking. I'm not.

And we went too just across the railway tracks to where the bowl of the Lovell Telescope tilted its ear at the sky. When we did I had with me a battered book: *The Story of Jodrell Bank* by Bernard Lovell, and on its flyleaf my late mother's familiar hand: 'Once more, with feeling . . . bought at Jodrell Bank, Cheshire, 4 September, 1978'. I was eleven then, and my father had nearly driven off the road when he'd seen that huge white dish appear over the horizon. We were visitors from Manhattan travelling towards Manchester. We had no idea it was there. And here I was again with Alan and

Griselda. Everything happens as it must. This book is called *First Light* thanks to Alan ('I can be quite good at titles,' he wrote to me, when I was at a loss) and in tribute in part to that great listener in the next field over from Toad Hall. All our contributors have listened to Alan Garner's work, and have heard his stories – and through them, their own.

That is my story, and that's why I am here, editing this tribute to Alan and his work. It's being published by the wonderful Unbound because one of its founders, John Mitchinson, and his wife (one of Unbound's editors) Rachael Kerr, have their own tales of connection to Alan and Griselda, one that goes back further than mine. But publishing with Unbound has brought a very special benefit: and that was to truly understand, as the funding for the book motored swiftly up toward 100 per cent, just how much Alan's work meant to so many people. Whether subscribers pledged £10 or £100 or more, I heard stories of passionate attachment to Alan's work. Some began at the beginning, with Alan's first book, *The Weirdstone of Brinsingamen*. For some it was *Red Shift*, or *Elidor* or the dreaming voyage of *Strandloper*. Many mentioned *The Voice that Thunders*, his revelatory collection of essays which blends the analytical with the personal. But to each of these readers it was clear that Alan was speaking to them and to them alone: that is what every one of the contributors of this volume clearly feels too. 'I believe the first feeling that overwhelmed me was one of being trusted,' Stephen Fry writes of discovering Alan's work. 'At no stage did the writer of this story explain to me what I was supposed to feel, or what was the meaning of the story I was reading.' Ali Smith recalls how Alan's books alerted her to the possibilities of language when she was only a little girl: 'I knew what "weird" meant, and what "stone" meant, but what did they mean together and how was it that putting those two words together like that made something somehow bigger than just the sum of what the two words meant separately?'

Alan Garner's words make something very big indeed. They create worlds which connect – as you'll discover in this volume – not only with the work of artists such as Ali Smith and Stephen Fry, but scientists, archaeologists, historians. I have always known that Alan

Garner's work touched many lives and crossed many disciplines: but with this collection I can demonstrate the real reach of his art and his thought. 'A book, properly written, is an invitation to the reader to enter: to join with the writer in a creative act: the act of reading.' So Alan writes in 'Hard Cases', one of the essays in *The Voice that Thunders*. All that is left for me to do is invite you to enter in.

AT THE EDGE

David Almond

I first met Alan Garner not on Alderley Edge but in the metropolis. He was there to be made a Fellow of the Royal Society of Literature. He used Byron's pen to make his mark on the list of the finest authors writing in English over the last 200 years. His was a brief visit. He'd arrived that afternoon. The morning after, he was taking an early train back to his home. He told me to visit him there. I haven't done so yet. But I've been there in his books, especially in *The Stone Book*.

Garner lives and works close to the Edge, and is neither metropolitan nor provincial. He's closer to being parochial, in Patrick Kavanagh's sense, never being 'in any doubt about the social and artistic validity of his parish'. But he's more than that. He goes under the parish to fetch out stones, he cleans them, he inspects them, he shapes them with exquisite care, he turns them into steeples and into walls, he lifts them to the stars above. He turns the stones to words. He is the first of his line to use words not things. And within them, like Blake looking at a grain of sand, like the scientist looking into the atom or the cell, he finds the universe.

He hasn't sought glory or acceptance. He doesn't seek to be classified. 'I've no interest,' he says, 'in being compared with other writers or their work.' He doesn't act from ego or even from will. He's written few books, sometimes very slowly, sometimes with long gaps between. His work seems more to be an act of dedication and passionate acceptance. Finding himself uneasy in a culture in which 'we sacrificed the numinous for our other greatness, the intellect,' he turned back to the place where his family have lived and worked for generations. 'The physical immobility of my family was my lifeline. My family is so rooted that it ignores social classification by others. On one square mile of Cheshire hillside, the Garners are.' So Alan Garner is, as that signature on the RSL Fellowship scroll shows, as the name on his book covers show. But at the best of times, there's no Alan Garner at all. 'The feeling is less that I choose a myth than the myth chooses me; less that I write than that I am written.' Of rereading passages from *The Stone Book*, he has said: 'I ask myself who could possibly have written them, because "I" certainly didn't.'

Early in *The Stone Book*, young Mary is released from her father's side and carries her candle deep into the mines beneath the hill. She finds that the dark and silent place is crowded with all that's gone before: footprints that seem as fresh and sharp-edged as when they were first made; the outline of a hand that fits in hers; the figure of a bull, and beside that, her father's maker's mark. But it isn't her father's mark. It is the mark of their ancestral father. None of this will last forever. Mary's purpose, like Garner's, is to come back out and tell the tale of what's been down there and is down there, to turn the places and the objects and the places into symbols, into words. 'We pass it on . . . you'll have to tell your lad, even if you can't show him.' And a single stone itself, like the dark and hidden place that it comes up from, tells of time. Her father has the craft, the stonecutter's secret of how to crack the stone, to polish it: 'It was black and full of light, and its heart was a golden, bursting sun.' And it contains the remnant of ancient seas and ancient sea urchins and of questions that transcend the empty tales told by the parson in the parish. But they are religious, such sacramental moments of revelation that edge the character and the reader to the borders of mystery. 'A true story is religious, as drama is religious . . . "religion" describes that area of human concern for, and involvement with, the question of our being within the cosmos.'

Each stone comes out from the dark and hidden spaces. Each stone must be valued. Some would cast them aside, and in the field they can seem a heap of dull and heavy things, but carefully chosen and opened and shaped they are shown to be unique. The best can be turned to walls, if they are hard enough, if they have enough of time in them, if the craftsman has the skill. 'I'll not put me name to it,' says Grandfather of a stone that isn't good enough. Stones are laid in careful lines like sentences, walls constructed like paragraphs, chapels like stories, homes like books. And so the words that are used are those that would often be discarded by others, unaware of their potency. They are words that speak with the lovely clicks and vowels and rhythms of the common tongue, each word set in place, in proper order, so poetry and music and power can be released. Just as his ancestors' lifelong struggle was to turn the things of the earth into constructions of strength and grace, Garner's has been to turn the words of the earth into such constructions, into art. 'All my writing has been fuelled by the instinctive drive to speak with a true and Northern voice integrated with the language of literary fluency.'

Just as there is a hidden cave in the earth that can be explored, there is a secret cave in the sky. Young Robert climbs into it, the beautifully formed steeple, to where the birds are, and the birds accept him, and make space for him. Again, it is filled with the footprints of an invisible crowd that has entered here before. As the cave beneath fitted Mary, so this cave fits him. 'He was wearing the steeple all the way to the earth.' These burrowing, climbing, written children link the earth and sky. Just as in the earth, there is a maker's mark. It is Robert's own name, but of course it is also the name of the ancestor who worked here long before. A secret place, hardly ever seen, that some might consider to be unimportant to the whole structure. But it is a sacred space, and here, just as on the visible lovely outside of the steeple, the stone has been properly worked. 'The stone was true though it would never be seen.' So it is with the writer. Each word matters, no matter how obvious it might be, if the structure is truly to be a thing of beauty. The invisible matters. It vivifies everything we see.

Between the cave beneath and the cave above, there is another chamber: the dark forge, with the fire at its heart; a fire surrounded by tackle, presses, anvils, bellows, firebricks, hood; a fire that is tended and controlled; a thing of destructive potential turned to a centre of creation; a place where the apprentice is brought to learn creation's 'art, craft and mystery'. And all around these caves and chambers, the parish is operatic. It is filled with voices, with music, with rhythm, with things beautifully formed by human hand. The characters speak in lovely dialect. Their feet beat out tunes as they step across the earth. 'Who-whoop!' is called across the fields throughout the book. Looms rattle and swish. Hammers and chisels chick and clink. Songs accompany them, riddles and hymns and soldiers' songs. The whetstones strike the scythes and bring out tunes. The men swing scythes in unison, 'scythes and men like a big clock, back and to, back and to, across the hill they walked.' Musical instruments are played: the ophicleide, the cornet. Even the cleaned and oiled barrel of a gun is turned into a pipe. Things made in the forge glint and shine: the horses' shimmering bridles, the turning weathercocks. The importance of proper making is everywhere. Ordinary things are made to be extraordinary: the hammers and scythes themselves, the sledge, the horseshoes, milk cans, brass fenders. The gun, with its 'catches, magazine, levers, bolt and barrel'. Things are precisely geared and balanced: the yard door and the long handle of the bellows, both of which can be moved with a single touch. The clock, with its wheels and cogs and pendulum, things that 'Stop. Start. Day and night, for evermore, regular.' Such things matter if the parish itself is to properly work, if the book that embodies it is to properly work. For the parish and the book must also embody the workings of the universe. 'We're going at that much of a rattle, the whole blooming earth, moon and stars, we need escapement to hold us together.'

The writer, Alan Garner, is at the heart of all this. He draws us, his readers, to his hill and he makes it real for us. He writes us down into the earth, climbs us into the steeple, leads us into the mysterious forge, causes us to see and hear the individual and gathered voices of his parish. He helps us touch the extraordinary ordinary objects, helps us experience the sacred places, the sacramental moments. He exposes the reality of the known world, and he leads us to the Edge, to something beyond the parish, beyond the stones, beyond the words, to something that is not the writer or the reader. And we are enthralled by this world made so very real, and by the mystery that lies within and all around it.

David Almond is the author of Skellig, The Savage, The Tightrope Walkers, A Song for Ella Grey *and many other novels, stories and plays. His books are translated into almost 40 languages and are widely adapted for stage and screen. His major awards include the Carnegie Medal and the Hans Christian Andersen Award – the world's most prestigious prize for children's authors. He is Professor of Creative Writing at Bath Spa University and lives in Northumberland.*

THE COSMIC LIGHTHOUSE: ALAN GARNER AND JODRELL BANK

Teresa Anderson

I work at Jodrell Bank. The Lovell Telescope, a huge white radio dish the height of Big Ben, towers over us here. As it turns and dips it is a constant reminder of our place in time and space.

It picks up radio waves rather than visible light. Radio waves that travel at the speed of light, for years (sometimes billions of years) across the cosmos to reach our receivers.

Alan Garner is our almost-neighbour. His house is separated from Jodrell Bank by a couple of fields and the train line between Manchester and Crewe. He's an old friend, or a new friend, depending how you see it. It's Alan's fault that I used to mark invisible crosses on our washing machine every night when I was a little girl, so I feel that I've known him for a lot longer than he has me.

Jodrell Bank is the home of UK Radio Astronomy and, lately, the new headquarters of the great radio telescope of the future, the SKA. The site is a huge collaborative endeavour. Engineers, scientists, students and support staff, all toil like bees to achieve a common purpose – to work out what is out there in the skies – and to understand where we fit, on our tiny blue rocky planet, alone (so far) in the ungraspable vastness of space.

I say ungraspable – but of course, science knows a lot, and we can reel off many facts and numbers about our Universe:

It's just under 14 billion years old; there are around 100 billion stars in our own galaxy (most of them with their own system of planets) and about 300 billion galaxies in the visible Universe. Our galaxy is around 100,000 light years (that's 1,000,000,000,000,000,000 kilometres) across.

Almost all the hydrogen in the Universe was made in the Big Bang.

For those of you who are wearing gold rings – it's interesting to consider that every atom of gold was made in an exploding star. And that many of the atoms in your body have been part of other bodies, other planets, other stars. Most of the matter in you is many billions of years old – you're just a new configuration of it all.

And alongside the facts are the concepts. For example, sometimes, here, we talk in terms of 'look back time'.

If light from a star takes eight minutes to reach us, we always see the star as it was eight minutes ago – a 'look back time' of eight minutes (our Sun is eight light minutes away). If it takes eight million years to reach us, we see it as it was eight million years ago. As I mentioned, some of the signals picked up by the Lovell Telescope have travelled for billions of years, at the speed of light, to get here. We are always looking back in time.

This produces some interesting intellectual gymnastics. The Crab Nebula is the (vaguely crab-shaped) cloud of dust and gas that blew out into space when a star was seen to explode by Chinese astronomers in 1054. It's visible with a normal telescope.

Here at Jodrell Bank, we point our radio telescopes at the dark region left at the heart of the Crab when the star exploded. There, invisible to the eye, but 'visible in the radio', is the collapsed core of the exploded star, a pulsar, which spins around 30 times per second, producing regular 'flashes' of radio waves as it spins, like a cosmic lighthouse.

The mental gymnastics then begin, when we remember that the Crab Pulsar is around 7,000 light years away. When we observe it we are looking back in time, to see the pulsar as it was 7,000 years ago, following observations made by Chinese astronomers, who observed it exploding 960 years ago.

If he reads this, Alan will be laughing by now.

He sits in his house, at a place he has occupied since 1957, the year that the Lovell Telescope first moved into operation, and watches the telescope from his windows. Sometimes he asks exactly what it is observing (he has been known to telephone the Jodrell Bank Control Room) and he writes in parallel with it as it works.

I read his early books – the *Weirdstone* series – as a child, books that he wrote as the telescope was tracking Soviet and American rockets in the early days of the space race.

As I grew older I found *Red Shift* – in which Alan holds place and people as anchors as time dislocates – and *Elidor*, in which he writes about a doorway which becomes a point of contact, a portal between worlds and through which the energy of a threat begins to leak. As he wrote, the Jodrell Bank telescopes scanned distant galaxies, observed pulsars and zoomed in on quasars. The dislocation of time and space permeates his work.

I finally met him for the first time around 10 years ago, here at Jodrell Bank.

One of my early heroes, he was circumspect at our first meeting. He sat and observed and listened for almost an hour, which was nerve-racking, to say the least. Since then he and his wife, Griselda, have often worked alongside us, helping us make explicit the fact that Jodrell Bank is a point of connection between many worlds. A site where people not only do science and create superb engineering, but also consider their place in the Universe, in time, in relation to others – a location where science is part of the human story, of culture as a whole and where the history of science elides with the history of humanity.

The first time I visited Alan and Griselda at home, I felt I recognised the house and the place. They both spoke eloquently of its history, of the people who had walked the floors, touched the walls, set fires, cooked and ate, lost things between floorboards, were born and died.

And one small thing was more shocking than any other. One

thing made an electric connection between me and those people of other times, one that I still feel today.

When I was very young, anxious and religious (a heady combination), I invented my own secret way of warding off the threats of the outside world. Invoking what seemed the strongest source of protection I could find at the time, I would sneak around our bungalow in Durham every night, surreptitiously marking invisible crosses (I said I was religious) on door and window frames. It was superstition at its most basic level, a response to my fear of the unknown and my growing sense that the Universe was a lot bigger than I'd realised. I had a panic one night near Christmas when it dawned on me that I'd forgotten about our chimney. I had to creep out of bed when everyone else was asleep to make sure it was included in the protective ring so that nobody but Santa could get in.

As Alan showed me around his house, he pointed out marks scratched, centuries before, in the timbers around the ancient chimney.

He mentioned, casually, that these were in fact known as apotropaic marks, were intended to ward off evil and could be found all over the house, on window and door frames, as well as the chimney timbers. He pointed out crosses, scratched into the darkened wood, apparently unaware that the hairs were standing up on the back on my neck and that there was a rushing sound in my ears that made it hard for me to hear him speak. A memory was unfurling itself in my brain. Something I'd forgotten I'd forgotten, and a sign of the way that Alan's writing connects with his readers.

In his book, *Elidor*, an ordinary suburban door becomes a connection between worlds, an entry point for a threat that leaks energy into even household appliances, animating them so that they run without being plugged in.

After reading it, I found myself including not only our fireplace and chimney, but also our Hotpoint Twin-Tub in my nightly round of cross marking. Other white goods worried me over subsequent months and soon I was creeping around each night marking not only windows and doors, but also anything electrical with my invisible apotropaic signs. I think I kept it up until we moved when I was 11.

I had forgotten the process – forgotten, even, that *Elidor* had such an impact on me – until I met Alan and was standing in his house. Alan's immersion in the academic underpinning of his fables and narrative had led him to provoke something universal in me as a child. My own secretive, private invention is 'a thing': something I now hold in common with people from many cultures across the planet.

It's a small example of the way that Alan has bridged worlds and times, anchoring them in places and in people, as the Lovell Telescope moves on its tracks, slipping between looking in different directions and back to different ages, every day.

Alan's work is woven through with ours, and in 2012 he made that link explicit. *Boneland*, the concluding book of the *Weirdstone* series, locates Colin, its main protagonist, here at Jodrell Bank.

And as the eve of the 70th anniversary of the founding of the Observatory approached, we launched our 'Garner Lecture Series' here with 'Powsels and Thrums', a lecture by Alan himself.

Alan has said that this will be his last public lecture (we will see, of course) but the lecture series will continue, interleaving with our astrophysics lectures, so that we bring these ideas to light, rehearsing and reinventing the links between worlds.

Teresa Anderson is Director of the University of Manchester's Discovery Centre at Jodrell Bank. A physicist by training, she also has a doctorate in electrical engineering – and now works on the boundaries between science and culture, welcoming over 160,000 people to Jodrell Bank each year. The Centre runs an eclectic programme: including education sessions that attract 18,000 school visitors per year; the 'Live from Jodrell Bank' science-music festivals; the 'Lovell Lecture' series (on the latest in astrophysics research) and the 'Garner Lecture' series (launched by Alan Garner in 2015).

THE FULL MOON SHOPPING MALL

Margaret Atwood

Once upon a time, a long, long time ago, say two or three weeks as the news flies, in the vast but horizontal city of Toronto, there was a mother who loved to shop in shopping malls. She would get so caught up in shopping that she would forget the time, and would be late for dinner; so her two children, Krystal and Kyle, had become very good at cooking hot dogs and macaroni and cheese, so they would not go hungry. Their father was in the Futures market and was easily distracted, and never noticed what was going on, so it was no good asking him anything about cooking.

One day the mother wandered into a shopping mall she had never seen before. It was called the Full Moon Mall. You will not be very surprised when I tell you that it was in fact the night of the full moon, but the mother was not attuned to the phases of the moon.

Inside this mall there were a lot of cheese shops, butcher shops, shoe shops, and fur shops. The mother wandered here and there, looking at this and that. She was very taken with a fur shop, so she went inside and tried on fur coats. The saleslady had a long nose, sharp claws, pointed teeth, and reddish eyes; she kept urging the mother to try on yet another coat, and saying how fine they looked on her. And indeed they did look fine.

But then the full moon rose, and all of a sudden the mother saw that the saleslady was not a human woman, but a large, fierce raccoon. With a scream she ran for the door, but the raccoon was there before her, and turned the key in the lock. 'You have been trying on our skins,' growled the raccoon, 'and turn about is fair play. So now I will try on yours.' Then the raccoon killed the mother, peeled off her skin, and put it on. It fitted quite well, except for the tail, which had to be stuffed inside; nor could the sharp teeth and claws and the reddish eyes be disguised. Over the mother's skin she put on the mother's clothes, and if you hadn't been paying close attention you wouldn't have known the difference.

With the help of the other animals in the Full Moon Mall – for all of the shops were run by animals, who sold things made from themselves, because why pay the middleman – the raccoon stashed the mother inside the freezer of the butcher's shop, to eat later. All the animals locked up their shops and went out the main door of the mall, and the raccoon went out last, for she was the CEO, and locked the door behind her with her magic Full Moon key.

She placed the key inside the mother's handbag, so as not to lose it, since there was only one key, and without it she would have to stay in her raccoon shape all the time, wandering around in alleyways, which would not be so delightful as the Full Moon Mall. Then she found the mother's address and house keys and car keys inside the purse, and got into the mother's car in the parking lot, and drove to the mother's house, being careful not to run over any of her fellow raccoons along the way.

Krystal and Kyle were making macaroni and cheese and hot dogs for dinner.

'Hi kids,' growled the raccoon. 'Sorry I'm late.'

'What's wrong with your voice?' said Kyle.

'Where'd you get that manicure? Cool!' said Krystal.

The family sat down to dinner. The father, who was thinking about pork bellies, did not notice anything unusual, except that his wife's bum seemed to have grown quite large – this was because of the tail – but Krystal and Kyle found it peculiar when the mother took her hot dog over to the sink and washed it, and then stuck her head down into the macaroni dish to lick it clean. 'Got any eggs?' she growled then. For there is nothing raccoons like better than fresh eggs.

'No,' said Krystal. 'You were supposed to buy some, remember? At the shopping mall.'

'Oh,' said the raccoon. 'Got any frogs?'

'Kyle,' whispered Krystal. 'Don't say anything out loud, but that's not our mother.'

'It's not?'

'No. It's a raccoon.'

'Don't be a goof,' said Kyle. But then he looked hard, and right enough, their mother's teeth were never that pointy.

By this time the raccoon mother had shoved her head into the refrigerator and was gobbling up some grapes. 'What'll we do?' said Kyle. 'Where's our real mother?'

'We need to get that animal out of our house,' said Krystal. 'She'll rip everything to shreds, and maybe us, too!'

'And make her tell us where she's hidden our mother,' said Kyle.

'Run like the wind to the corner store,' said Krystal, 'and buy a dozen eggs.' She looked inside her mother's handbag for some money, and what should be in there but a strange-looking key. 'This might come in useful,' said Krystal to herself, and she slipped it into her pocket.

Kyle ran like the wind to the corner store, and was back in a flash with a dozen eggs, extra large, organic. Krystal, meanwhile, had armed herself with a baseball bat. The raccoon mother had thrown a lot of things out of the refrigerator onto the floor, and was helping herself to a pound of butter.

'You're not our real mother,' said Kyle and Krystal together, in their loudest voices.

The raccoon mother wiped the butter from her whiskers, which by this time were poking through her skin. 'No, I'm not,' she said. 'Whoop-de-do, clever of you. So what? I like it here.'

'We'll trade,' said Krystal. 'Give us our real mother back and you can have a dozen eggs, extra large, organic!'

'No deal,' said the raccoon mother. 'Here I am and here I stand, with all you have at my command.'

Krystal knew that once anyone started rhyming it was best to reply in the same way, so she said, 'Very well then, we shall see; and by the way, I've got your key!'

'My key!' shrieked the raccoon. For without the key she could never get back into the Full Moon Shopping Mall, and would have to stay in her raccoon shape all the time. She dropped to all fours and advanced on the children, teeth bared, but Kyle waved the baseball bat and she backed off.

'Now, take us to our mother spit-spot,' said Krystal, 'or I'm flushing this key down the toilet.'

So the raccoon mother drove the children to the Full Moon Shopping Mall, and Krystal used the key to unlock the front door, and then the door to the butcher's shop, and there was their mother, hanging up on a hook without her skin. She didn't look very healthy at all. But when the raccoon peeled off the mother's skin and slid the mother back into it, she came to life again, and once she had all her clothes back on she was as good as new. 'My goodness, children,' she said, looking at her watch. 'I lost track of the time!'

'What else is new?' said Krystal. 'Don't you know you got skinned? Go outside and get into the car, and wait for us there. It's important!' So the mother did.

Krystal broke all the extra large organic eggs into a bowl and set it on the floor. The raccoon lapped them up with pleasure. While it was doing that, Krystal slipped the key to Kyle. 'Run like the wind,' she said, 'and hide the key in a trash bin. Then get into the car. Fast!' So Kyle ran like the wind.

The raccoon finished the eggs, and stood up on its hind legs. It was indeed a very large raccoon. 'Now,' it growled, 'my key, my key! It belongs to me! Then we will see what we will see!' Its eyes were redder than ever, and Krystal knew that, since raccoons are no respecters of deals, once it had the key it would surely jump on her and bite her to death.

She stood on her tiptoes, ready to run. 'Your key is hidden in a bin. When you find it, you will win, and can always get back in,' said Krystal. She scooted out the door with the raccoon right behind her, snarling with rage. But the car was ready and waiting, with Kyle and the mother inside, and Krystal hopped into it, and they sped away, back to their house. And the mother was never late for dinner again.

And that is why, from that day to this, you will see the urban raccoons in the vast but horizontal city of Toronto tipping over trash bins and rummaging through the trash inside them: they are looking for the key to the Full Moon Shopping Mall. And if they ever find it, take my advice: don't go in. Or you too may find that you've been skinned.

Snip, snap, my thread is spun, but other tales have just begun.

Margaret Atwood is the author of more than 40 books of fiction, poetry and critical essays. In addition to the classic The Handmaid's Tale, *her novels include* Cat's Eye, Alias Grace, The Blind Assassin – *winner of the 2000 Booker Prize – and the* MaddAddam *trilogy:* Oryx and Crake, The Year of the Flood *and* MaddAddam. *She is the winner of many awards, which, in addition to the Booker, include the Arthur C. Clarke Award, the Prince of Asturias Award for Literature, France's Chevalier dans l'Ordre des Arts et des Lettres, Italy's Premio Mondello and, in 2014, the Orion Book Award for Fiction. In 2012 she was awarded the title of Companion of Literature by The Royal Society of Literature. Margaret Atwood lives in Toronto, Canada.*

READING TOGETHER, READING APART

John Burnside

To any child from the lower echelons of society, nothing seems so casually elegant as a middle-class childhood. I say this because I am such a child: born to a casual labourer and a former shop assistant in the mid-fifties, I was, from the beginning, taught to focus on advancement, in any available field, which meant hard work, deliberate study and, most important of all, a complete, hard-nosed eradication of any imaginative tendencies. A child autodidact with an ambitious mother, I had gone straight from catechism to 'The Classics' without stopping on the way for what would now be called Young Adult writing, or worse still, low fantasy.

In fact, from the very first, comics, magazines and 'silly' books were banned in our chilly post-war prefab on the edge of Cowdenbeath. I remember slipping out early on Saturday mornings and letting myself into my friend William's house, to read the comics and trashy magazines his father brought home from his job as a delivery driver; the family were rarely awake before noon, so I had hours to myself with *The Dandy* and *The Victor* while they slept. This was, however, strictly a clandestine pursuit and I was always aware of the fact that, for my mother, any kind of fantasy was a path to hell: not just religious, but intellectual. Reading the classics, (which we borrowed from the library, or occasionally bought on trips to Edinburgh), along with carefully selected educational texts, like the Ladybird 'How it Works' series, was edifying and informative – a first, decisive step towards university and, that ultimate grail, a professional career. Anything to do with fantasy, anything aimed at idle children, anything that did not improve me in some way, was out. (The one mysterious exception to this was *Gormenghast*, which my mother bought me in the Penguin three-volume box set after I passed my first set of O-levels. I never knew whether this was a concession on her part, or because Mervyn Peake – unlike, say, J.R.R. Tolkien – was someone whose work she considered instructive.)

I didn't quite fulfil my mother's ambitions and proceed satisfactorily to one of the major universities (for reasons of social class, Oxford and Cambridge were assumed to be beyond even our wildest imaginings, though Edinburgh or St Andrews would have been more than acceptable). I did, however, go to a college in Cambridge, known then as Cambridgeshire College of Arts and Technology and, for the first time, I began to mingle with people who had enjoyed what I took to be the privilege of an English middle-class upbringing. This being the ostensibly class-free 1970s, I was even tolerated, if not exactly welcomed, at University events – the most memorable being readings by such American poets as Michael McClure and Ted Berrigan. Yet what struck me most, at the time, was how little my new acquaintances had read of the classics and, even more surprisingly, how little they cared. By then, I had read Catullus and Ovid in the original, and I knew what the poets were doing these days, not only in Ghana, but pretty much everywhere else. I could get by in Old French, I was adept in Middle English and I knew more about science than any other Humanities student I had encountered. I was, at times, rather impressed with myself; everyone else found me mildly, though not at all interestingly, absurd.

Which did not matter at all because, after a while at least, I didn't much care for the people I met in Cambridge any more than I had for my classmates in Corby and Kettering Tech. I had my books, and poetry and – well, I'm told that there's a song about it. The one thing I did care about was meeting women – which, disastrously, I did, several times through my first and second years of study. When summer came, I would retreat to Corby, where I worked in factories and spent my time with the kind of women I was used to: i.e. girls, some of whom found my clumsy erudition attractive. So it wasn't until my third year that I was afforded the opportunity to fall in love with someone from outside my own culture – though when it happened, it was like learning a new language, a new code that made the world and everything in it subtly different. Richer. More fantastic. Falling in love with this woman – whom I shall call Helen – revealed to me what infinite vistas of nonsense I had been carrying around in my head. About class, for example. From her, I learned – implicitly – that it wasn't what cutlery you used, or even how you spoke that mattered in social situations (well, sometimes it did, but the people who cared about such things weren't worth bothering about). No: what mattered was the self-assurance that others had and I lacked, a self-assurance that depended on a sense of entitlement that could not be faked. A self-assurance that made people feel comfortable when my awkwardness provoked boredom and, eventually, that slight annoyance you might allow yourself for the one person in the room who can't play bridge, or charades, or whatever game it was that, in certain circles, is taken for granted. This revelation cured me, eventually, of the worst aspects of my own class prejudices (I had supposed that, because my social clumsiness made people uneasy, they must be snobs or idiots). But the other, more important revelation was the immense gap in my education that, until then, I had never suspected.

'You've never read *The Owl Service*,' Helen said, one day, when an allusion she made went straight over my head. 'Really?'

'What's *The Owl Service*?'

'I don't believe it,' she said. 'I thought you'd read everything.'

'Who wrote it?'

'Alan Garner,' she said – and I understood, then, that she really was surprised, that she wasn't just pretending. Over the next few minutes, she proceeded to give me a rough outline of the book and, to be frank, I thought it sounded utterly preposterous, but I was in love and, because she said I would have to read this book, I did. In fact, she read it again to keep me company, comparing page numbers and impressions whenever we met, the way I had once done with a previous girlfriend, a student of French and Spanish language whom

I had persuaded to read Cocteau's *Les Enfants Terrible*. That woman dumped me shortly after the scene where Dargelos throws the snowball – though whether the decision was romantic or literary, I couldn't have said. Some time later, we met in the street and she introduced me to the new love of her life, an engineering student from Bristol called Tim.

So I read *The Owl Service*. In fact, we read it together – in different places, though occasionally, I should think, we overlapped in time. Of course, given the theme of class, I was drawn to Gwyn as a sort of kin figure – but I did not identify with him, as I might have done had I read the book years earlier. What struck me most about this novel was the way it combined realism and the irrational, how it made the pagan world seem, not some distant, misty realm of dragons and princes or, for that matter, women made of flowers – but something emotionally, psychologically and spiritually immediate, as much a part of day-to-day life as exams and adolescent rivalries. Till then, I had kept the fantastic in a separate box from the 'real' – yes, imagination was a good thing, but it wasn't part of how one lived in this world. It was, in fact, my deep misfortune to have been brought up to render unto Caesar, not only in silver, but also in credulity, and I was quite sure that Fancy was not valid currency in the public sphere. That world was fairly mechanical, rational, to be navigated – and negotiated with – in terms that made practical sense. I could read the poems of Blake, I could study the *Mabinogion* and Arthurian legends, but everybody knew that we would eventually have to come back to the Newtonian, the literal, and the imaginatively diminished in a universe that – while not actually made of cogs and wheels – was best likened to clockwork. Even the huge and most exciting discoveries of twentieth-century science and philosophy – incompleteness, uncertainty, cosmic background radiation, quantum theory – seemed to happen in an abstract, almost imaginary space, far away from 'the real world' and no matter how much we were obliged by new information to revise our ideas of how the cosmos actually worked, that real world still ticked over in the old way: apples falling from trees in linear time; the unscrupulous and the cunning filling their coffers at the expense of others; great corporations destroying the land, regardless of the earth spirits and dryads and river gods who might live there.

Suddenly, I saw that this was wrong. It wasn't just *The Owl Service* that opened my eyes to what was going on – I read other books by Alan Garner, rejoicing in the way he made the pagan world so immediate, so contemporary, without ever resorting to smoke and mirrors, and I was reading deeply in a wide variety of mythologies during that final year of college – but it played a huge part. I'm not saying it was just 'objectively' wrong to believe that the clockwork world was, if not all there was, then all that mattered – clearly, those who did take that stance could go through life more or less unscathed (if you can say that of someone who never gets to teeter at the edge of the world in joy and wonder at its beauty and seeming impossibility); what I am saying is that it was morally wrong.

Not to yield to Fancy was a form of collaboration. To deny magic was to be a fifth columnist for the forces of reductionism. To claim to observe the separation of powers and not insist on Steiner's social threefold model (i.e. a separation of powers in which the cultural plays as significant and independent a role as the economic and political) was to be a traitor to the imagination. It was time to acknowledge that the imaginative, the magical and the creative were just as important as the rational, the scientific and the analytical – that the ultimate purpose of society was not money or war or conquest, but culture. My mother's ambition had numbed that impulse in the child I had been: I thought fantasy was just a distraction from the real business of getting on, or getting by, in a world that, from the first, had always seemed to belong to others – and of course it did, in one sense, just as it still does if you assume that what Caesar has is 'the world'. That I no longer do so has something to do with Alan Garner and, now that my world is at least informed by the pagan, in the old and true senses of that word (that is, one shamelessly inclined towards and basically informed by all manner of non-Newtonian, fanciful and (re)generative country matters), I am immensely grateful to his imagination for that.

I am still in touch with Helen. I even see her now and then, when circumstance allows, but even when it does not, I am aware that she is there, somewhere in the world – and I like to think that, quite by chance, we may be reading the same book, in different houses and different time zones, turning the pages or lingering over a particularly choice phrase, equally enchanted, together and apart.

John Burnside teaches literature and ecology, creative writing and American poetry at the University of St Andrews. Recent books include the T.S. Eliot and Forward prize-winning poetry collection, Black Cat Bone, *and a third volume of memoir,* I Put A Spell On You.

IN THE SAME ROOM AT THE SAME TIME

Susan Cooper

Alan Garner is unique – an observation that's likely to be made in every contribution to this book. As writers, most of us start off along a well-trodden road; some of us turn on to side roads that attract few other travellers, and some even end up on tracks marked only by a bruising of the grass. But Alan, having started down a side road, then strode away from it altogether and climbed an unscaled mountain. He's still up there, going from one peak to the next.

We first met in 1983, in Llanbadarn Fawr, a village where Aberystwyth University has a campus. We were at a conference. By this time, Alan had reached *Red Shift* and *The Stone Book Quartet*, and I had followed a five-book sequence called *The Dark Is Rising* with a novel called *Seaward*. I remember happily the way that Alan and Griselda and I, having met, got along famously, and I remember the fact that once Alan and I started talking we seemed never to stop. While everyone around us was speaking English or Welsh, we were speaking something else: a dense, allusive language full of leaps and assumptions, the language of writers fed by the same sources, writers generally published for children but writing only for themselves.

Between lectures we talked and talked, sitting, walking, making pilgrimage to the sixth century church of St Padarn which stands like a small cathedral looking down at the sea, a lofty, haunted place where six centuries ago Dafydd ap Gwilym sang as a boy.

At some point Alan said to me, 'When were you at Oxford?'

'Fifty-three to fifty-six,' I said.

He said, 'I knew we'd been in the same room at the same time before.'

I wrote later, 'It was like meeting a long-lost twin, with whom I could speak a language that I had never before heard spoken except inside my own head.' And I added, 'We both write fantasies which travel over the horizon of myth – but Alan is by far the more intrepid traveller.'

We did have some basics in common. Alan and I were born seven months apart, and our childhoods were moulded by the Second World War and certain other difficulties. We were deeply rooted in our respective places – Cheshire for Alan, Buckinghamshire and North Wales for me. Through the good offices of the Welfare State, we had each gone from what's known as a modest background to an excellent grammar school, and then to the University of Oxford, where our minds found elbow room and we became suitably bilingual in English dialect. And all the time, our lifelong reading had focused on folk tale and myth. When we began to write, we both headed up the same side road.

When Alan listed, in the Author's Note to *The Moon of Gomrath*, the fairly arcane books that had been of most help in his 'grasshopper research', I had only to raise my own grasshopper head to see most of them on my own shelves. For our two earliest sets of books we had used the same elements, but for our own ends; each of us, for instance, distinguished between the Old Magic and the High Magic, but not in the same way; and each of us had a particular and only partly similar use of the Wild Hunt, and of its leader, who has half a dozen names and none of them definitive. Originality, as Alan said in that same note, is really no more than 'the personal colouring of existing themes'.

Small wonder that we've always had a lot to talk about.

But Alan's originality goes way beyond his own description. Certainly we all dip into old Tolkien's Cauldron of Story and choose whichever theme we want, but my intrepid friend then flies up to his mountain, into the rarefied air that most of us can't breathe, and gives his theme far more than a personal colouring. There's no other writer in the world who could have created *Red Shift* and the three major books since.

Strandloper, *Thursbitch* and *Boneland* aren't so much novels as explosions of mythic energy: wonderful, demanding, uncompromising books. The words may be simple but the narrative is not; its roots go deep into place and through time. As Ursula K. Le Guin said when reviewing *Boneland*, Alan is 'more myth-maker than fantasist'.

And the myth that he makes is carved out of the land to which he belongs, the land from which he and his people came, the land in which he lives. And expressed, of course, in its language. He is above all a writer of place, of a very particular place, and of the music that is its speech. That's one of the two most powerful – out of many – reasons why I love his work.

The other major reason is hard to describe. It has to do with the *nature* of one's response to his books over the last 20 years. 'I am a writer, a maker of dreams,' Alan once said. Sometimes I think life has been subtly transforming him from a storyteller into a poet. These later books don't draw you gradually into a woven web of narrative; they batter your subconscious with bursts of images, words, incident, whirling you into a labyrinth whose centre is only glimpsed. Until the end, when you do find yourself there at the centre, stunned by the power of metaphor, staring at light, at white snow come from a black cloud. A great poem can do that – not, often, a novel.

I haven't said this very well. My intrepid friend could do it better.

Many happy returns, Alan *bach*. May you keep on following the malachite, and making dreams.

Susan Cooper was a reporter for The Sunday Times *until she married an American and moved to the United States. She has been writing novels and picture books set in Britain ever since. Her books include the fantasy sequence* The Dark Is Rising, King of Shadows, Victory, *and most recently,* Ghost Hawk.

WHERE THE STARLIGHT SINGS

Frank Cottrell-Boyce

I know the geography of a dozen magical lands, but the location of only one.

I was in my teens when my family got its first car. It was barely in the drive when I started pestering my dad to run us down the M56, to Junction 6, pick up the Macclesfield Road, park at the Wizard Inn and walk 'by Seven Firs and Goldenstone . . . to Stormy Point and Saddle Bole'. I wanted to see for myself the Fundindelve of Cadellin. I found the great stone barrier within half an hour. Narnia, Middle-earth and Earthsea are impossible collages of myth and reality. But Alan Garner described Alderley Edge exactly as it is. It's all there. You can walk the paths that Colin and Susan walked. But to do so after reading the books is to tread an invisible other path, in a parallel Alderley – older, more enduring and somehow more real than the suburban beauty spot which the rest of my family was enjoying that day. Even now when I drive around Cheshire, I can feel in the dips and twists of its lanes the sinews of a hidden network of caves and caverns. It's a two-storey county with a double reality.

Alan Garner did this.

So to walk again from Seven Firs to Stormy Point, this time not with my dad but with Alan Garner himself, felt a bit like going to visit the Giant's Causeway with Finn mac Cumhaill. I hesitated to ask, worried that he would find the idea intrusive, or just too tiring. In fact he was energetic and energetically generous. His wife

Griselda was sweetly protective of him and he was sweetly dismissive of her protection.

This is how we walked:

1 SEVEN FIRS AND THIEVES' HOLE: Money is a force of nature in this part of Cheshire. It shapes the human landscape as clearly as glaciation shaped the Pennines. In the car park of the Wizard you are in the world of getting and spending. There's an information board outlining the walk, including a dashing black and white photograph of Alan. It makes me uneasy that he's become part of the branding of the place. But we're only 100 yards or so up the trail when that world begins to melt away. Alan points out a long depression under the trees – Thieves' Hole. It's part of a medieval hollow way. This is the route the farmer with the white mare was travelling in the Legend of Alderley. From here to Stormy Point, the way was clear and short. In the days before commercial forestry, you would have been able to see it. So why did the farmer go 'by Goldenstone and Saddle Bole'? Alan leaves the question hanging. As he's talking he draws a cross in the earth with a piece of branch, saying this is where the meeting happened. It's electrifying, this sense of his that something happened here, that the story is part of the land. Alan had the legend from his grandfather. He's carried it around, cared for it, puzzled over it, played with it all his life. It's a precious thing – like Susan's tear. He's sure that in the folk tale and all its retellings, in children's books and ballads and even in the pub sign, there is a faint resonance of something real, some echo of a remote, significant moment, when we were first trying to find our place in the world.

2 GOLDENSTONE: A little way off, at the side of the path is the 'Goldenstone' – a hefty chunk of conglomerate. It's not a natural outcrop but a boulder that has been dragged here for a purpose. Alan begins to speculate about its origins and tells me the story of how, when he was 19, he sat here puzzling about the Goldenstone in the story. He started to dig and uncovered this boulder. 'Wait a minute,' I say. 'You dug this up?' 'Yes. It was in the story so I knew it must be somewhere.' I'm struck by two things. The first is his

belief that stories contain or even predict truth. The second is how his life is punctuated by these enormous acts of self-confidence. He walked out of a hard-earned place at Oxford because he was sure he was going to be a writer. Although he was barely out of his teens, the local branch of the Society of Oddfellows gave him the mortgage which enabled him to buy Toad Hall – the house he still lives in and which he restored himself. But perhaps confidence is the wrong word. Maybe sureness of purpose is better. His trajectory as a writer, for instance, is extraordinary. From the brilliantly written but fundamentally generic *Weirdstone*, pushing through the nerve-jangling, febrile *The Owl Service* and *Red Shift* into the limpid perfection of *The Stone Book Quartet*, it's hard to think of anyone who moved so far and so quickly from their beginnings and with such a strong sense of direction. Where does this assurance come from? From parents? From Manchester Grammar? From this place?

3 Stormy Point: We follow the path up through the woodland. At the point, the cover lifts like a curtain to reveal the whole plain shining below you, rising up toward the Peak District. At our feet is a narrow gully called The Devil's Grave. You're supposed to see the Devil if you walk around it three times widdershins. In fact it's an old copper working. Saddle Bole – just a few yards away – gets its name from smelting. This has been an industrial landscape since the Bronze Age. The underground pathways of the stories are mine workings. The flashes and meres that jewel the plain are the result of subsidence. To the left is a little patch of heather. That's what the whole place would have been like before the forestry. When Alan talks like this, you can almost see the flicker-book of history playing across the Edge. He tells a story about how his cousin got the fright of his life just here when he heard a sound like bagpipes passing just below his feet. Alan and Griselda start by discussing what could have caused it but end up discussing the cousin. He still lives in the house, not very many yards away, that Alan's family has lived in for generations. But now the house is worth a fortune and money may finally take from the family what wars and the Depression couldn't.

4 Castle Rock: Alan reads the landscape to me as we carry on up to Castle Rock, picking out meanings where I see only mud and stone. *That rock shouldn't be there. That dip is man-made. This was an old path.* It becomes clear why the farmer in the Legend took this slightly circuitous route. We've been following a boundary. Goldenstone marked one corner of it. These pathways delineate the rest. Boundaries are neither one place nor the other. That's why thieves are buried on boundaries – for instance Thieves' Hole. And this rock sits right on the boundary. It is liminal. It hovers in the gap between two places. Between the reality of trade (payments were made on borders) and that other reality of the story. The story skirts the edge of the material world. That's why the best bit happens on the way back from the fair – when it's late and the light is fading.

It's a very short journey. The Edge is a tiny plot of land. Yet the *Weirdstone* trilogy feels huge. A bonsai epic. Like Alan's life – with its massive artistic ambition and its tiny geographical reach.

5 Druids' Circle: Another family connection. In the woods, between Stormy Point and the Beacon, there's a small stone circle. It's not ancient. It was put here a couple of hundred years ago, probably by Alan's great-great-grandfather Robert, who simply had some stones left over and wanted to do something memorable with them. It was Robert who carved the face on the Wizard's Well. Garners have always left their mark here.

Alan tells stories about overhearing coach party guides talking about ley lines and Druids here. He's impatient of anything too mystical. He's searching these stories and places for something true.

He tells me about talking to one of the archaeologists who was working on the excavation of the Lindow Man – an Iron Age bog body found in Lindow Moss (which appears in *The Weirdstone* as Llyn Dhu). The archaeologist said to Alan, 'You knew about this, didn't you? Before we found it. He's Grimnir.' The story excavates the truth.

There's also an impulse to leave a mark on the Edge, the way his grandfather did. For centuries the mine workings here were tiny individual claims – exploited by individual families. Much the way families still have claims on areas of bog in the west of Ireland. The Legend of Alderley is Alan's claim. Passed down to him. He has been working away at its details, its faults and fissures. 'Why is it always a mare in the story?' he asks, 'Why would a knight want a mare?' Somewhere in Giraldus Cambrensis he has found an account of a fertility ritual that involved a king copulating with a white mare. Surely that's it. That's the truth which continues to resonate in the classic novel and the pub sign. He tells me this, and then he and Griselda fall to talking about the time when he revealed this story and tried to warn someone in the audience that it would not be suitable for children. How cross they were that people let their children come in anyway. I want to hug them both for their delicacy of feeling.

6 Church Quarry: They saved this for the end of the walk, as a treat for me. We swerved away from the car park behind the pub and entered a deep declivity. The layers in the rock are clearly visible. But dug into the face is an adit – a test digging – as round and dark as a full stop. This is the spot where Colin's *bergli* hut stands in *Boneland*. It turns out that a troubled young man – John Evans – did live here, in much the way that Colin lives here in the book. 'Bloody hell, you never made anything up did you?' I laugh. 'Not that I know of.' But then I think of that mitten with its thumb stuck in the glass hill in *Elidor*. I don't believe I've seen that anywhere else. But most of all I'm moved by how delighted they are to see the shock and pleasure of recognition on my face when I see that stone, full stop.

7 Toad Hall: The walk over, I drive Alan and Griselda back to Toad Hall where they live. This is the house that Alan found while out on a bike ride after he left Oxford. Next to it is the Old Medicine House – a beautiful half-timbered house which he found over the border in Staffordshire and had moved here, in sections, like a giant Ikea flat-pack. It's the heart of the Blackden Trust – the educational charity they founded to protect this place and its history – and they eagerly share its treasures with me. Because I'm a Catholic, Griselda is keen to show me the coded references to Mary

and her angels carved into its roof beams, relics of the Persecution times. The fireplace, set right in the centre of the main room, is a wonder in itself. But by far the most remarkable thing about the two buildings is their neighbour. Toad Hall and the Medicine House nestle into the hill just behind the Lovell Telescope at Jodrell Bank. The radio dish hovers over them like an inverted cathedral dome. A charge seems to flow between the two places, between past and present but also between this little patch of Earth and the vastness of space.

Alan shows me some of the archaeological finds that have been uncovered around the house. Just as on the walk, just as in his stories, he saves the best until last. He puts in my hand a piece of stone so black and smooth it feels like a solid absence. 'Now close your hand over it.' My fingers find natural resting places and I know instinctively that I'm holding a made object. It's a Palaeolithic axe, the one that appears in *Boneland*. The minute I know this, absence turns to presence. My fingers are closed over the trace of thousands of fingers over thousands of years.

The Legend of Alderley isn't an Arthurian story. The Arthurian bits are decorations it has picked up on the way. The story of a sleeper under the hill – a top man – who will come back at the end of time is something far, far older. Alan talks about the report of Demetrius in Plutarch's *Concerning the Failure of Oracles* which says that there is in Britain 'An island in which Kronos is imprisoned with Briareus keeping guard over him as he sleeps. For, as they put it, Sleep is the bond forged for Kronos. They add that around him are many divine beings, his knights and his soldiers.' But it's older than that too. The story is a piece of mental technology – as old as the axe. It expresses our need for a beginning and an end and a connection between the two. This is what the Lovell Telescope is doing too, of course, scouring the universe for evidence of our velocity, trying to locate our starting point – the Big Bang – and predict our finishing line – the Big Crunch. It converts radiation to sound. It's where the stars sing. This is why the bonsai epic of Alderley feels huge.

I let go of the axe head, hand it back and say thank you and I'm struck by another force acting on me, as directly as the gravity and velocity which Tom outlines at the beginning of *Red Shift*. Kindness. I've been struck all day by the way that Alan and Griselda have the measure of each other, and how welcoming and generous they've been with these precious objects. I'm surprised that I haven't noticed before just how much kindness flows through the novels – from the all-embracing hospitality of Gowther, through Mary's father's sharing of knowledge in *The Stone Book* to the teasing tenderness of Meg in *Boneland*. I'm aware too of the greater generosity shown in sharing their story and protecting their plot of earth. What connects the axe head and the radio dish is a current of generous acts, of sharing.

I don't know how to say this so I just say, 'Thank you for a lovely day.'

And Griselda of course says, 'Do come again.'

Frank Cottrell-Boyce is a children's novelist. He won the Carnegie Medal for his debut novel Millions *and the Guardian Children's Fiction prize for* The Unforgotten Coat. *His most recent book is* The Astounding Broccoli Boy. *He is also the screenwriter of, among others,* Millions, The Railway Man, *and* 24 Hour Party People. *He's probably best known as one of the co-creators of the London Olympics Opening Ceremony in 2012.*

THE STILL FOOT OF THE COMPASS: ALAN GARNER'S SIBLINGS

Amanda Craig

When we think of the protagonists of classic children's literature, they are very often a boy and a girl – or a family consisting of girls and boys. The reason why seems obvious. Having protagonists of both sexes widens a book's potential appeal; the clash between male and female can provide comedy, drama, energy and even the stirrings of romance.

Alan Garner's first four novels – *The Weirdstone of Brisingamen*, *The Moon of Gomrath*, *Elidor* and *The Owl Service* – were not specifically written for children, but are best known as children's literature partly because they contain many of the features of this genre, not least in choosing children as protagonists. That these children are always siblings may also seem unremarkable, until you consider that the author is himself an only child – and that what he does with the concept of the sibling is worth noticing.

In the days when large families were the norm, brothers and sisters were commonplace both in fairy tale and children's literature. Much like Jacob's brothers in the Old Testament, they began as foils for the hero: doomed to failure through moral flaw or, as in the case of Jacob and Esau, lack of wiliness. By the time of the Grimms' collected fairy tales, sibling relations have undergone considerable improvement – especially between the sexes. Brothers tend towards loyalty and protectiveness ('Hansel and Gretel'). Sisters endure terrible ordeals in order to rescue their brothers from enchantment ('The Seven Swans').

During the first golden age of children's literature, the sister is both friend and mother-substitute to her brothers: literally so in the case of Wendy Darling in *Peter Pan*, and less obviously in E. Nesbit's *Five Children and It* trilogy, whose Anthea is resourceful at gaining food or tending wounds. Whether in C.S. Lewis's *The Lion, the Witch and the Wardrobe*, Arthur Ransome's *Swallows and Amazons* or Eve Garnett's *The Children of One End Street*, brothers and sisters display loyalty, affection and conventional gendered roles.

If you read *The Weirdstone of Brisingamen* and *The Moon of Gomrath* with this in mind, it is interesting how this convention is turned on its head. Susan is neither motherly nor passive, and by the second novel she has become something extraordinary: a Maiden capable of defeating the children's powerful enemy, the Morrigan. Although both Helen in *Elidor* and Alison in *The Owl Service* are more passive, sibling loyalties mean each sibling must fight real danger to save the other.

The *Weirdstone of Brisingamen* is the most conventional of the four. Colin and Susan are sent by their parents to live in Cheshire with Susan's mother's former nurse, Bess, and her farmer husband Gowther. Lacking children of her own, Bess gave Susan's mother the 'Bridestone', passed down generations from mother to daughter, and Susan's mother gave it to Susan. Unknown to them, the 'Bridestone' or 'Tear' (as Susan calls it) is the lost 'Weirdstone of Brisingamen', stolen hundreds of years ago from Cadellin Silverbrow, the wizard at the centre of the tale. Without the Weirdstone's protective magic, both the wizard and the knights sleeping under the hill until Britain's hour of need, are in mortal danger from the forces of evil. Those forces, led by the Morrigan, are alert to Susan's bracelet and steal it from her; the children steal it back, and after a long ordeal underground, battle ensues.

The drama and mystery are enthralling, but the children themselves barely individuated. While Gowther, Bess, the Morrigan, Cadellin and the dwarves are vividly described, we have no idea about Colin or Susan as people – not even which is the elder. (In

Boneland we learn that they are twins.) Colin seems slightly more dominant, logical, humorous and is the one who works out how to escape the goblins (or 'svarts') by running counter-intuitively uphill. However, there are none of the disagreements that usually occur between fictional (and real) siblings. You almost wonder why there needs to be two of them.

With their macs, bicycles and lemonade they are as bland in the first book as any nice child out of Enid Blyton, tidily eating sandwiches even when being hunted deep underground; if you consider C.S. Lewis's Eustace and Jill in *The Silver Chair* and their quarrels, the difference is notable. Though we feel for Colin in his claustrophobia, there is more character in the ore-stained tunnels of their distressing journey. Yet with the recapture of the bracelet comes a shift.

For the first time, Susan acts alone ('I don't care; I've got to try. Are you coming? Because if not, I'm going by myself,' she tells her brother). It's a turning point and, even if Colin saves his sister during her crossing of the Plankshaft, Susan is never dependent on him again.

It is when Susan receives the second bracelet, the 'Mark of Fohla' which unexpectedly protects her by destroying the monstrous Mara, that she begins to become the more powerful sibling, linked inextricably to magic and the moon.

Cursed or magical objects are a familiar feature in Norse and Celtic myth. Both Wagner and Tolkien exploited the *Volsunga Saga* and its doom-laden ring 'Andvaranaut'. Yet heroines do not tend to be the bearers of such talismans. In children's literature before Garner, the only one I can think of is the Princess Irene in George MacDonald's *The Princess and the Goblins* (1872) – who is given a magic ring by her great-grandmother, and who also travels underground to rescue a boy trapped by goblins which are unmistakably the inspiration both for those in *The Hobbit*, and, with their slapping feet and giant fiery cave meeting, *The Weirdstone*'s own svarts.

Susan's new bracelet has the ability to open the gates to Fundindelve, enabling her to escape the dark creatures sent to capture her, summon the Wild Hunt and defeat the Morrigan. For a child to encounter Susan, growing in confidence and potency in the 1960s, was surprising and enthralling: you have to wait 30 years, until Philip Pullman's Lyra, the heroine of *His Dark Materials*, to see a heroine get her hands on such a powerful magical object again.

Colin does not resent her powers, or (as in *The Moon of Gomrath*) try to stop her exploring them, but subsequent siblings are not so accommodating. Magical objects are a repeated theme in all four of Garner's early works, and they become increasingly sinister and divisive.

Those in *Elidor* come, of course, from the four treasures of the original Tuatha Dé Danann ballad about Child Roland and Burd Helen, which in turn demands that there are four Watson children not two. In *The Owl Service*, the love triangle between Alison, her stepbrother Roger and Gwyn is also dictated by myth, although the haunted dinner service is Garner's own invention. Traditionally, such objects transgress the boundary between the human and the non-human: indeed, like the 'Apple of Discord', they often have a will to impel protagonists towards bad choices.

The Weirdstone of Brisingamen's other sibling relationship is, of course, the secret one between the wizard Cadellin and his identical twin Govannon, who has become Grimnir, a foul-smelling hooded monster, 'like Grendel of old'. At the climax, Grimnir chooses to return the Weirdstone to Cadellin and defies his dark master. It is a brilliant twist, later echoed by Darth Vader in *Star Wars*: what this, and Colin's desperate search for the lost Susan in *Boneland*, suggests is that the sibling relationship is effectively that of a mind divided against itself, seeking unity.

Though instantly captivating to a child, *The Weirdstone* has not yet achieved the mastery that allows Garner to shift so seamlessly from naturalistic language to the intensity and mystical lyricism that came with *The Moon of Gomrath*. It is partly this dualism that makes him of such enduring interest to the general reader. Unusually for fantasy, Garner's novels are not set in an imaginary land but are local and particular to the part of Britain in which he and his ancestors have always lived. Alderley Edge and its surrounding landscape are real places, steeped in legends that include echoes of the *Mabinogion*. The Welsh valley of *The Owl Service* is somewhere the Garners have stayed, and the original dinner service was shown to the author by his mother-in-law. Many great children's authors explore the interplay between the magical and the mundane: the transit between the two is suggestive of many states – between sleep and wakefulness, between childhood and adulthood, between the poetic and the prosaic. Traditionally in children's literature, the magic ends when puberty arrives: a reflection perhaps on the way that the instinctive creativity of childhood may not survive the discovery of sexuality. Yet in Garner's work, we are persuaded that magic reveals itself as a part of the landscape, elements, weather, history or an emotional state involving stress, distress or ecstasy.

By *The Moon of Gomrath*, Garner's voice has become that of a truly remarkable writer. Again, he uses many tropes of classic children's fiction: it is interesting to consider whether he might have been influenced by a now forgotten children's classic of 1944, William Croft Dickinson's *Borrobil*, in which a brother and sister also enter a magical world after finding Beltane fires lit in a wood. However, Garner's shamanistic use of Celtic myth, his language and the drama that unfolds, is of a wholly different order of literature.

Colin and Susan never express their feelings for each other except through their actions. Their perception of the numinous is what gives them an emotional life, as emotions of extreme joy or terror saturate the landscape through which they move. That the places mentioned (apart from Fundindelve) really exist adds to the story's fascination, because one feels this magic is intertwined with the living landscape and its past. The passages in which Colin runs along the Old Straight Track to find the Mothan flower by moonlight, the siblings' fiery ride with the Wild Hunt, and Susan's rescue of her brother, are not so much derivative of myth but new-minted, and charged with extraordinary feeling; so is the death of Findhorn in *Elidor*, and the shower of flowers at the end of *The Owl Service*. Great fantasy literature can give readers a strong mental image of what, say, a dragon might look like (which is why it often translates so well to film) but Garner is outstanding at showing us what magic might actually feel like: marvellous, terrifying and pretty much like mania, in that it is an ecstatic state that its victims do not wish to leave.

That such magic might be literally irresistible is one of Garner's profoundly original touches. Traditionally the escape into a magic world is within safe parameters: the protagonists will always return, heartened and enlightened, in time for a dinner that is still hot. But Garner's magic is akin to a fugue state – we feel its loss as a tragedy. Colin and Susan ache to re-enter Fundindelve, or ride with the Wild Hunt. Roland does not want to be in a Manchester slum, but in the shining lands shut out of reach. Perhaps – in the most gloriously ambiguous ending of all – Alison does not want to be flowers but an owl, even if it is killing her. It can be no coincidence that the author was later diagnosed, as he recounts in *The Voice that Thunders*, as manic depressive.

Why, though, did Garner choose to give his heroes siblings? The effect of Susan's departure beyond the stars will be devastating for Colin, as we learn in *Boneland*, which, perhaps, questions Susan's very existence. It's an intriguing and poignant twist.

In *Elidor*, the relationships have turned fractious and a good deal more realistic. Roland is the youngest of three brothers, and the one who suggests they find the liminal street that connects damaged 1960s Manchester to the embattled land of Elidor. Energetic and enthusiastic, Roland retains the enthusiasm of childhood but is sneered at repeatedly by the eldest brother, Nicholas, for 'imagining things'. True to the fairy tale, Roland kicks a ball out of sight, and when his siblings do not return from their search for it, he is the one who saves them from their enchanted captivity. As the blind fiddler tells him, he is 'stronger than any of them' because his imagination has real power in *Elidor*.

Garner's use of the old ballad of 'Childe Rowland' is marvellously done, not least because it shifts between details of ordinary life and the sinister beauty of the supernatural so smoothly that we can laugh at the Watsons' father trying to counter the effects of magic with his screwdriver, even as our spines crawl. The four objects which the children retrieve are strongly reminiscent of those associated with the Holy Grail – a sword, a cup, a spear and a stone – and another wonderful touch is that, back in our own world they look like pieces of rubbish – two laths, a cracked cup, an iron railing and a brick – even though their energy disrupts every electrical object at home.

But the relationship between Nicholas, David, Helen and Roland is just as charged. Roland is the true believer who does not want to forget Elidor and what they must guard. He is the one who goes alone to retrieve the Treasures from their old home, and who mentally creates – then destroys – the door between the two worlds. Initially supportive, the two elder boys try to explain away their experience of Elidor as a form of mass hallucination. They are determined not to remember, whereas the gentler Helen is closer to Roland in her sense of sadness and responsibility. It is she who unwittingly helps the prophecy come true: like Susan and Alison, her maidenhood has a magical power which Roland's energy, faith and imagination alone can't summon. In the end, they all have to act together, and it is Nicholas who redeems himself by realising that they must throw the Treasures back into the golden land that they have succeeded in rescuing, but from which they will be forever shorn.

The Owl Service is a much more complex book, and one that is deeply interested in relationships. Its families are fractured: Alison and Roger are uneasily related only by their parents' second marriage, and Gwyn is the son of a single mother in a rural Welsh valley. All three find themselves re-enacting the myth of Blodeuwedd, the maiden made out of flowers who betrays her husband when she falls in love with another man and is turned into an owl.

This is no children's book, and its supernatural happenings need attentiveness to work out. It begins with Alison being asked by Gwynn how her 'bellyache' is: given that she is a teenager, the adult reader may deduce she is suffering from menstrual pains and has just become a woman. Indeed, the whole story throbs not just with mounting family tension (in addition to class war) but sexual electricity. The fact that it's Roger, not Gwyn, who persuades the dying Alison to become flowers, not birds, at the climax, stroking her face, suggests that he may become her true lover not her stepbrother.

Given the Welsh myth on which it is based, the undercurrent of sexual jealousy and rivalry between the two boys seems unmistakable.

Roger himself is one of the most repellent characters Garner has created, similar to but far worse than Nicholas in *Elidor*. His gratuitous jeers at Huw ('You're not so green as you're grass-looking, are you?') and his bullying of the friendly Gwyn, his snobbery and aggression, make his volte-face a surprise. Alison is clearly unhappy and uneasy. All the adults in the novel are unpleasant, class-obsessed and seem to have ruined their lives; the question is whether Gwyn, the bright grammar-school boy, will escape this fate.

This magic is not ravishing but almost wholly unpleasant. The more Alison traces obsessively over the owls on the dinner service, the more she becomes ill. The two boys, who start as friends, are increasingly hostile. Gwyn, through whose eyes we see most of the story, is reminded that he is employed by Roger and Alison's parents in a scene of toe-curling condescension. Gwyn's mother is savagely unkind to her son. The past invades the present, and the ambiguity of the Welsh people and language emphasises it. The build-up of frustration and sinister magic is superbly conveyed in taut sentences and dialogue; only when the flowers fall at the end, releasing Alison from the spell, do we see the lyrical beauty of Garner's prose return.

Yet it is interesting that of the two boys, it is Roger who calls Alison back. Although he is a stepbrother not a blood-brother, he seems to be part of a recurring pattern in Garner's first four books in which the sibling is the one who keeps those afflicted by magic anchored in this world – the still foot of the compass, as it were.

Real life is never as attractive as that promised by magic, or indeed mania. It is fraught with difficulties, and may even take place in a Manchester slum. But it is nevertheless where human beings belong, and Garner's genius is that he conveys the extraordinary, the mythical and the hair-raising with unique conviction, while showing us that it cannot last.

Amanda Craig is the author of six novels, including In a Dark Wood *(short-listed for the MIND Book of the Year Award) and* Hearts and Minds *(long-listed for the Bailey's Prize). Until 2013 she was the Children's Books critic of* The Times. *She reviews literary fiction, non-fiction and children's books for numerous national newspapers and magazines, and is currently finishing her seventh novel,* The Lie of the Land. *She lives in London.*

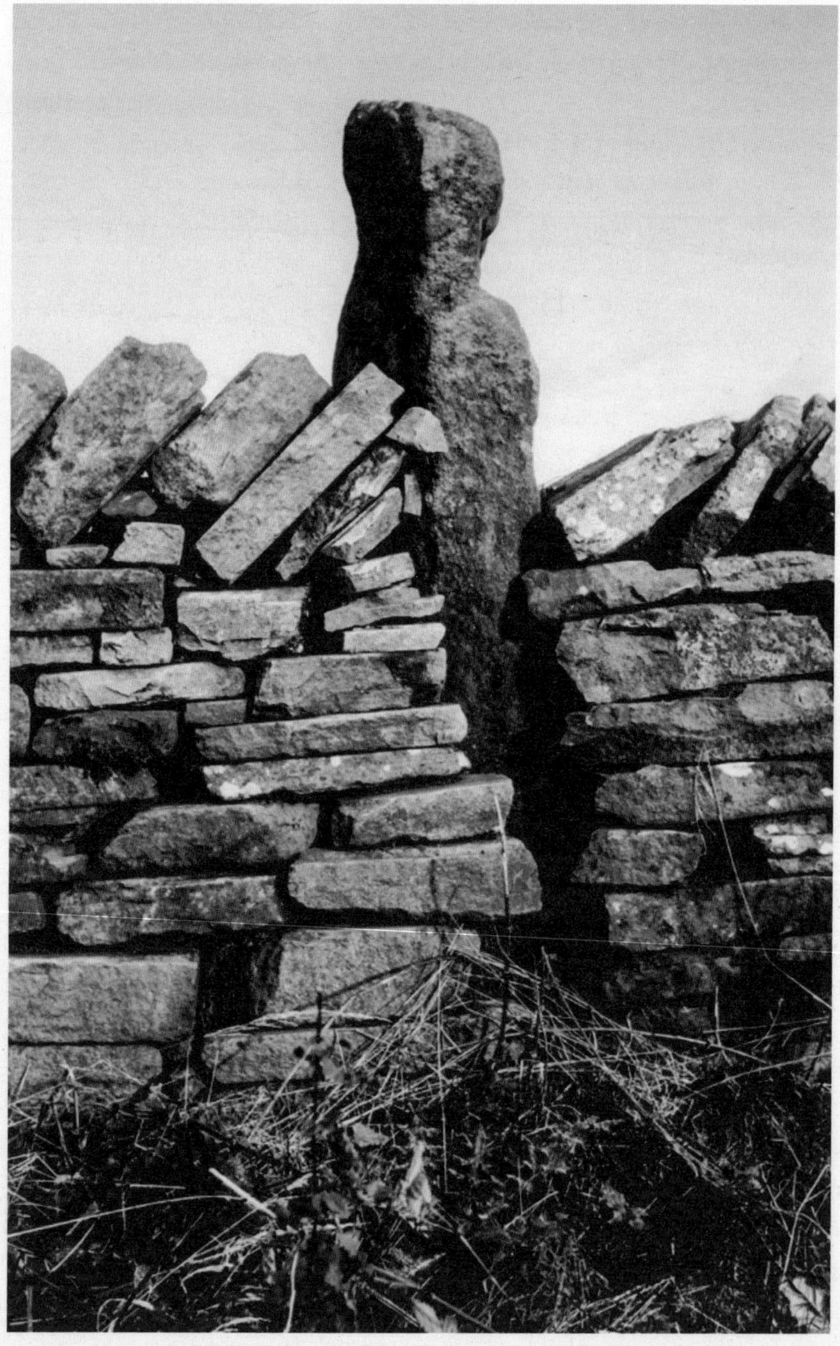

The gatepost without a gate, on the Causeway at Pole Moor.
(Photo © Bob Cywinski)

THE GATEPOST

Bob Cywinski

I found Alan on the Causeway, an ancient unmade track as wide as a road that runs from just behind our house, rising straight and high over Worts Hill before dropping steeply down to meet the Rochdale Road on the moors near Nont Sarah's. He was studying a well-worn irregular millstone grit 'gatepost' that stood in the drystone wall that bordered the Causeway, abruptly interrupting the gently undulating flow of the neat horizontal courses of cleaved Yorkshire stone.

'What is that?' he asked, looking at the 'gatepost'.

'A gatepost?'

'So where is the gate?'

Indeed there was no gate. Nor was there a second gatepost. The drystone wall abutted the vertical monolith on both sides and, on inspection, it appeared that the stone had been in its place long before any wall had been built.

'I think it might be a standing stone,' said Alan. 'It could be medieval or considerably older. There should be others.'

We began to look. Within a few minutes we had found a second similarly shaped stone lying in the grass beside our own gate, not more than 20 feet away from the first. A third was lying the same distance away in the field over the drystone wall by the spring; a fourth standing just across the road serving as one of a pair of gateposts; and a fifth recumbent and hidden in the grassy triangle at the meeting point of the six moorland roads that appear to converge at our house.

It was then that I began to understand why Alan seemed so

happy to visit Pole Moor. Like Blackden, where Alan had lived for so long, this was a special place.

Pole Moor: perched high on the hill over 'Slawit' and the Colne Valley, next to Marsden Moor with its Mesolithic flint workshops in an area devoid of flint, and a few hundred yards from the recently discovered path of the Roman road from Chester to York that twists and turns around Wholestone Moor by the rocking stone before passing the Roman *vicus* and fort of Cambodunum at Slack. Nearby, high on the hill alongside the early coal workings on Worts Hill, the remote eighteenth-century Pole Moor Chapel stands at the convergence of several packhorse routes, one of which crossed over Pole Moor as it made its way from Halifax to Marsden and to Lancashire.

We were also not too far from the place where John Wesley first approached Huddersfield, declaring somewhat unkindly that 'a wilder people I never saw in England'. We had to be wild to cope with the even wilder weather. Weather that always arrives horizontally, chilling our bones and soaking our houses and probably giving us the place name Pole Moor: the wet or marshy moor. Where Alan and I were standing on Laund Road was marginally less wild. A laund, from the Celtic, is a grassy plain or glade, and not many of those were to be found on the high moors, at least before the introduction of nitrogenous fertilisers three-quarters of a century ago.

So, our house was firmly planted on a grassy glade on the moors where six roads converged, watered by a spring and surrounded by standing stones, in an immediate landscape shaped by and preserving ten thousand years of human history. It was a very special place and Alan saw that, and easily convinced me of it, too.

Thanks to Alan my own sense of place had been developing for some time. It had begun almost a decade before when we first visited Blackden, shortly after we had been introduced to Alan by our mutual friend and colleague, the historian and archaeologist, Richard Morris.

Knowing that Sue and I had an interest not just in archaeology but also in what emerging scientific techniques could do for it, Richard had arranged for us to visit Dominic Powlesland at his

Landscape Research Centre in the Vale of Pickering. Alan was also there, and the five of us, an unusual collaboration of two academic physicists and three archaeologists, had a breathtakingly fascinating afternoon that extended well into the evening. We pored over Dominic's extensive geophysical survey of the Vale, with its crescent barrows, pit alignments, Iron Age ribbon developments and Roman villas – all revealed in highly detailed monochrome. We handled Bronze Age Beaker ware. We discussed how neutron scattering and neutron tomography could use the wave-particle duality of the neutron to provide new information on the structure, substance and manufacture of ancient artefacts. And, despite our very different academic backgrounds, or perhaps even because of them, our conversation flowed easily; though all too soon it was time to leave.

Fortunately, a few weeks later, Sue and I were able to continue the conversation, sitting with Alan and Griselda in front of the log fire in the comfortable parlour of medieval Toad Hall. We had been at Blackden all day and our hosts had enthralled and educated us with the history and archaeology of the place and what had been unearthed there. Every period of human history from the Mesolithic to the twentieth century was represented in the finds. Alan carefully explained that the juxtaposition of these finds was not coincidental, but a consequence of the place itself. It was a place that had been chosen carefully by each one of its occupants over millennia, precisely because of its particular location, the lie of the land and the resources, both spiritual and material, that it provided. As much care had been taken over the siting of the Bronze Age barrow found under Toad Hall as that taken in siting the Jodrell Bank radio telescope a few hundred yards across the railway line.

It was clear that Alan did not own this place. The place owned Alan. He was the proud curator, protector and narrator of this special parcel of land and what he told us that day helped us understand that archaeology is about more than what is in the ground. It is about more than the lives of the people that walked upon that ground. It is about the relationship between those people and the ground itself. My sense of place began to gestate.

As we sat around the fire after dinner, Alan and Griselda told us yet more about Toad Hall and its companion, the Old Medicine House, a rescued and very beautiful sixteenth-century timber-frame apothecary's house that had been saved from demolition in 1970 and painstakingly rebuilt at Blackden using the still clear carpenter's marks as an Ikea-like guide to its reconstruction. We spoke about the people who had lived there and their beliefs and superstitions, and about the apotropaic objects and symbols found in the structure of both Toad Hall and the Medicine House. In this context Sue mentioned in passing that she had noticed owl-like figurines throughout Toad Hall and The Medicine House. Perhaps they too were apotropaic. Alan replied simply that he had once written a book about owls, and since then he has been receiving gifts of owls from around the world. The conversation moved on.

Much later that evening, in the car on the way home to Yorkshire, Sue wondered whether Alan might be an ornithologist. However something, somewhere in the deeper recesses of my brain, began to stir uncomfortably. An author of a book about owls living near Alderley Edge? With sudden and embarrassing clarity I realised that our friend Alan Garner – the archaeologist and possible ornithologist – was not just an Alan Garner, but *the* Alan Garner: Alan Garner, the author of *The Owl Service.*

Fortunately the painful embarrassment soon healed. We had become friends with Alan and Griselda because of our shared interests, our respect for each other's ideas and, most importantly, because we simply enjoyed each other's company. Not because we expected to bask in the bright light of a particularly wonderful and world-famous author who happened to share the same name as our new friend.

I realise now that there is a particularly interesting aspect to this friendship between two people that many might consider to represent the extreme and opposing ends of the cultural spectrum.

Almost 60 years ago Alan the author and classicist was taking up residence in Blackden whilst a few hundred yards away that iconic symbol of the excellence of British science, Jodrell Bank's Lovell Telescope, was nearing completion. Although contemporaneous these two events were geographically and, as it transpired, symbolically separated by a railway embankment. Almost simultaneously, and as if in response to this symbolic separation, C.P. Snow was bemoaning the deep and ever growing rift between scientists and 'literary intellectuals' in his lecture entitled 'The Two Cultures'.

Over the decades, C.P. Snow's concerns have metamorphosed into hard prophecy – and his concept of 'Two Cultures' has evolved into dogma. The apparently irreconcilable separation of science and the humanities into two distinct and unrelated intellectual pursuits is almost universally accepted as truth.

Almost.

Because from the moment of our first meeting, it has been very clear that neither Alan nor I respect, or even acknowledge, the wholly imaginary boundaries between these equally important and interwoven threads of our culture.

Around the fire, or over a glass or more of wine, either at Blackden or Pole Moor, our conversations often continue far into the early hours of the morning. They are like gentle waves on a beach, lifting and turning scientific pebbles and artistic shells in equal number as they wash back and forth. Particle physics gives way to the etymology of place names; Roman bronze to special relativity; quantum mechanics to bog people; Gawain to alternative nuclear futures; tachyons to votive offerings; and cosmological red shift to literary *Red Shift*. Alan introduces to me the mythology of Cheshire, of Mow Cop and of Thursbitch, while I tell him of the half-remembered characters from the folklore of Huddersfield, and so we breathe a new life into Walker Treacle, the healer tramp from Holywell Green, who could cure anything but jealousy.

And always we talk of man's place in the landscape, and how, for thousands of years man has shaped that landscape whilst, in turn, it has shaped both his science and his art – from the flint knapping at March Hill, to Bronze Age copper mining at Alderley Edge, and from Celtic stone carvings to Lowry's visions of urban life. We marvel together at how science, art and the landscape were all brought together half a million years ago by an almost-man who expertly shaped a beautiful and beautifully functional Palaeolithic hand-axe and I marvel alone at how this object has itself led to the literary masterpiece that is *Boneland*.

We do not lament the separation of the 'Two Cultures' because for us that separation does not exist. I learned from Alan, and probably he from me, that the intellectual process of creating a novel, and the characters and landscapes within, is almost identical to that which underpins scientific methodology. Both author and physicist seek to create an internally consistent model universe that can be poked and prodded with questions of 'what if?', and if our literary and scientific model universes respond in a way that is externally consistent with our observations of the real universe, we claim success.

Alan and I speak of 'Melting Snow', not as a coded attempt to reconcile science and the humanities – for they do not need reconciliation – but a recognition, demonstration and exploitation of their existing oneness. 'Melting Snow' became a significant thrum in Alan's beautifully woven inaugural Alan Garner Lecture which, as an act of conscious symbolism, was delivered at Jodrell Bank in 2015 to complement, but not contrast with, the Lovell Lecture Series on science. Jodrell Bank, like Alan and me, does not see boundaries.

It was the height of summer when Alan and I looked for the gatepost's companions on the Causeway. Winter comes early on the moors and that winter brought snow which, like all Pole Moor snow, arrived from across the fields in drifts of 10 to 15 feet deep. The gatepost was hidden for weeks but, as the snow melted, I was drawn to it once again. I noticed, for the first time, that a deep, smooth groove had long ago been cut along the full length of its upper surface. A few calculations showed this groove aligns directly with the position of Polaris, not in its current position but where Polaris had been four thousand years ago when men were starting to extract copper from the mines at Alderley Edge.

Is this alignment a coincidence? Very probably.

Am I over interpreting? Definitely.

But, thanks to Alan, I am at least trying hard to understand man's place in the landscape.

Bob Cywinski is a physicist, living on the moors just outside Huddersfield with his partner, Sue, who is also a professor of physics. He studied at Manchester and Salford, and has held professorships at St Andrews, Leeds and Huddersfield Universities and science advisory roles around the globe. He is passionate about public engagement in science, photography and music and has performed at Glastonbury, but unfortunately with nuclear physics rather than with his guitar. In 2015 he was awarded a D.Sc. and Professor Emeritus by the University of Huddersfield.

– GO, IN THE FORM OF A BIRD

Maura Dooley

‘I’m up here and down there . . . which is me? Am I the reflection in the window of me down there?’

The Owl Service: Chapter Fifteen

I glimpse her sometimes,
the girl whose face was made of flowers.

Summertime without school,
days shook their wings,
and the room was full of petals.

In search of mystery
I emptied the dresser of
Aynsley, Willow, Burleigh,
too familiar to be magical,
Doulton, a garland of blooms:
none of them right.

On scraps of paper I traced
the transferred patterns of
broom, meadowsweet, flowers of the oak,

a flutter of shreds
caught and coloured,
concentration, incantation,
breath and a wish for breath
for change, for transformation.

Summertime without school
and petals, flowers falling.
Today, my daughters, growing,
are a sweet absence in the house,
and all about them a fragrance,
tawny shriek of girlhood,
flight of silverbrown feathers,
rumpled bedclothes, a swinging door,
the trace of something efflorescent in the air.

Daughters in Summertime,
their faces fresh as may blossom.

Summertime without school
my days were fullempty
not knowing then what I waited for

– the feathers to scatter,
and petals to fall like breadcrumbs
as I made my way through the forest.

Maura Dooley's most recent collection of poetry is Life Under Water. *Anthologies she has edited include* The Honey Gatherers: Love Poems *and* How Novelists Work. *A new book of poems,* The Silvering, *will be published in 2016. She was recently Poet-in-Residence at the Jane Austen House Museum, Chawton. Her poems from the residency are published as a pamphlet:* A Quire of Paper. *She teaches at Goldsmiths, University of London and is a Fellow of the Royal Society of Literature.*

THE OWL SERVICE: CROSSING THE THRESHOLD

Helen Dunmore

> '. . . She is hurt too much she wants to be flowers and you make her owls and she is at the hunting –'

When I first read *The Owl Service*, in my teens, it seemed to be all about barriers. The story takes place in a valley hemmed in by mountains. To leave the valley is difficult, dangerous, sometimes impossible. As the novel opens a young girl is confined to bed, and in the loft above her something potent and magical is locked away. The bolt is rusted in and painted over. No one has been up there for years. In the billiard room an exquisite life-sized wall painting of a woman clothed in flowers has been hidden behind pebble-dash. Immediately it becomes clear that the dynamic of the novel involves the uncovering of what has long been concealed, and also that this uncovering is in itself a force that will propel all the characters into places where they have never been or wanted to go.

There is a brilliantly airless quality to the opening of *The Owl Service*. No one has room to breathe, because each character must tiptoe up to the barrier set up by another, test it, retreat. The language of the novel – and language itself – embodies further barriers. The Welsh language is a subterranean current that informs every word spoken by the Welsh characters, even when they are using English. Welsh is also used very deliberately as a means of preventing the

English characters from understanding, and as a means of asserting that there are realities here which cannot be 'put into English'. The language barrier defeats translation until the very end of the book. Huw Half-Bacon's lyrical, hypnotic invocations are not understood, but are taken as evidence that he is eccentric, possibly deranged. Nancy rages at her son Gwyn for using Welsh when she wants him to use English. Clues are missed and evidence is misplaced because the characters so often use language not to communicate with others but to separate themselves. Clive, for example, attempts to explain away the tensions within the household by using a register of suburban English which is often comically out of place: 'A fiver cures most things. She's dead set against some plates or other – I didn't understand what any of it was about.'

Clive also embodies the theme of class that is so vital to the novel, because it sets up boundaries between the characters which substitute anger, resentment and pretence for understanding. Nancy and Huw Half-Bacon hide their complex, violent past behind a façade of servility. Nancy is also a snob who finds Clive wanting because he is a self-made businessman, not a gentleman. The mysterious unseen Margaret, Alison's mother, spies on the family and dictates proper behaviour to her daughter. She mocks her husband's former wife, the 'Birmingham Belle', and disrupts the growing relationship between Alison and Gwyn as much as she can, on no other grounds than class.

Clive at first appears somewhat of a caricature, failing to see what is under his nose and smoothing over difficulties with money and bluff good humour. However, he is a more subtle character than at first appears, and his task is a complex one: he wants to draw together the disparate fragments of two families broken by divorce, dissolve the barriers between them, and make them one. 'And it is the first time we've all been together – as a family, and … and … you know?' The mystery of why he has married Margaret is never quite solved, and there is a comical element to her persistent absence. Forever resting, sunbathing or spying on the rest of the family, she lurks behind the barriers she has set for herself and alone of all the characters undergoes no change during the course of the novel.

As the novel progresses, barriers do begin to dissolve, but not in the way that Clive hopes. Past and present are no longer separate, but instead they revolve together in an obsessive and repetitive waltz of destruction, tuned to the noise of a motorbike, the thud of a spear or the scratching of an owl's claws. Alison is pinioned by this dissolution of time: 'Nothing's safe any more. I don't know where I am. "Yesterday", "today", "tomorrow" – they don't mean anything. I feel they're here at the same time: waiting.'

The whole novel is in one sense an argument for setting bounds on the past. Long before the phrase 'post-traumatic stress' was common currency, Alan Garner explored in *The Owl Service* the way that intense, tragic events affect generations because they go on recurring in flashback, unresolved and invincible. The death of Bertram on his motorbike refuses to be 'held' within the past and Nancy's bitterness over the loss of her lover is as acrid as it ever was. Huw Half-Bacon and his ancestors have been locked into an unsuccessful struggle to set a boundary against what they perceive as their doom. They cannot prevent a vengeful, bloody love triangle from forming and re-forming. The spear that kills Gronw still whistles through the air centuries later; except that 'centuries' are not a reality when the past refuses to be divided from the present.

So while Garner suggests that some barriers are meant to be broken – for example, the barriers of class or those thrown up by misunderstanding – there are others which must be in place if human existence is to be fruitful. The past must become truly the past, and it can only do so if there is a redemptive alteration of destructive patterns. When Roger deliberately chooses to break out of the circle of abuse by accepting Gwyn's abuse of his mother, he frees not only himself but also Alison and Gwyn. Alison is rescued not by a dramatic or knightly gesture, but by the crossing of a more intimate threshold. Adolescent boys fear ridicule and loss of face, and in accepting Gwyn's insult, Roger liberates in himself the necessary tenderness that will turn owls to flowers.

Reading and rereading *The Owl Service* over the years, I've come to believe that it is as much about thresholds as it is about barriers. Gwyn longs to escape the confines of the narrow future envisaged for him by his mother, but for most of the novel he beats himself against closed doors, becoming more and more furious with himself and everyone else. He cannot cross the threshold alone, and at the climax of the novel he refuses to do so. But because Roger does succeed in crossing the threshold to maturity, then Gwyn too can be healed. Huw is still repeating the mantra of doom '... and so without end without end without end ...' but Roger has reached another place as he says to Alison: 'You're not birds. You're flowers. You've never been anything else. Not owls. Flowers. That's it. Don't fret.'

In these short, simple sentences Roger becomes Alison's brother. At this moment Gwyn is effaced, although throughout the novel he has been the most vivid of the three adolescents. He cannot break through the spell of his own inherited trauma. Someone else must do this on his behalf, not by force or magic, but by growing up and out of the story.

The Owl Service begins with an adolescent girl lying in bed with a 'bellyache', which some commentators have interpreted as the onset of her first period and the threshold of sexual maturity. In this passage Alison embodies both major themes of the novel: she is restricted and confined, but at the same time she is undergoing a liberation as she crosses into a new stage of life. When the novel ends, the same girl is lying on a table, covered with Huw's jacket, her flesh scored by owl's claws and her body covered with feathers. She is victim, sacrifice and live, terrified girl. Huw Half-Bacon cannot help her with his fatalism, and neither can Gwyn, who is full of hate. The three of them are transfixed within the myth and it looks as if the cycle is going to turn yet again. The 'woman made of flowers' who has taken over Ali's existence is also the 'woman made of owls' who will destroy it. Her myth has lorded it over a valley and its individual lives for generations, and while Garner gives full weight to the beauty of this myth he never romanticises it. The valley is infertile. The emotional lives of Huw and Nancy are stunted, and they look all set to stunt the next generation in Gwyn. But at this key moment comes Roger's intervention and the cycle is broken. *The Owl Service* can now end on a note of victorious lyricism as it returns to the source of the Blodeuwedd myth, unmaking and returning to her elements the woman made out flowers for the sole purpose of satisfying a man.

'And the room was full of petals from skylight and rafters, and all about them a fragrance, and petals, flowers falling, broom, meadowsweet, falling, flowers of the oak.'

The most extraordinary thing about this extraordinary book is that while it gives to myth every ounce of the power and enchantment that is its due, it also suggests that sometimes myth must be unmade. It may be a threshold that must be crossed, if the human is to flourish. This is the triumphantly liminal quality of *The Owl Service*, and what makes it a novel to read and reread for a lifetime.

Helen Dunmore is a poet, novelist, short story and children's writer. Her novels include Zennor in Darkness, *awarded the McKitterick Prize;* A Spell of Winter, *awarded the inaugural Orange Prize and* The Siege, *shortlisted for the Whitbread Novel of the Year Award and the Orange Prize. Her 2010 novel* The Betrayal *was shortlisted for the Orwell Prize. Her poetry collections have won the Alice Hunt Bartlett Award and the Signal Award; her poem 'The Malarkey' won the National Poetry Competition. She is a Fellow of the Royal Society of Literature and her work is translated into more than 30 languages. Her latest novel,* The Lie, *was shortlisted for the Ondaatje Prize and the Walter Scott Prize.*

POSSESSIONS

Mark Edmonds

Alan's writing grabbed me when I was 12 or so. Awkward and inarticulate (me, not the books), I escaped into his novels in the way I did when reading about Odysseus and Fionn mac Cumhaill, or when following the exploits of Dan Dare and The Amazing Wilson. But there was something about Alan's work that made me follow him through the library and out into the hills. His novels had a mythic quality, but they were rooted in a world that I knew. And they hinted at a depth to the landscape, a numen, which seemed to matter even if I didn't fully understand it. Something I tried to catch a glimpse of on the walks that carried me through the school holidays. Then I found *Red Shift*, and my familiar landmarks were pulled into shadow.

I didn't get it first time round, not properly. I wasn't used to dialogue doing so much work, or the bitter honesty with which human frailties and relationships were handled. Things left unsaid or unresolved, things that mattered. It was shocking. What I do remember is that time made sense in a way it never had before. Not as succession but as a collapsing of ongoing moments, a now in which past and present were combined. And then there was the needle that pulled those threads together, a strange stone axe with a weight beyond measure. Time and the stone didn't grab me; they found me.

When I eventually stumbled into the archaeology of landscape, Alan was on the reading lists I gave my students. By then there was a lot more grist in the mill, *The Stone Book Quartet*, *Strandloper* and

Thursbitch – the latter perhaps the closest thing to a sibling for *Red Shift*. And all of them brought home just what it meant to belong to country. Landscape was not just out there, an object held in distanced regard. It was a story learnt by heart, on the move and around the hearth. A narrative with depth and with darkness too, told as much by the land itself as by those who worked across it. From the Dreamtime of Australia to the Rough Magic of William Buckley's Cheshire, *Strandloper* maps the common spiritual ground where kinship with the trail meets affinity with one's own square mile. In *Thursbitch*, where time folds back upon itself and memory seems so grounded, the world beyond the valley still washes in on convoluted currents; even the most stubborn boundaries are permeable. Alan's argument was both simple and seismic. The landscape is not a book, with chapters layered neatly one upon another. So it needs writing that takes seriously the poetics of our involvement in the world.

But what about that axe? Alan is one of our most eminent writers of place, working with language that is almost a part of the geology to which he belongs. Yet in all of his work, objects play powerful roles. In *Red Shift*, the axe is the votive weapon that flips Macey to another state of being; the thunderstone that Thomas Rowley gives to Margery; the 'Bunty' that Tom and Jan find up the cottage chimney on Mow Cop. Three times, three couples, pulled in by the gravity of the thing. It's a powerful presence, all the more so because it has deep roots. Long before it fell into Macey's second-century hands, the Bunty was a blade, a protection and a weight to give relationships duration. It is the product of a tradition with roots in the Neolithic, when axes were tokens of identity and value as much as they were tools. Even then, they were turning and talking in the hand, and even then, they could be thunderbolts. Some of the most dramatic and well travelled axes that we have from that time were pulled down from the clouds, from precipitous quarries near the tops of mountains. The links to lightning that lit up medieval and later imaginations have very deep roots indeed. And all of that brought into focus by the handling of the blade, the cold weight of it, the turning of it over and again upon itself. Handling that brings a story into focus, about the name of the stone and the hands through which it has passed. Throughout *Red Shift* it is the heft of the axe that matters. That is what makes Tom's decision so traumatic. When he sends the Bunty to the glass-bound oblivion of the British Museum – 'You can go and see it. It has a label and everything.' – the connection is broken.

It isn't just a matter of time. The *longue durée* may give certain things their weight, but so does travel, and objects shift their shape and meaning as they move. Tricksters taking advantage of each new pair of hands to turn a different face to the world. It's a kind of Chinese whispers that Alan's made good use of in his work, and in this he's in good company. Many of our oldest stories are full of objects that gain potency from the journeys they've made. *The Odyssey*, *Beowulf*, the *Orkneyinga Saga*, they all bristle with things changed by their passage from one world to another. Like Jack's 'Whizzler' in *Thursbitch* or the 'Swaddledidaff' in *Strandloper*. Drawn from the rainbow, the Swaddledidaff's a gift from Het to Will, their special stone that holds them: '. . . from me to thee'. When William is transported to Australia, the stone goes with him. But once there it is transformed, part of the dreaming that recognises William as Murrangurk, an aboriginal elder returned from the dead. When he finally comes back to Cheshire, to find that Het has moved on, the crystals lose their light. The stone has become a 'lifeless wallung'.

Like the Bunty, the Swaddledidaff is a protagonist. It moves the story forward and has an involvement, a responsibility, in what happens to the people it collects along the way. And when the thing is done, when the relationship is over? Well, the stone moves on, falls from the hand and back into the flow of things. Waiting for another chance to reconcile the brief span of a life with the deeper field of cosmological time. For a discipline obsessed with origins, Alan's handling of the way that objects play with time is little short of revelatory. Archaeologists divide the past up into slices and specialise within the close horizons that their periods create. But like the landscape, artefacts stubbornly refuse to stay in the boxes that we make for them. They have biographies that run from then to now, and some of them will still be collecting people long after we have gone. These afterlives are as much a part of their story as

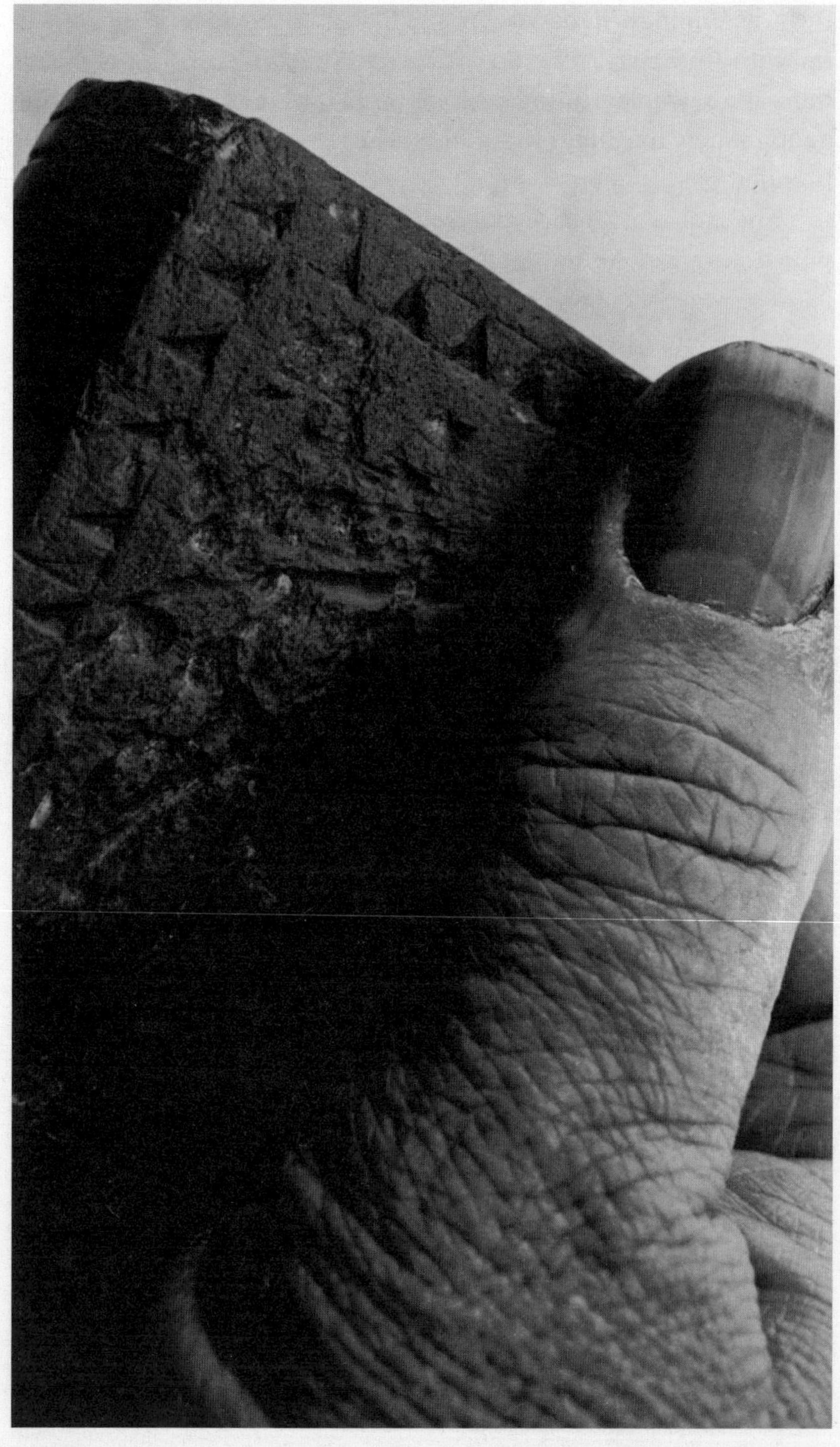

their beginnings. It has taken a while for the discipline to catch up with this. But as we do, we're finding that even in prehistory, there were people pausing, picking up old stone and making it anew, giving it new meanings to suit their time. Passing on the story of the thunderbolts.

The archaeological literature has yet to match the clarity with which Alan gets the argument across. And that's a real challenge, because we generally deal with stuff that gets taken for granted, with the clutter that shapes our lives without us even noticing. That is what makes *The Stone Book Quartet* so remarkable. Just as it distils what it means to be owned by land, so it also catches how we tell the stories of our lives through the tools we make, the tokens we exchange and the stuff that hangs around. Through the possessions that possess us. It even manages to blur the line between our bodies and the things we use; in the rhythm of a task, in the practised lifting of a stone or in the flicking of dust from a swage block. Identity shaped by habits we are hardly aware of. That this comes across so powerfully here is in no small part because the material is drawn from the Garner family chest. Even so, each book catches with poetic clarity the quiet guidance of small things forgotten.

The way this works across the four novellas is deceptively simple. Four generations, down 80 years or so, each one seen from the vantage of girls and boys trying to understand their place in the world. Through them we see how understanding comes from learning how to work, from polishing a skill with stone or metal, or in settling to the rhythm of the loom. To work 'without waste and easily' is to know where and who you are. That learning takes many forms. In *The Stone Book*, Mary watches her father make his mark upon the stone he sets – always at the back or on the bed, save once. She sees the mark again in the cave that only children can reach; the bull, the hand, the time behind the simple lines. 'We pass it on.' In *Granny Reardun*, when Joseph chooses the path of a 'hammerman', his hesitancy in taking the first step has little to do with his aptitude for the 'art, craft and mystery of the forge'. What matters is his obligation to his grandfather, and to the stone that Robert is a part of. It is only when he sees their connection, in chisel mark and weathercock, that he fully understands. Metal is not asking him to turn his back; it just wants him to know where and how he fits. Once he does, it's down to the anvil with a barrel.

These are signal moments, an object, a mark or a material snapping sharply into focus. But there are many other things that we only catch a glimpse of: the clay pipe returned as a gift to the earth, the bobbins and discarded threads, the fittings of the home where Mary sits and watches as her father pulls a Bible from a pebble. Like the donkey stone and the cornet in *Granny Reardun*, and the clock in *The Aimer Gate*, objects fall in and out of our attention, carried from one book to another almost without us noticing. And it is precisely because they are taken for granted that they resonate. They are part of the fabric that a child recognises as home, the hammer that rings down across the years. They're the clock that keeps the Hough in step or the instrument around which the community sometimes dances. A community that also finds itself in mutual patterns of work, those moments when it all just clicks; when scythes move 'back and to, back and to' in line, while others pull the fallen stalks together in their wake.

For the bull in the cave, 80 years isn't even a blink. But across that span we get a vivid evocation of simple objects shaping people and drawing one generation into another. An arrow in the steeple, a key worn thin, a pipe in the garden. Pulled down from the chimney or more properly handed on, some things hold their stories. Others get forgotten or remade. Memory only keeps so long as there's someone to apply a bit of polish or to trace a carved line in the darkness. It's this mix of remembering and forgetting that is so persuasive. And nowhere is that brought home more clearly than at the end of *Tom Fobble's Day*, when William has a sledge made for him by his grandfather, Joseph. The frame and rails are a composite of the forge that Joseph has stepped back from, and the loom used by William's namesake many years before. As he flies full tilt downslope, it all condenses. 'There was a line and he could feel it. It was a line through hand and eye, block, forge and loom to the hill. He owned them all: and they owned him.' It is only a moment, but it is enough.

I began this essay by describing how the stone axe found me

when I first fell into *Red Shift*. That sounds like an origin myth if ever there was one. In fact, I'd had my moment in the Pitt Rivers Museum, a year or so before I read the book; that may be why it struck such a chord. And it resonates still, as do all the novels that I've mentioned here. Read for pleasure and for inspiration, Alan's work is some of the most profoundly archaeological writing that I can think of. By which I mean that it is profound and that it bears the hallmark of careful archaeological research. But where many archaeologists are content to document the process of recovery and description, Alan takes this as his point of departure. It has to ring true to the materials, that much is given. But archaeology is an act of the imagination, a creative bringing of the past into the present, and there are very few who work that magic more powerfully than he does. It's a function of the language, the place-specific dialect and the craft of writing that makes poetry of the prose. But it's ultimately about the landscapes that Alan takes us into. Landscapes that are close-grained but never simply period pieces. There's a darkness, born of inequality and suffering, that we catch in glimpses of evictions, hard graft, disease and transportation. There's the tangle that connects his communities to currents turning round the world, the interwoven biographies of people and materials. Things are never just local. And at the back of all of this, there's our relationship with time. The time that people make in the pattern of their lives, the time of memory and that other, sublime and properly terrifying sense that keeps us awake at night. Catching all of that in the weight of a stone, as Alan does in *Boneland*, takes us to the heart of what it is to be human.

Mark Edmonds is Emeritus Professor of Archaeology at the University of York. He has published a number of books on prehistory and on the archaeology of landscape, and has a particular interest in arts-based approaches to interpretation. His most recent book, The Beauty Things, *is a collaboration with Alan Garner. He lives in Orkney.*

OF THE EARTH, EARTHY . . .

Stephen Fry

Was I ten or eleven when my favourite godmother sent me *The Weirdstone of Brisingamen* for my birthday? In her card she told me that she knew the author and that she believed I would enjoy it. She spoke a mouthful.

Deep in the Norfolk countryside one late summer, then, I curled up in bed with this strangely titled book. I was entirely and permanently captivated and read the whole thing through in one go. I believe the first feeling that overwhelmed me was one of being trusted. At no stage did the writer of this story explain to me what I was supposed to feel, or what was the meaning of the story I was reading. I was somehow almost as collusive in the adventure as Susan the Stonemaiden and Colin her brother. The narrative was complex and the good and the bad were not as clearly delineated as I was used to, but the language was simple and exquisitely accurate, nailing every detail with the precision of poetry.

More followed: *The Moon of Gomrath* (a sequel to *The Weirdstone*), *The Owl Service* and my favourite, *Red Shift*. When I came across fellow Garnerites at school and elsewhere, I discovered that we all believed ourselves to be members of a very fine and exclusive club. Fine because something in this author's writing and storytelling made us better, more observant and watchful people and exclusive, I suppose, because we couldn't help hugging ourselves for being in on this Great Secret. I felt the same about another scandalously undersung literary figure, Russell Hoban.

One of Alan Garner's most lauded qualities is the deep and

abiding connection in his works to the land of England. That splendid world 'chthonic' could have been coined for him. Out of the soil emerge power, life, vitality – and danger, too. Like Cadmus, Garner sowed seeds in the earth and horses, soldiers, creatures, wizards, dwarfs, living plants sprang forth. His use of a real, living, Google Earth-able landscape – the Edge in Cheshire – might at first glance seem risky. So parochial (literally so, for the Edge covers a scattering of parishes) a setting might limit the scope and reach of the stories. Far from it, of course: the authentic local detail makes everything credible and all the more universal.

Alan Garner gave me the ability to look at the land and natural world around me with new eyes. All my excitement and attention hitherto had been devoted to the world of Greek gods and heroes. I had never known that there were stories and creatures all around in dull old England. Garner awoke me and countless other children to the inner life of the earth and the inner life of the imagination. His precise, perfect writing and fiercely intelligent and knowledgeable mind showed me what writing could do and I cannot think how I could ever repay him. Or my dear godmother, of course.

Stephen Fry is an English actor, screenwriter, author, playwright, journalist, poet, comedian, television presenter, and film director. His acting roles include Jeeves in Jeeves and Wooster, *with Hugh Laurie, the lead in the film* Wilde, *Melchett in the BBC television series* Blackadder *and many more. He has written and presented several documentary series, including the Emmy Award-winning* Stephen Fry: The Secret Life of the Manic Depressive, *and is also the long-time host of the BBC television quiz show* QI. *In addition to all this, much more and everything else, he has written four novels and three volumes of autobiography,* Moab Is My Washpot, The Fry Chronicles *and his latest,* More Fool Me.

STORYTELLERS, SHAPESHIFTERS . . .

Cornelia Funke

Cornelia Funke is a prizewinning author and illustrator. A former social worker, who supports many children's charities around the world, she tells her stories for all ages – as storytellers do – and both for book-eaters and those who don't succumb easily to printed magic. She is the author of Dragon Rider, Thief Lord, *the* Inkworld *trilogy and the* MirrorWorld *series. She lives in Los Angeles, California, in a house full of books, but she mostly works outside, surrounded by hummingbirds, toads and dragonflies. Not forgetting Marley and Mozart, her Alexandrian parakeets.*

THE WORLD AND THE WORLDS: SOME MUSINGS AND TWO BOOK REVIEWS

Neil Gaiman

It all started with *Elidor*, for me. I do not think I understood how important *Elidor* was at the time. I was seven. *Elidor* was not my favourite book. It was barely on the shelf of books I loved, but it changed the way I saw the world. I mean this, without exaggeration and without poetry.

Until then, when I encountered fantasy it was discrete: fantastic worlds were accessible through a portal, be it a wardrobe or a mirror, but the world was the world and the fantasy was the fantasy. It was contained. You could travel to Narnia, but you did not have to fear that Narnia would come for you. There was a gulf between here and there. People like me in stories were not like me: they were Victorians or Americans, they lived in another time and another place, and moments of recognition were far and few.

I had never been to Manchester, but the world in which *Elidor* was set was a place and, just as importantly, a time that I understood. It felt real, it felt like it was a story happening to real people and happening now. I had known what an abandoned building was like, to walk in, to explore. Now I knew that I could encounter a unicorn there, that the gap between the world I knew and the worlds I did not understand, was paper-thin, dust-thin. It was urban fantasy before anyone knew that we needed our fantasies to be set, sometimes, in the fields and streets and back alleys we knew.

I went from *Elidor* to a borrowed copy of *The Weirdstone of Brisingamen*: I loved it and its sequel, *The Moon of Gomrath*, but they felt familiar: they were set in caves and woods and on high hills. I already knew that there was magic in the Earth, that landscape was enchanted already. (*The Owl Service* and *Red Shift*, read a few years later, were too grown up for me. I read them, and wished, in each case, that I hadn't: I knew that they were stories I would have to come back to when I was ready for them, on the other side of puberty, when the puzzling adult emotions would finally make sense to me.)

There are moments without which we literally would not exist, we would not be ourselves: we would be other people, who would look the same, but with a different inner landscape, with different dreams and hopes and, most importantly, different ways of looking at the world. There are alternate universes in which I became excited by numbers, or by the texture of paint, or by death, and became another kind of writer entirely, or something that was not a writer at all. Reading *Elidor* was one of those moments for me.

The freight of fantasy is the freight of the unrevealed. When it is at its most powerful, it shows us the world we know through another's eyes, in a way that we can never unsee. Garner's eyes and his ability to build a bridge in his fiction that takes us there and back again: these show us the shape of what is unrevealed, of what lies under the covers or is buried beneath the ground. Some car parks, after all, are the burial places of kings.

I've been fortunate enough to write publicly about Alan Garner's work twice now. I discussed his *Collected Folk Tales* for the *Guardian*, and *Boneland*, the final book in the sequence that began with *The Weirdstone of Brisingamen*, in *The Times*.

Boneland was, to put it mildly, a surprise. *The Moon of Gomrath* had always felt like the second book in a trilogy, and Garner had previously stated in interviews that he had thought about writing another book, but found that he no longer cared for his protagonists, had learned too much as a writer, and did not want to go back. I did not know what to think when I heard he had written the third book. And then I read it, and thought, He didn't write the third book. He wrote the one after that.

This is what I wrote:

BONELAND

Over 50 years ago Alan Garner wrote *The Weirdstone of Brisingamen* and its sequel, *The Moon of Gomrath*, two books of magic and myth, featuring the children Colin and Susan. They encounter a wizard who guards sleepers beneath the hills – Arthur and his knights, perhaps – sleepers who will wake to save us in our time of greatest need. The children encounter elves and dwarfs, goblins and killer cats, battle the evil shape-shifting Morrigan, and make their way through a patchwork of mythic events and battles, culminating, at the end of *The Moon of Gomrath*, with a Herne-like Hunter and his men riding their horses to meet the nine sisters of the Pleiades – leaving Susan, who needed to be with them, behind, wanting to go the stars, and Colin only to watch.

(There are well-drawn characters in those books, but they are not Colin or Susan. And the landscape of Alderley Edge is the strongest character.)

Garner continued creating mythic fantasy out of the matter of Britain, building, reimagining and recreating tales from the *Mabinogion* and from a hundred other sources, and then he began writing novels intended for adults, stories hewn and chipped from the past. (The past is always with us in Garner. The stones have stories.)

There was to be a third novel of Colin and Susan, but for 50 years Garner did not write it.

In *Boneland*, he also does not write it, although he describes it, implies it, tells us its shape. Instead he gives us, what? A fourth book? A coda? Either way, it is an adult novel about loss and history and memory and mind, a link between the present and prehistory, a place where everything Garner has made before comes together.

Colin has grown up to be a brilliant, but extremely troubled, astrophysicist. Susan is not there. Colin is autistic, has problems with memory (he remembers everything after the age of 13, nothing before), cannot relate to other humans, is searching the sky for intelligent life, and hunting for his sister in the stars. As the book begins he is being released from a hospital after some kind of breakdown.

Boneland is a realistic novel of landscape, inner and outer, past and present. It becomes a novel of the fantastic toward the end: perhaps old magics have risen to show Colin the way out, perhaps he has conjured them himself as he confronts his demons and his pain. I do not know if the conclusion of this book makes sense if you have not read the first two books, and I am not entirely certain whether reading the first two books will make it easier to read this one. *Boneland* demands a lot of the reader, either way. But it returns more than it demands.

The characters are well drawn – Meg, the too-good-to-be-true therapist and Bert, the salt-of-the-earth taxi driver, linger in the memory long after the book is done. The Watcher, who provides the novel's alternate point of view, gazing out from the caves of prehistory, gives us an affecting and powerful look at a mind ten thousand years away, and a way of looking at the world that is not ours, or Colin's. As the Watcher story intersects with Colin's story, the *Weirdstone* novels also conclude (although they conclude in negative space, as if we are seeing the after-effects of events in a book unwritten) and Colin's story concludes with them.

Trying to express how and why Alan Garner is important is difficult. He does not write easy books. His children's books were powerful and popular, but never simple or comforting; his adult novels are lonely explorations of present and past. He is a master of taking the material of history, whether myths and stories or landscapes and artefacts, and building tales around them that feel, always, ultimately, right – as if, yes, this was how things were, this is how things are. He is a matter-of-fact fantasist, who builds his fantasies solid and real. *Boneland* feels like the book you write when you can no longer muster the belief in magic to write about elves and wizards in caves, but you can write about the older magics, the flint knapping workings of ancient times, and you can believe in the power of the mind, and the crags and caves and outcrops, you can believe in the landscape, because the landscape is always there. And you can still believe in sleepers under hills, believe in the legend of the wizard buying a horse that began *The Weirdstone of Brisingamen*.

The words Garner chooses, carves, inserts into his prose are perfect. He deploys short, accurate words better than anyone else writing in English today, and he makes it look simple.

Boneland is the strangest, but also the strongest, of Alan Garner's books. It feels like a capstone to a career that has taken him, as a writer, to remarkable places, and returned him to the same place he started, to the landscape of Alderley Edge and to the sleepers under the hill.

. . .

I don't review many books. I know that I ought to, because literature is a process of conversation with itself, and if the people who are making books don't talk publicly about the books they read and what they think, then the conversation dies. But there is never enough time to write about books, and there are always other things that need to be written.

But then the *Collected Folk Tales* arrived, and brought back with it a forgotten slice of my childhood, and I wanted to talk about what this book was, and why it was good. After all, I remembered reading *The Hamish Hamilton Book of Goblins*. I could even remember where in the library I sat, when I read it.

COLLECTED FOLK TALES

'There was a hill that ate people,' begins the first story. Just like that. No room for argument or dissent.

'Far away, and a long time ago, on a high mountain, without trees for shelter, without body or arms for anything, on spindly legs, ran Great Head,' begins another story.

We are in the realm of folk tales, where we are told what happened, and we must simply go along with it. We have no other option.

There is something of the national treasure about Alan Garner. He has been writing excellent books for more than 50 years. He was, I suspect, the first person to write what now we would describe as Urban Fantasies. He is, moreover, a remarkable writer – his prose at its best (and it is pretty much always at its best) seems inevitable, and pushes reviewers into using similes that compare Garner's words to rocks and gorges and unchanging natural formations.

My experience reading the *Collected Folk Tales* was peculiar: there was a feeling of happy familiarity from the first, a peculiar *déjà vu*, as if I knew them, these stories, some of them intimately. My assumption as I read was that I had encountered most of them in other forms and other places (folk tales are told and retold, after all), but then, when I finished reading, I looked at the copyright page, and realised that over half of the stories had been published in 1969, as *A Hamish Hamilton Book of Goblins*, and I thought, yes. I could remember the cover. I read it when I was nine, and reread it often, and was glad I had. I could remember it in my local library, remembered taking it off to a quiet corner and reading it, remembered how much I had loved it (and how much I loved Ruth Manning-Sanders's folk tales with their Brian Jacques illustrations as well). And the *Book of Goblins* had been a Puffin book, too, and they had it in my school library.

It is peculiar to encounter a book half of which was assembled up to 40 years after the rest and not to be able to see any obvious difference in the writing or the writer. The prose in the old stories feels as inevitable as the new. The stories, old and new, are written in a variety of voices, emulating the places the tales came from, but the prose is always spare and hard, not a word wasted, not a word out of place.

Here we have stories from Britain and Ireland and all over the world, retold with assurance. Some of the high points that were not in the original collection include 'The Flying Children', a story of lies and sex and supernatural revenge and murder I had first encountered in Neil Philip's *Penguin Book of English Folktales*. It is a story that makes authors want to retell it (I fell in love and shoehorned it into *Sandman*) and a tale Garner calls 'Iram Biram', which Neil Philip called 'The Pear Drum' when he collected it as a folk tale, and which is a curiosity in itself, because it began as a nightmarish Victorian short story by Lucy Clifford called 'The New Mother'. Garner strips it down to its elements. It's an act of literary ventriloquism that illuminates the oral and folk tradition. Two girls named Blue-Eyes and Turkey are tempted by a wild girl to be naughty, with the promise of a gift of a mysterious 'pear drum'. They are not naughty enough to get the drum, but are still so naughty that their mother leaves, and a new mother comes in her place.

Lucy Clifford's story ends with the children living out on the moor, occasionally looking into the window of their old house, where . . .

> '. . . still the New Mother stays in the little cottage, but the windows are closed and the doors are shut and no one knows what the inside looks like. Now and then, when the darkness has fallen, Blue-Eyes and Turkey creep up near to the home in which they once were so happy and with beating hearts, they watch and listen; sometimes a blinding flash comes through the window and they know it is the light from the New Mother's glass eyes; or they hear a strange, muffled noise and they know it is the sound of her wooden tail as she drags it along the floor.'

It's a literary voice. The Neil Philip *English Folktales* version, collected in 1955, ends:

> 'There were no lamps lit, but in the glow of the firelight they could see through the window the glitter of their new mother's glass eyes and hear the thump of her wooden tail.'

Same story, but reduced to its essentials. Garner takes that ending and goes beyond it, first taking the tale into the oral tradition, playing with the sound and the meaning of words:

> 'There were no lamps lit, but in the glow of the fire they saw through the window the glitter glitter green glass of

a mother's eye. They heard the thump; thump; thump of a wooden tail.

> 'Iram, biram, brendon bo
> Where did all the children go?
> They went to the east, they went to the west
> They went where the cuckoo has its nest.
> Iram. Biram. Brendon. Bo.
>
> And the Wild Girl wept.'

Garner makes up a poem, and adds the haunting image of the Wild Girl weeping as a way of closing the tale, and moves it somewhere entirely new, away from Victorian nursery horror and into the realm of the twice-told tale.

The book itself has a core of Goblin Stories (but a goblin can be anything, and Garner's own preferences seem to be for moments of the inexplicable. So many of the stories lack explanation for the events in them, as if the stories are the lyrics of folk songs, and the true meaning is in the music). There is an essay in here on the roots of the fairy folk, and who they really were, or might have been. There are a few dialect pieces, written, Garner says, in the voice of his blacksmith grandfather. There are poems – some collected from Anon. and the dead, others by Garner himself – my favourite being 'R.I.P.', which begins:

> 'A girl in our village makes love in the churchyard.
> She doesn't mind who, but it must be the churchyard . . .'

and continues, lusty and honest to its bitter-hopeful end.

There is a telling of Valmiki's *Ramayana* in this book, the inclusion of which, we learn, guarantees Mr Garner his place in heaven. And there are Norse Gods, and Algonquin revenge magic, and a hero's odyssey from Ireland to a series of magical islands.

This *Collected Folk Tales* is, by definition and by temperament, a patchwork, and reading it is like entering a rag and bone shop in which every object has been polished up and repaired and made fit for use, while always leaving in the cracks and dents that show that the goods have had years of use already. With the exception of some of the poems, there is nothing new or shining here, and the book is all the better for it. If I had small children, or a classroom, I would read to them from it.

And if, by the time I have grandchildren, there are still public libraries, as I hope there still will be, I trust that they will find this book themselves in one – for it will be all the better for not being given or suggested or recommended to them by an adult – and take it to a quiet corner, and read.

★

It is almost fifty years since I read *Elidor*, since I read *The Hamish Hamilton Book of Goblins*. The ingredients that form us, that make us who we are, are difficult to identify. I grew up to write folk tales and fairy tales, to write stories in which there is, somewhere, often buried deep, a resonance with myth.

I was a child who loved Narnia, because it offered escape, but Elidor, which offers little in the way of reassurance, seems to have formed me more deeply. Alan Garner gave us a real world, and another world only a broken window away, with no feeling of escape from either: worlds, inner and outer, reflect each other, and the magical world, now barely a dream away, will always be the streets of Manchester, filled with houses from which the owners have been forced out, partly demolished. Ideas of Alan Garner's – that we walk in myth and re-enact it, that some things and people are dangerous but that rocks and stories and the past matter and give us something to hold on to – are things I have grown up taking for granted, that furnish the inside of my head and my world view in a way that Lewis's cosy magic never could. And for that, as for the stories, I am utterly grateful.

Neil Gaiman is a best-selling author and creator whose books for adults include The Ocean at the End of the Lane, Neverwhere, Stardust, *the Hugo and Nebula Award-winning* American Gods *and* Anansi Boys. *Among his children's books are* The Wolves in the Walls *and* Coraline;

The Graveyard Book *was the first book ever to win both the Newbery Medal and the Carnegie Medal. He has worked widely in film and television, and uses social media to promote the good causes he believes in and to celebrate literature and literacy. His latest book is* Trigger Warning, *published by Headline.*

THE GIVEN

Elizabeth Garner

I was born alongside a book.

I cannot remember a time when I did not know this.

The first evidence of my existence is not the usual photograph of mother and baby, cocooned in a hospital bed. Instead it is a series of numbers in the margins of a manuscript. My mother's contraction times, set beside the emerging words of my father's novel *The Stone Book*. I was on the page before I was in the world. But that's just the start of the story.

The midwife proved to be a cousin. She had a nineteenth-century photograph of the Garner family – one which included all of our relations – standing outside their cottage in Alderley Edge. When my father saw the photograph, he realised the book was more than a single volume. There were tales of generations to be told. *The Stone Book* became *The Stone Book Quartet.*

My father refers to such moments when the real world provides irrefutable evidence to support the fiction as 'The Given'. For the writer, it is proof that you are on the right track and the book will be written. This was always talked about as practical fact, not superstition or romance but quite simply the way that things are. So, the myth of my birth was both the confirmation of a theory and a tall tale of coincidence. It was impossible for me to separate the two elements.

But these were not the only kinds of tales that I grew up with. My parents' house was full of books. I remember thinking, as a child,

The photograph that Alan Garner's cousin Rita, who attended on Griselda at Elizabeth's birth, had inherited the week before, which instantly precipitated *The Stone Book Quartet*.
Standing: second from left, Alan Garner's grandfather Joseph; far right, his great-grandmother Mary.
Seated: Alan's great-great-grandfather Robert with his wife, Anne.

that if all the timbers of the house were removed the shape of the building would be left standing, held by the stacks of literature that lined the walls.

It's credit to my parents that none of the books were forbidden. We were free to read anything we chose to pick from the shelves. So when my friends were submerged in the more conventional childhood literature, I was working my way through the Andrew Lang fairy tales, Kevin Crossley-Holland's myths, Arthur Ransome's *Old Peter's Russian Tales*. This didn't make for easy conversation in the playground, but it gave me a belief that old stories mattered, and were true – more true than tales of boarding school larks or plucky gangs of children fighting smugglers in coves. After all, the home that I grew up in had once stood 20 miles away. That was a fact. So when I read of Baba Yaga's house running around on chicken legs, this was completely plausible – it was something I already knew.

Then there were also the stories that were held within the fabric of the building. When the timbers of the Old Medicine House were dismantled, treasures came spilling out. A child's handwriting exercise in immaculate copperplate; marbles; broken bottles that had once held mysterious ointments. And, perhaps most magical of all, the summer after the house was resurrected in the garden, poppies sprang from the ground. The building was originally the home of an Elizabethan apothecary and the seeds had been shaken out of the beams. The house was aptly named: it brought its own medicine with it.

If you are born into a writer's family this is what happens. Anecdote becomes story, story becomes myth, myth becomes retold until it is set in stone. But these were my father's myths, not mine. I found my own stories in the Old Medicine House when I was eight years old.

I have a clear memory of a van driving into the garden and three people emerging from it. They were the Company of Storytellers. They came carrying drums and bells and whistles. One of them even had a harp. But most intriguing to me was their suitcase full of horns, of all shapes and sizes. I was told that if you blew them hard enough they could move the dish of the Lovell Telescope at Jodrell Bank. I saw no reason to doubt it.

A timber-framed house carries sound in a way that bricks and mortar do not. So, when I was sent to bed, I crept into my favourite den, where the top of a wardrobe nestles against the side of the chimney. The run of the chimney up the heart of the house magnifies the sound like the trumpet of an old-fashioned gramophone. I hid and I listened.

There I heard the tale of the impossibly long trials of a lovesick hero, where time was charted by the flight of a bird past a mountain, the feathers brushing the rock once every 100 years. Only when the side of the mountain was worn away would the hero gain his heart's desire. I realised that this must have been how the cliff side of Alderley Edge was formed. The stories in the books that I loved became living things. In that moment, I understood Once Upon A Time was also Here and Now.

That was over 30 years ago, and it is a memory that has sustained me throughout my career as a writer. Growing up in a creative environment was a blessing, in many ways. When I talk to fellow authors they often say that they always knew they wanted to write, but had to find the courage to do it. They spent years in 'proper' jobs before they gave themselves permission to put pen to paper. That was never the case for me.

But a blessing never comes without a curse. A family name carries weight and expectation. It took courage to step out of the margins and to put my own words on the page. The two things that sustained me through that process were my love of traditional stories and my belief in The Given.

The more I discovered my own voice as a writer the more I realised that I was writing with the assurance of that eight-year-old moment of realisation. The folk tales are there, in the backbone of my books. Perhaps not always obvious, but there nonetheless. For those tales are true: we do fall in love with mirages; we do fly too close to the sun and we do make creatures out of clay and expect them to live.

Then there were The Givens. Whilst writing each book, there

The hiding place mentioned is on top of the wardrobe.
(Photo © David Heke)

was a moment where I encountered a piece of evidence in the real world that was undeniably part of the fiction I was grappling with: the discovery of a piece of graffiti on the wall of a squat party in London; a nineteenth-century photograph found in a museum archive; the purchase of a random bundle of books at a charity shop, amongst them a handbook on early twentieth-century medicine.

Writing is a long and difficult process. It is easy to allow self-doubt and discontent to get in the way. The Givens allowed me to believe in the world I was wrestling onto the page. Perhaps this can be explained as selective perception, but I have never felt a need to rationalise it.

If the story of my birth cannot be separated from the story of a Given, then the family I was born into, the home I was raised in, and the people I encountered there, have also given back to me, and continue to do so. The Old Medicine House is not a museum; my family name is not a thing that should be preserved in aspic. The Blackden Trust is a place of creative development: a place to understand the stories of the past, allowing them to be retold, rediscovered and rewritten as stories for the future.

Elizabeth Garner is a novelist and editor with 15 years of experience of story-development in both film and publishing. She has written two novels: Nightdancing, *and* The Ingenious Edgar Jones. *She is currently working on her third book. She also teaches Creative Writing for The Oxford University Department of Continuing Education. She is a founder Trustee of The Blackden Trust.*

THE OTHERING: DOWN FROM OXFORD, FINDING MY PLACE

Joseph Garner

My Nan – nigh on six foot and not
    ninety pounds with change –
Took my hand with a drowning grip:
'Ye're awreet lad – there's nommuch
Garner in thee. Ye're Stuart at 'art'.

Like the Garner craftsmen, she was
    Stuart, but still
quick to chide and slow to bless.
All her hopes now wrapped up in me.
The pictures on her stairs stopped
    when he broke the tape in the
    220 yards, under 21.

The 220 yards – I was maybe 12 when old Ian Bailey
in Master's gown, shook my hand, looked
far beyond me, shining:
'Oh Garner, to see your father
accelerating out of the bend in the 220 yards
– it was a wonder to behold!'

The Garner Library,
The Voice that Thundered,
The white-hot crucible of creation,
The silent presence that must never be disturbed,
    The absence.

The Garners that made things that last:
Stone walls an' cobbled streets,
Spires an' punches for letterin' milk churns,
220 yard records on cinder track,
An' sacred stories learned but n'er wrote down.
Aye, an' yet a Stuart left to keep the faith for 'em.
Oh, them Garners could naught be trusted with what's reet:
Yer werd, Yer craft, Yer place,
It's all ye 'ave.

It's all that matters, and to her mind he'd
    kept on running
    through the tape,
    running, running, a wonder to behold,
    so far, and so long, that he'd forgot.

'So now lad, back to them books, but
dawnt forget,
ye dawnt wont sum 'apeth
'undred years yon, cum upon it
an 'ee says "What fool made tha' codge?"'

She weren't no fool, she weren't on aboot
owt that could be wrought in stone, and the pictures
    of 'im as a lad, it took werk

    To arrange them perfectly,
With the last at the bottom of the stairs.

To be raised a Garner, you know one thing for certain: we are craftsmen. In older generations we were weavers, stonemasons, and blacksmiths. My father may barely know one end of a screwdriver from another, but a craftsman finds the material that sings to his touch, and he weaves, carves, and forges in language and story. Two generations ago, craftsmen were still the centre of rural life – at its simplest a village without a blacksmith could not shoe horses, plough fields, or hang doors. Craftsmen held a mystical power in their knowledge and skill, they kept secrets and they chose very carefully who to pass them on to, if at all. A graduating apprentice held an equally sacred responsibility – for a master to name an apprentice as a craftsman meant that the master was willing to accept the craftsman's work as his own. A failed apprentice might have some basic skills, but the mystical knowledge was never passed on. In the language of our family (if nowhere else), this is the meaning of the word 'tinker'.

In my father's medium the same is true – the storytellers of two generations ago would rather have their stories die with them than pass them on to a tinker. Thankfully they saw what they needed to in my father. So when he talks of a writer as a channel to the numinous, or a vessel for a yet untold story, he is keeping the secret of the craft: to explain a story is to betray it and its source. Similarly, the care and beauty in the final piece, be it a bolt of cloth, a cornerstone, or a bridle, is what matters, not the material from which it was wrought. When my father says that it doesn't matter if something did happen, just that it could have happened – the real point is that the fine craftsmanship of the story always trumps the fine detail of the facts.

You don't grow in an apprenticeship through platitudes – good master craftsmen care for their charges as a true mentors, but at the same time set them tasks just outside of their comfort zone, judging their achievements by the final tasks they cannot yet complete. Thus a true craftsman is always quick to chide and slow to bless – with the final blessing being the sending of the apprentice out into the world as a craftsman representing his master. This system of learning sadly is largely lost, although ironically the one place it does still persist is in academia. Even as Professors, we have mentors pushing us to take on a task we do not yet know how to complete, and judging us as potential peers or successors by our ability to do so.

That is the first thing I wanted to say – that my father is a craftsman, and would be recognized and honoured as such by any of our forbears. He has made things as permanent and as perfectly crafted as the stone walls in Alderley Edge.

The second is more personal – that I see both my father, and myself as Others (in the philosophical and sociological sense). Furthermore, we both grew up with the ingrained creed that you are only, and forever only, 'your word, your craft, your place'. The Angry Young Men, of which my father is very much one, may not have been the first individuals to experience or describe Othering, but they were the first movement to do so. To be the Other in a place, either in an autocratic system such as a conscripted officer corps, or as a student in a supposedly meritocratic university, is a psychological meat-grinder. But to finally return home, to discover that you are now also an Other, and to realize that you will be a perpetual Other, is a life-changing amputation from the one constant fundamental creed of our craftsman's upbringing. It is no surprise that my father's work is infused with themes of class, betrayal, and alienation. Nor that he treats writing as a craft imbued with the same mysticism with which his blacksmith grandfather imbued his own work. Nor is it surprising that themes of generations-long relationships with landscape and place permeate his writing.

However, this narrative of Othering as a way to understand my father, or the Angry Young Men, misses two fundamental points. Namely, that Othering is a chain reaction that ripples through families. My Nan was Othered in her own way by the changes in my father, which she struggled to understand. It took my own experience of Othering and my own resolution of how I could hold onto the creed of 'your word, your craft, your place', to see a much deeper complexity in their relationship. Her pride in my father as a young man, was I believe, her way of expressing her acknowledgement of his achievements throughout his life. The photograph of breaking the tape in the 220 yards was not a literal full stop, but a metaphor, and a continued expression of pride.

Second, this pattern of creed and Othering is played out anew, generation after generation. Just as my father connects with the third part of the creed through his lifelong commitment to the stories, magical places, and history of Cheshire, my attempt to redefine my connection to my roots has been to work in advocacy of one kind or another. In working with underrepresented students, I have been come to appreciate that a creed that one might think of as being one unique to Northern English rural craftsmen is also shared by first generation American students, be they from white Appalachian, or African American inner city communities. Similarly, the interaction of these three values ('your word, your craft, your place') with the Othering of a university education, is a common shared experience and language that unites students across the spectrum of diversity. In particular, while the reality and experience of being an Other never goes away, there is a basic psychological survival instinct to turn it into a strength and a force for positive change. As Others we have a unique opportunity to perceive, explain, and find solutions to disparities, inequities, and biases throughout society. In particular, Others educated in a system (be it academia, medicine, or the arts) can use the language and media of the majority and the privileged to expose and address issues that they might not otherwise see in a way that they can understand. The Angry Young Men, including my father, and their impact on class and the new valuing of rural and urban culture, are a particularly effective example.

This brings me to the third, and most personal thing I wanted to say. Which is that surviving the internal conflicts of Othering, and transforming them into a positive forward force, requires a pilgrimage of sorts. In the experience of Othering, we can find ways to keep our word, and to find a new craft to stay true to. The internal conflict of Othering comes from the fear of being severed from our roots. Thus to come through the experience of Othering with a new sense of self, we have to go back to our roots and find a way to make peace, and to reconnect our new selves. In one way or another, I have seen this as the most difficult time for so many of the students I have worked with. In my case, this pilgrimage was spending time with my Nan. I had no concept of the Other at the

Alan Garner, 1952.

time, I simply knew I had to spend some time with her. I didn't leave with a grand vision for my future, but I did leave with a sense of identity, and a reconciliation of the family lore.

I have no idea what my father's pilgrimage was or what it meant. Few of us share our pilgrimage, and we know better than to ask. But I do know that the notion of a shared human experience rippling and repeating across space and time is one my father would appreciate.

As for how much of this story is true? Most of it. Particularly the picture on the stairs.

Joseph Garner is an Associate Professor in the Department of Comparative Medicine, a Courtesy Associate Professor in the Department of Psychiatry and Behavioural Sciences, and a member of the Child Health Research Institute at Stanford University. He is an internationally recognised expert in the behaviour and welfare of laboratory mice; he also works extensively in human health, both as a researcher and an advocate. His advocacy work includes serving on scientific advisory boards for the Trichotillomania Learning Center, the Tourette Syndrome Association, and the Beautiful You MRKH Foundation.

MR GARNER'S READING LESSON

Ben Haggarty

Man sucking thumb! Two o'clock –
Otter chasing fish at ten.
Small figure confronts large figure at nine. Combat to ensue.
Are Peake and Doré with us in the cumulonimbus?
Yes, 100%!

A work of art is successful if it transforms the way you perceive things. Through his art, Alan Garner taught me to read. Not words, but what lies, as he might say, 'aback' of them.

I first encountered Alan's approach to seeing through *The Old Man of Mow*. In 1968 a children's book illustrated entirely with photographs was an attractive novelty (even if it was part of a rather patchy geography education series). To my ten-year-old burgeoning ego it clearly starred none other than me and my brother, Sam, scrambling over northern rocks. I'd been given it for Christmas by my grandmother and though she lived in a Sussex hamlet, her family was northern through and through. Every summer we stayed with elderly aunts who took us to Higgar Tor and the other fierce peaks and moors which surround Sheffield. These great aunts, Eppie and Gag, had used their industrialist father's wealth to buy and donate land for the Peak District National Park and been instrumental in establishing the Council for the Preservation of Rural England. They endlessly mocked our southern accents and carthorse names and told us we were made of harder stuff.

So here we were, Ben and Sam, on a wild goose chase, wearing our best school mackintoshes, gallivanting over walls, staring into a hell jaw of fiery brick kilns and tearing down lanes in search of . . . an old man (and if you're unfamiliar with the book, you might want to skip the rest of this paragraph because it contains spoilers). The story shares something of the circular quest of *The Conference of the Birds* and ends with a superb anthropomorphic pareidolia and a practical display of Alan's unending celebration of immortal stone. Harder stuff indeed. The book caused me such intense mirror neuron tingling that no rock, tree or cloud has since been spared the scrutiny of possible alternative readings. At 56 I still try to avoid being duped by craggy old men.

Garner's pareidolia (the ability to see multiple forms in things) is pivotal to his work – most famously in the choice between reading a decorative plate pattern as either flowers or owls, and most strikingly in the crown of oak leaves depicted in the windows of the Church of St James and Saint Paul in Marton, Cheshire, which gave birth to the Shick-Shack rituals that envelop *Strandloper* and its ecstatic final act.

Perceptions of surface form altered by acts of autosuggestion, lucid revelation and even synaesthesia, can act as a troubling shock, launching questions and doubt – leading to a search for truth.

A story is not the words, it is the 'what happens' communicated by those words. Words are a medium of communication whose reach is dependent on a common understanding, but the images and events they convey can sometimes evolve into an independent language of tropes and motifs. When a narrative holds such powerful appeal that it warrants myriad repetitions by multiple voices, it gradually etches itself a mythic outline. The factors generating such an appeal are working at a level of fundamental metaphor whose objective significance can only be understood by subjective exploration. If a story becomes embedded in a series of iconic images rather than words, it is then free to journey unbound by linguistic, geographical and temporal borders. However, if a critical object in a story is perceived in different ways during that journey, then the subsequent versions of the story may vary markedly, depending on the storytellers involved. And when that happens, things can get really interesting.

Alan's world is one in which it is assumed that one thing hides behind the form of another. He says he wants to 'make the patterns clear'. With each book his mastery of his art evolves, and his books, collections, talks and essays offer those who would put themselves in a relationship of study, a training, or perhaps, a tuning.

In order to make the patterns clear, Alan has had to be attentive to that which obscures. His element has become a liminal world of half-light and shadow: he, himself, has become the strandloper. So, paradoxically, his work intentionally ambiguates from the outset. He understands that the Trickster is the storyteller's god. Nothing valuable ever comes easily. Everything should be doubted.

The Guizer, published in 1975, was decades ahead of its time and remains an unsurpassed anthology of trickster tales. Plant a name as juicy as Sam Blowsnake on the first page of it and you send a sixteen-year-old running into the woodlands and straight into the chaotic flailing of Wakdjunkaga – a proto-man with a wakening conscience.

When *A Bag of Moonshine* appeared in 1986, few spotted that the book is exactly what it says on the tin. Though claiming to be a collection of folk tales from England and Wales, several are glorious smuggled goods, translocated from far overseas and not 'British' at all.

And while publishers cashed in on the bicentenary of the publication of the Grimms' *Household Tales* with gift editions, or persuaded bankable authors to rework the stories, Garner, ahead of the pack, quietly slipped a stunning version of 'Faithful John' into the 2011 augmented republication of his collection of international Goblin tales, *Collected Folk Tales*.

Alan's pareidolia expands from multiple perceptions of a single object into understanding the dance behind an entire action. He once took me up to Alderley Edge during an archaeological open day. The grim tunnels of the hollow hill are the oldest large copper mines in England and, on that day, a couple of experimental archaeologists had recreated a Bronze Age furnace. As they incessantly pumped a pair of leather bellows, the register in a small thermometer crawled painfully upwards. The mix of ore and charcoal grunted and snorted for many hours while the men sweated ale. Alan stood behind me patiently and then, an exact and objective temperature reached, the furnace shot its blazing wad precisely and fully into the trough at its base. The flaming copper ejaculate halted at the end of the course and lay there smouldering. The archaeologists keeled over spent and happy . . . and Alan said calmly: 'There, Ben – that's what they meant by drawing the sword from the stone.'

A skeuomorph is an architectural term meaning a redundant practical feature that continues to be remembered in design – for example, contemporary street bollards unwittingly honour the cannonballs that were once jammed into the muzzles of obsolete naval guns, planted upright to be used as mooring posts. The legend of the sword in the stone is a perfect example of a skeuomorph held in the iconography of oral tradition. The oral tradition deploys instinctive dramaturgical processes of composition and performance to compel audiences to listen. In this way, half-grasped or misheard information, gossip, rumours and memories are inevitably engineered by storytellers into narrative forms to maintain some semblance of sense. In this case, knowledge of the whereabouts of an ore supply, coupled with the know-how to extract its metal, would help anyone defend, or win, a crown. Unravel this a little more and the legend of King Arthur's sleeping army under Alderley could be rationalised as a skewed (likely) or coded (less likely) memory indicating the whereabouts of an ammunition dump.

This masterly insight sent me sifting for further fresh levels of pragmatic meanings amidst the already multiple layers carried in the imagery of folk tales and myths. In the kaleidoscope of fantastical motifs, many mask memories of literal facts as well as containing symbolic truths. These run the gamut from the prosaic, such as the hero-challenge of fetching water in a sieve bearing a practical memory of Mesolithic basket bucket making; to the legendary, such as the Griffin being a Silk Road marvel deduced from fossilised eggs and bones lying exposed in the Gobi desert; to more mysterious, secret and sacred matters, such as Ariadne's thread hinting at a

Palaeolithic initiate's aid for navigating cave passages to meet the bull in the wall.

You've set this boy running, he's supercharged with excitement, but Mr Garner knows you can't simply stop with an ammunition dump! You have to hop, skip and hurl yourself at the heavy, impermeable world of stone and break on through to the vibrating, finer materialities of consciousness and subconsciousness – a world which could be called the myth world or even 'the dreaming'. Never mind the sword that makes a king: what about the monstrous sleep which has overcome the king and laid the land to waste?

For me today, joy lies in the presence of ambiguated figures lurking at the junctions where mythology meets the evidence of the archaeological record. These figures mark the whereabouts of bridges between worlds. Sometimes between our world and the myth world, sometimes between two, or more, myth worlds. Navigating these bridges is a perilous undertaking and mapping them will always be approximate – but we can peer across the abyss . . . then stride into the unknown.

The great Irish epic *Cath Maighe Tuireadh*, anglicised as 'The Battle of Moytura' and recorded in two sixteenth-century manuscripts, holds a Bronze Age ur-myth common to a world transformed by metallurgy. In essence it tells of an all-consuming one-eyed ogre who threatens the existence of everything and must be defeated with a special weapon obtained by a special hero. In this case the monster is the Fomorian King, Balor – but let his silhouette play on the shadow screen of skeuomorphology, and it could equally be Polyphemus, Humbaba, Goliath, Khumbhakarna. The hero here is Lugh – the Samildánach – master of all arts.

The fourth branch of the Welsh *Mabinogion* – which provides the template for the tormented triads of *The Owl Service* – seems at first glance to be an entirely different narrative, yet the two epic cycles juggle taunting images between them, luring us into the matter not just of Britain, but of the whole age of metal.

Both these stories centre around a skilful hero-deity, Lugh Lamfada in the Irish and Lleu Llaw Gyffes in the Welsh. That the story of a hero or god with variants on this name, was known throughout Europe is attested in place names the length and breadth of Britain (Carlisle, Leominster, Ludlow, Loudon) and far across the continent in Lyons (France), Leiden (Holland), Legnica (Poland), Lugones (Spain) and in hundreds of other places. Storytellers – and priests – have always found it expedient to mould their stories onto their local landscape. The Irish *Battle of Moytura*, with its associated text fragments and still extant oral traditions, remains woefully unfamiliar to the British for reasons of historical bias, yet it clearly belongs not only to Ireland but to all Europe, and preserves a cultural iconography elsewhere obliterated by the Romans. Though the manuscripts of the Irish epic are later than the Welsh manuscripts, they are recensions and scholars suggest the language they contain dates it as the earlier tale.

We can ponder what the mono-visioned devourer in the ur-myth might represent; what the nature of the weapon that can destroy it is: and how it can be found and by whom. We can ask what qualities such a person must possess – and so on. Subjective exploration of the metaphorical meaning of stories by seeking to intuit understanding of their symbolism, particularly when internalising such a tale of sovereignty, is by its nature a private activity taking place in the unbound, soft, intangible world of consciousness. After all, whose inner king is not sick?

So, such questions present themselves for contemplating rather than answering. Instead, let us step onto another mythological bridge. Although the Welsh narrative lacks a one-eyed monster, it has in its place a standing stone with a hole pierced through it. It seems pretty clear that a spear cast by a skilful hand through that eyehole remembers the defeat of the ogre and is thus a king-making ritual. Crossing back to the tangible, hard world we can find many such holed standing stones scattered throughout Europe. If your imagination goes so far as to bind a sacrificial victim behind one of them, then you will hear a scream when an arrow meets it mark … you could call them 'king stones'.

More bridges appear. In the Welsh tale the magician, Gwydion, traces the outline of a human with flowers on the ground and she becomes Blodeuwedd, the woman of flowers. In the Irish tale a human outline – also formed of flowers – appears on the ground, but in this case it is the outline of a boy buried beneath. This boy, Miach, was a magical youth brutally slain by his jealous father because the son had proved to be a more able physician than he. The boy had rendered the maimed king, Nuada, whole again by coaxing his severed arm back to life – thus releasing him from the use of a silver prosthetic limb and allowing him to regain his rightful throne. And yet the father's filicide is forgiven by the corpse in the grave. Miach's spirit reveals the secret of all healing herbs by causing them to sprout in the soil above him, showing their effective correspondences to the human body. The father, feeling himself mocked, destroys the flower pattern and thus the gift of the knowledge of healing plants is muddled forever. Witness to this scene is the boy's sister, Airmed. Put a lamp behind this extraordinary passion play and it casts a silhouette similar to Gwydion's creation of Blodeuwedd as a wife for Lleu, with Arianhrod as the unseen bystander . . . put the light before it and it shows a completely different story . . . yet a tantalising resonance remains. It's all about healing a wound.

Another figure, another bridge. A silver amulet of a man holding a large fish in his hand and inscribed 'Nodons' was unearthed in the remains of a Romano-British temple at Lydney on the west bank of the River Severn. Silver fish . . . or silver arm? Is this talisman a key that reveals King Nuada's silver prosthetic limb to be a skeuomorph for the Salmon of Knowledge – especially considering the various legends of the salmon which swim both Rivers of Life – the Boyne in Ireland and the Severn in Britain – and that Nuada is the maternal grandfather of Fionn mac Cumhaill? Or perhaps it's vice versa! Did arm become salmon?

Now we're in the realm of profound ambiguity and the wound of that mysterious Arthurian figure, the Fisher King – emasculated and guarding the Grail – begins to gleam and beckon. Could we really be talking about penises? However, if the Fisher King epithet is recalling the archaic iconography of the King/God Nuada/Nodons, then he's guarding spears and cauldrons which long predate the story of Christ, and his punitive emasculation might simply be a red herring placed there by chaste Christian storytellers. In a post-

Freudian world, to consider our silver salmon as primarily a symbolic embodiment of knowledge rather than as a phallus is, ironically, the more challenging and shocking option. Wisdom or willies? Irish and Welsh mythology both hold the salmon as the most ancient and sacred of creatures – wise, perhaps, because it knows the place of its birth and death.

There's plenty else to discern in the jumble of stories and plenty more bridges (some more rickety than others): the spear-making of Irish Goibniu and Welsh Gronw; the theft of pigs and cows; rapes; wizardry; incest; disguise; gods of youth; cauldrons of rebirth; abandonments to the waves; the nonsense chants of Lugh and Lleu … but let's leave this game of divination there.

Garner is the master detective of such hauntings, he can sense the ghosts behind the visible – and know which ones are worth tracking. His works are fractal songs of the Great Song he learned on a childhood sickbed, which knows this is a causal universe where every single atom of everything existing is permeated by a numen. Nature and human artifice is guized (disguised) – meaning and purpose are there to be found (garnered) and unriddled by the very act of searching for it. Perhaps the action of seeking is more important than the finding. At the very least because without the searching, there is no story.

Returning to that craggy Old Man of Mow – you look for the truth of him, only to discover he was there all along. He tells you that Truth has many sides … both in and out.

Ben Haggarty has been telling traditional tales professionally since 1981 and is widely credited as a key pioneer of the worldwide oral storytelling revival. His versions of traditional narratives are full-blooded and include East European wonder tales, adult epics such as Gilgamesh *and* Midir and Etain *and modern myths such as Frankenstein and Mister Sandmann. He is Artistic Director of The Crick Crack Club and is patiently working towards realising his vision of a permanent venue for storytelling in London. He has also created, with illustrator Adam Brockbank, two volumes of a graphic novel,* Mezolith, *which explores the archaeology of the imagination. Ben has known the Garner family since 1984.*

THE SLEEPING KING AND THE BODY OF THE WORLD

Nick Hennessey

An ambulance was on its way to Macclesfield General at the back end of January. The sun had not yet risen, as the Bedford engine revved against the steep hill that cleaved the night. Inside a pregnant woman lay panting as the yellow of the streetlights pulsed by. Just as the vehicle heaved over the crest of the hill of the Edge she felt a sudden surge inside her, a force from the nameless beyond, as if the unseen itself were pushing through her into the world. She clamped herself tight like iron. 'Not your time,' she hissed, 'Not yet. Not now. But soon.' The ambulance picked up speed and hurtled on through the night.

Shortly before sunrise, at six o'clock in the morning on 31st January 1968, in Macclesfield General Hospital, the iron gates were at last unlocked, and I was born.

It's a fantasy I know, this story of my birth. All my mother actually said was 'You nearly came out in the ambulance on the way.' The rest is the product of an overactive imagination and a strong sense of self-importance. Although perhaps it isn't so much self-importance as self-doubt, an answer to the age-old question, 'Who am I?' It is a story that strives to locate me in a landscape, a landscape of myth, to 'place' me. We all do it, build our stories into places, but to my mind it is a risky business. For if there is one thing I have learned from the work of Alan Garner it is this: place is dangerous.

I grew up with Garner's books; I can still see them now in my mind, neatly lined up on the shelf above my pillow in my childhood bedroom, their spines chiming with significance. Significance because, I was told, Alan Garner lived nearby and wrote about the Edge. I have to confess, however, that in those days I never read them. I never got that far. The cover and the opening pages of *The Weirdstone of Brisingamen* were as far as I got. The cover because it shows a man with a goblet in his hand, sitting by a small stream, with owl-like, piercing eyes that seemed to say to me 'Who do you think you are?' – and the opening pages because in them Garner tells a story he heard from his grandfather, of the Legend of Alderley Edge.

I think I remember when my mother first told me the story, long before I could properly read it from the book. But very clearly I remember going up to the Edge soon after and feeling very dislocated. The story, existing then only on my mother's breath, contradicted, or rather contested, what I saw: namely the explicit, clear, open, physical experience of being there. Suddenly there was something beneath the surface, beneath the skin of the place, something that left me asking, 'What is this?' So this is why place is dangerous: because place is where two truths collide. We might say that in a place like the Edge we find two different orders of truth: the ordinary and the poetic, or perhaps the personal and the mythological, and because they are of different orders they cannot reconcile and they meet like climatic pressure cells. In meteorological terms, an occluded front is where high pressure meets low pressure, and the weather starts to get rough as one cell is forced up and the other down. The singular splits, irreconcilable realities diverge, and as language stutters impotently, the gap between them can't be ignored. It is these dynamic forces that move through us when we deeply encounter a place, and it is our task to hold them both within ourselves.

One of the things that has always excited me in Alan Garner's fiction – yes, now in my mid-forties, I can confidently say that I have read nearly all his work – is that the characters are always on the edge, struggling to pick out a precarious path between breakdown and clarity. At any moment there is for them the very real possibility of complete psychological meltdown, an implosion of the mind under sheer pressure; yet at the same time there is within our grasp a sudden, synaptic explosion of profound understanding. This is place, its danger and its paradox.

One might argue that this is nothing more than the consequence of Garner's own internal wiring and says nothing about the actual world, and that would be a fair point – and yet that would mean choosing one truth over another, and so something wonderful would be missed.

The cover of my 1965 edition of *The Weirdstone* was created by George Adamson, and it too has stayed with me. In particular the eyes, piercing, unwavering, owl-like. Terrifying, in fact. Thirty years after staring in them for the first time, I met them again in Eiheiji, the Zen monastery in the mid-west of Japan. On the wall of the Welcome Hall is a vast ink painting of the Zen master Bodhidharma, credited with bringing Buddhism from India to China in the fifth or sixth century. The style of practice that sprang from him is known as Chan (Zen in Japan), which roughly translates as 'emptiness', and teaches that our big troubles come from choosing one phenomenon over another, one truth over another. Bodhidharma is usually depicted (as he is on the wall in Eiheiji) with fierce, unwavering eyes, a gaze that fearlessly meets all things equally. A tool of Zen is the *kōan*, something akin to a riddle passed down through the lineage of the practice that forces us to directly meet our own paradox. In facing the *kōan*, it is said, we meet the masters directly and sit with them, so closely that our eyebrows entwine. Breath to breath. Their questions become our questions and we face the Great Matter of Life and Death. The *kōans* force us to stop choosing, and instead to inhabit the difficulty. Of course, this is difficult work because we stand to lose the most important thing we have: who we think we are. For the Zen tradition, the body is the way into the paradox, the Gateless Gate into the Great Matter. The body is place, where the mystery is encountered, and the key to entering is in not choosing.

To read the work of Alan Garner is, I feel, to sit with him, breath to breath, until his own doubt opens in us and we face the difficulty unflinchingly, without concession. You only have to read *The Voice that Thunders* to know how uncompromising a mind he possesses; his work is run through with struggle and paradox, and is full of the tension between internal and external, personal and mythological, place and self. It is my belief that the Legend of Alderley is aback of it all.

It's always worth going back to the spoken source of a story, to hear it as it comes springing from a local tongue, with all its musicality and cadence. I first heard Alan telling it a few years ago, and it struck me deeply that, as stories go it is astonishingly simple, as essential as any I've known. Small as a nut and as vast in potential, in little more than a handful of lines an entire journey is laid out. In its simplicity it is akin to *Noh* drama and, like *Noh*, pivots on *kenshō*, a revelation, an awakening that transforms us.

The pulse of the plot, rhythmic as the blacksmith's hammer and tight as a song, takes us in a few beats from the narrow, linear everyday world into a vast circle of time and back again. With each sentence no longer than a breath, there is the unmistakable visceral presence of the body in the language and the landscape, rooting the story in the world, in place. Each phrase unfolds like a petal, with an economy that feeds the listener with enough and no more. It offers no answers, but comes to us as sudden as a gasp and leaves us open.

There are only three characters: the Farmer, the Old Man and the Sleeping King. But who are they? We know who the Farmer is: he is everyone and anyone, an honest man of the soil, an ordinary who has fallen on hard times. He is you and me. Locally the Old Man is thought of as a wizard but, to avoid the hackneyed image, let us call him a guide, someone who knows the Old Ways.

Who is the Sleeping King? Variations of the story up and down these islands, from Scotland to Cornwall, are all very clear: he is Arthur. The Alderley Legend doesn't say. If we accept the consensus that it is Arthur, then who was he? Beyond the layers – twentieth-century fantasy, thirteenth-century romance, Dark Age post-Romano rebel, Iron Age war hero – what is his original face? Artus is believed to mean 'bear'. Could this be the root? A sleeping bear waiting to wake and rise with the sun?

In search of answers I travelled to Finland where I encountered

The Kalevala, the nation's epic. Within that epic-song tradition there is a story of Antero Vipunen, the oldest singer of all, asleep in the earth, who knows songs and spells from beyond living memory. Väinämöinen, the epic's hero, journeys down into his belly, fills himself with the glittering treasure of ancient song and returns to the world. Is this the same story? Could this be an answer?

On my way back from Karelia and the Russian border, near the town of Kuhmo, I met a guide who took me to see bears in the wild. I was very excited. After sunset we travelled to a small wooden hut in the silent, white forest and sat with our eyes fixed on an elk carcass some 30 yards out in the snow. Apparently the bears, waking hungry from a sleepy winter, would be unable to resist the food. An hour or so passed in the deepening night, as we stared out into what seemed like an infinity of pine trees. Suddenly I saw something move. I could pick it out in the shadows, a huge, lumbering shape, an unmistakable hulk rising onto its hind legs, sniffing the air. I watched, wide-eyed in wonder, then blinked and it was gone. There was nothing there. It was only my imagination. We sat on. But soon enough it returned, a great brown bear drawn to the easy feed, its massive head swaying with every padding step. I blinked. It was gone. Nothing, only the shapeless dark. Finally when morning came we hadn't seen a single bear (I thought I'd seen 20 at least), yet I felt it under my skin, knew it in an 'other' way, an intimate way. I knew bear by its not-thereness. And so it occurred to me that the key to the Legend is not found in knowing the characters' names: it is in *not* knowing them. Yes, the story is universal, similar to many stories found in cultures all over the world, but so too it is particular: particular in its naming of places on the Edge, but particular also because it does not name the Sleeping King.

So in returning to the very particular version, the version that springs from the local source as I heard Alan Garner tell it himself in the words of his grandfather, there is one phrase that stands out to me still – which I recall clearly even though it doesn't appear in the version printed in *The Weirdstone of Brisingamen*. When the Farmer leaves the cavern and the Sleeping King, leaving his horse and the Old Man, he steps out of the hillside into 'a night as black as a bag'. I love this phrase. It's a storyteller's phrase. It says nothing about 'a bag' but everything about the nature of bag: empty, potent, capable. The Farmer doesn't stand in the dawn, with the glittering sun of clarity in his eyes, he stands in the mystery, completely, wholly.

Like the Farmer we are all filled with questions about what we've just seen: who, what, where, how? They are natural questions, of course, but if we settle for answers then we miss something far more wonderful: a night as black as a bag. If we choose one truth over another we approach a kind of fundamentalism: the Iron Gates stay locked and the world is closed to us. Crusading is all that is left to us then, and that is dangerous in an entirely different kind of way.

As a performing storyteller I am acutely aware that the audience knows very well that the stories aren't 'real'. The art of storytelling isn't to convince the audience that what you say is true, but that it is possible. It is to move backwards and forwards between two worlds, the everyday world and the story world, here and not-here, supporting both. In doing so we hold them simultaneously and are awakened to our potential. So I am coming to believe that the King is not actually sleeping at all (after all, what would it say of us if the symbol for our collective subconscious was actually unconscious and oblivious?) but rather that the King is awake. Yes, he is inactive: but he is aware. Like the great Lovell Telescope at Jodrell Bank he is pure receptivity, a giant ear open to the world, neither picking nor choosing, but bearing witness to all. Indeed, the story says he is waiting, and 'to wait' originally meant 'to watch'.

To sit with Alan Garner is to sit with a root that goes extraordinarily deep into the soil, yet to keep an eye on the stars. To Alan Garner I owe a great deal. My work in storytelling and song can be traced through encounters with his work; but what I owe him the most for is not of him, but from him, through him. A story that continues to open like a flower, enriching my capacity to be open and present to this complicated and dangerous life, and to appreciate its extraordinary beauty. A story that begins simply: 'A farmer was on his way to Macclesfield market, at the back end of October . . .'

Nick Hennessey is an internationally acclaimed storyteller, singer, songwriter and musician. He has told stories for more than 20 years, performing at venues such as the South Bank Centre and Royal Albert Hall. He is particularly inspired by North European cultural traditions and has been awarded high honours in Finland for his work on their National Epic, Kalevala. *He is a sought-after artistic collaborator, working with top-of-the-field musicians and storytellers. He has broadcast documentaries for BBC Radio 4 and his musical work has featured on BBC Radio 3's* Late Junction.

POCKETS

Dougald Hine

There was a jigsaw we had when I was five, a map of Britain with illustrations of the places that matter. Two of these lodged in my imagination: the limestone wonder of the Cheddar Gorge, and the great dish of the radio telescope at Jodrell Bank. 'We know the people who live next to Jodrell Bank,' my mum told me, and this seemed a magical proposition. It was.

By the time I started piecing together the jigsaw, our families were just about in Christmas card contact, but for a while in the early seventies, my mum had been a regular guest at Toad Hall. Her friendship with the Garners began on a children's ward in Manchester, where she was nursing one of Alan's daughters. Later, their hospitality became a place to turn in a dark moment of her life. The pieces of that story have come out slowly over the years, but from the way she spoke, I had the sense that these people and this place had shown her a great kindness. And when I finally found my own way up the bumpy track to Blackden – by which time I must have been about the age she was when she found refuge there – I knew that I was arriving at a place of sanctuary.

Before that, there were the books. *The Weirdstone*, read for the first time on a rainy holiday in Swaledale, then racing on to the end of *The Moon of Gomrath* where the afternote was a first clue to the thoroughness behind the momentum of the telling. ('The spells are genuine,' Alan noted, 'though incomplete: just in case.') Like so many others, I was hooked, waiting for the arrival of the later books, returning to their pages and always finding more. There is something here that feeds a hunger in us, a hunger that is hard to name in the words our culture has to offer.

There are no favourites, but one book stands out because I find it hard to know who I would be if it hadn't turned up when it did. *The Voice that Thunders* was published the summer I was about to go up to Oxford and I carried it like a secret through the next three years. Under the bombardments of the graduate recruitment brigade, I would find shelter in Joseph Garner's quietly brutal careers advice: 'Always take as long as the job tells you,' and 'If the other feller can do it, let him!' (There was another spell, only this time with no safety catch, no words left out.) The effect of reading that book that summer was to awaken a sense of loss that was also a coming alive. As if a grief that had been a background greyness, taken for reality itself, was lifted into focus, could now be felt, honoured, lived through.

For a bewildered young man from the north of England, entering the unforgiving world of Oxford, this was a kind of armour. It didn't matter that I was unable to explain to my tutors or my peers why Alan's work mattered so much. My explanations would have been too personal, unintelligible within the language we were being taught to use. When I suggested to Craig Raine that I write on Garner for the twentieth-century paper in Mods, he said it was a touching thought, but I should really focus on authors of the first rank, which revealed his ignorance and saved us both a deal of pain. (Though another tutor, the great Shakespearean A.D. Nuttall, gleamed when I mentioned Alan's name.)

A first-rate academic education often resembles a half-complete shamanic initiation. The initiate's body of beliefs is cut to pieces, the head severed from the heart. She is taught to analyse or deconstruct anyone's way of making sense of the world, including her own. Yet the institution overseeing this operation scarcely recognises the reconstruction that must follow, if the young person passing through its care is to emerge whole.

In the depths of that initiation, little of what had come with me to Oxford still made sense, but these books did. They offered a refuge of meaning that I knew was not escapism. That their author had proven himself in the tutorial room and then chosen to walk away from this world was part of their power. What followed, in the journey from *The Weirdstone* to *The Stone Book*, was evidence that the severing need not be final, that head and heart could be brought back together, within our culture, even if the cost of this was indeed 'total war, by which I mean total life, on the divisive forces within the individual and within society'.

Later, by the fireplace at Toad Hall, Alan told me about the meeting with his tutor when he had made the decision to leave Oxford and try to write. 'Do it,' the tutor said, 'and if you find that you don't have what it takes, then come back next year, and no one will think the less of you. But if you find that you do, then you will have to create a Magdalen of your own.'

That was what he had done, I thought – he and Griselda – in the net of fellowship that gathers around their kitchen table and stretches to the corners of the world. I was drawn into the net after a talk that Alan gave at the Temenos Academy in London. I had asked a question that caught his attention, then stayed behind to pass on greetings from my mum to Griselda. When she recovered from bouncing with excitement and discovered that I was working on something called the School of Everything, Griselda decided that I must be enlisted to assist The Blackden Trust.

So I found myself bumping up that track to the house in the middle of a field, the telescope looming like a great white Grail behind it. As we walked from room to room, Alan told the stories of the place and handed me objects that I knew without ever having seen: the Stone Book, the little Whizzler, the Bunty. Just as awe was in danger of taking over, the thought struck that this shy, funny, brilliant man was also still the boy in the wartime photograph, that he was sharing these treasures just the way a small child will make friends by sharing his toys.

On the visits that followed, I got to know the Trust in action. It is a school in the truest sense: a place that offers the leisure to slow down, to deepen your attention, to notice the unexpected and to draw out its implications with rigour. Young people learn to look hard, to ask a question and follow where it leads, to test ideas and always to pursue the anomaly. They do so in the company of experts of the highest standing who are unafraid to display the limits of their knowledge or to explore their disagreements with good humour.

I have sat in its grounds as we knapped flint, under the guidance of a professor of archaeology, listening as the conversation gave way to silence, as the rhythm of our tapping fell into unison and the realisation spread among the group that this sound was being heard on this spot for the first time in three thousand years. Another time, when Ronald Hutton led a seminar on the Civil War and one of our group was moved to tears, I understood that it was possible to carry out the work of the historian, with all academic diligence, and at the same time to perform an older and more universal task: to honour the dead in such a way as to give meaning to the living.

Ivan Illich once described the climate which he had sought to foster in the meeting places he had helped to create, and it is a description that makes me think of Blackden: 'Learned and leisurely hospitality is the only antidote to the stance of deadly cleverness that is acquired in the professional pursuit of objectively secured knowledge. I remain certain that the quest for truth cannot thrive outside the nourishment of mutual trust flowering into a commitment to friendship.'

Around that table, you never know what field the conversation will enter next, and it was on one of those evenings that I first heard talk of 'cryptic northern refugia'. Once upon a time, a species like the oak was thought to have survived the last Ice Age only at the southern edges of Europe, from where it marched out again across the continent in waves, over centuries, to reseed the warming landscape. Now we know how fast that warming came – seven degrees in a decade, at the end of the Younger Dryas, the final glacial phase, around 11,500 years ago – and the palaeoecologists keep finding traces of plants and animals in times and places where they should not have been. So the old model has given way to a new hypothesis: in certain places, pockets of leafy woodland endured, protected by their own microclimates, harbouring isolated communities of creatures which would otherwise only have survived far to the south. These northern refugia were cryptic, so small as to barely leave a trace in the record, but the sites identified lie in steep-sided valleys, where high and low ground meet. Places such as Cheddar Gorge in Somerset, or Ludchurch on the Cheshire/Staffordshire border.

There is a path that leads from here to *Boneland*, but I want to turn back instead to *The Voice that Thunders* and a glint of that vein of creative anger that runs through Alan's work: an anger, by his own description, 'at once personal, social, political, philosophical and linguistic'. Addressing an audience of head teachers, invited to speak on 'The Development of the Spiritual', he issues a warning against the rise of a materialism which can see the world only through the lens of accountancy, which turns all to commodity, which appropriates competence in all fields of human affairs – from the classroom to the publishing house – and which, if unresisted, will usher in 'a spiritual Ice Age'.

Twenty years on, the ice has spread further across the social landscape, and few institutions are untouched. 'The new world economic order,' as John Berger terms it, is a totalisation of the process of enclosure that the land man brought to Thursbitch. What is the shape of hope in such a landscape? 'The shape of a pocket,' Berger answers in the book that takes its name from the phrase. 'A small pocket of resistance.' The image is borrowed from Subcomandante Marcos of the Zapatistas. Its smallness reflects the distance both men have travelled from the grand historical expectations of revolution, their Marxism tempered by the experience of the peasants of the Haute Savoie or the indigenous people of Chiapas. Perhaps because Berger writes in the same book about the cave art of the Palaeolithic, I hear a rhyme between the political and the prehistoric. If there is hope left, in this Ice Age, it is in the hidden pockets, the refugia too small to seem significant.

'Resistance is growing,' Alan tells the head teachers. 'Especially amongst artists.' The enclosure is never quite total; the hills will outlast the walls. That which is supposed to be lost often turns out only to be dormant, marginalised, walking the edges, or gone underground. In the darkest hour, that which is meant to be obsolete may yet make all the difference. The Trickster spirit will always get aback of those who only see the things that can be measured, counted and priced.

And in the meantime, there are always the pockets, the hidden corners of conviviality, the cryptic northern refugia, the places that matter. If that long-inhabited patch of ground across the railway tracks from the telescope at Jodrell Bank is such a place, the same is true of the pages of the magical books that have been written there.

Dougald Hine is leader of artistic development at Riksteatern, Sweden's national theatre, and founding editor of the journal Dark Mountain. *He is the author of* Uncivilisation: The Dark Mountain Manifesto, *with Paul Kingsnorth, and* The Crossing of Two Lines. *He co-founded the educational web start-up School of Everything and founded the utopian regeneration agency Spacemakers.*

ALAN GARNER AND ALAN TURING: ON THE ROAD

Andrew Hodges

On 11th November 2011, Alan Garner surprised the readership of the *Guardian* newspaper by his piece entitled 'My hero, Alan Turing'. Its 300 words did not offer any conventional sequence of splendid achievements: it was a first-hand, worm's-eye view of Alan Turing as a road runner 'with the aerodynamics of a brick', 'funny and witty' as he 'talked endlessly'. Only by allusion was Turing's status as the founder of modern computer science, and the chief scientific figure in breaking the codes of Nazi Germany, suggested in the account. Alan Garner's emphasis was placed quite elsewhere: it was on the 'fury' he felt on learning of Turing's criminal prosecution and punishment as a homosexual, and his own 'guilt that I did not, could not, help him, which lasted for decades.' In fact, a reader might well be puzzled as to why Garner was defining Turing as a hero at all, given that he was portrayed primarily in the role of victim, the last word being given to his suicide.

It puzzled me too, as Turing's biographer. News of a fresh witness to his life and death aroused excitement together with a certain self-reproach for having completely failed to locate such a vivid storyteller. When? Where? How? Like other readers, I also wondered how a writer who only emerged in the 1960s could be connected with the computer scientist who died in 1954.

But as I learnt from Alan Garner in 2012, when he generously invited me to visit, there were simple answers. The key point is that he was only 17, a sixth-former studying Classics at Manchester Grammar School, when this running partnership started. The meeting of the two Alans arose in 1951, simply as fellow amateur runners, rare in those days, spotting each other on the road. Garner lived as a schoolboy at home in Alderley Edge, Turing lived alone in his semi-detached house at Wilmslow. Garner was just developing as a strong sprinter, whilst Turing was well established in amateur athletics as a long-distance runner, but they found a meeting point in equal distances and speed over the Cheshire lanes.

This training partnership meant they met once or twice every week. None of Turing's friends and acquaintances knew of it, so if Garner had not come forward with this late, unexpected testimony, it would have vanished. From the biographer's point of view this would have been the loss of something very precious. Even on the central topics of the invention of the computer, the attack on the Enigma ciphers, and the prospect of Artificial Intelligence, Turing left little material to explain his train of thought. He left even less on his personal life: no diaries, and not many letters to friends, and of what he wrote, some has been destroyed. In particular, the true narrative of Turing's life in the period of the 1950s would be rather like an Iris Murdoch novel, except that we know only fragments of it from his isolated and laconic utterances. So anything that reflects on Turing's inner life is a vital contribution to the story.

The apparent generation gap, Turing being 39 in 1951, was not an obstacle. Turing was notably easy with other young people in general, but Alan Garner, with his experience of Manchester Grammar School's special ambience, was particularly conscious of being treated as an equal. It came as no surprise to Garner when Turing asked him if he thought intelligent machinery was possible. After running silently for 10 minutes, he said no. Turing did not argue. Why learn classical languages? Turing asked, and Garner said, 'you have to learn to use your brain in a different way': the kind of answer that Turing would have appreciated. Equality also was found in banter of the kind that would now be called 'no bullshit', full of word play and scurrilous humour.

Alan running on Alderley Edge in 1951.

As Alan Garner's *Guardian* piece revealed, there was an even more remarkable link. Their chat usually kept away from the personal: it was focused on sustaining the six or seven miles of running. But once, probably late in 1951, Turing mentioned the story of 'Snow White'. 'You too!' said Garner, amazed. For he connected it immediately with a singular event from his childhood. When four or five years old, *Snow White and the Seven Dwarfs* had terrified him with the vision of the poisoned apple. Turing responded with immediate empathy, and their shared trauma – as Garner saw it – remained a bond. 'He used to go over the scene in detail, dwelling on the ambiguity of the apple, red on one side, green on the other, one of which gave death.'

The significance of this imagery only became apparent in June 1954, when Alan Turing did himself die of poisoning with potassium cyanide, and with every reason to suppose that the bitten apple lying by his bedside had been soaked in the lethal solution. Some further background is necessary here. Back in 1937, Turing had conveyed to his pre-war boyfriend, James Atkins, details of a suicide plan involving 'an apple and electrical wiring'. He also told his post-war boyfriend, Neville Johnson, that he had once had a suicide plan. In March 1953 he did two things that strongly suggest he was reviving the pre-war plan. He set up a home chemistry laboratory, and made a point of using potassium cyanide in an electrochemical experiment, gold-plating a teaspoon. He also asked his closest gay friend, Nick Furbank (later a highly regarded literary critic and biographer) to be his executor; over the following year he drew up a highly unconventional will. The period around March 1953 was notable for what Turing described as a 'crisis' involving surveillance – a conflict that was inevitable given Turing's unrepentant gay life, involving wild trips abroad, and his status at the heart of national security.

In what sense was this a suicide 'plan'? Because it was intended to allow his mother, in particular, to believe that it was an accidental ingestion of cyanide while involved in a chemistry experiment. In the event, it worked; she did convince herself of this, and others have also managed this feat. How did *Snow White* come into it? The 1938 British premiere, which maybe both Alans saw in the same week, came after this plan was formulated. It must have struck Turing very forcibly, that the apple, his practical means of kindly deceit, was both an icon of folklore and fairy tale – and of this landmark film. His economist friend David Champernowne, who went to the cinema in Cambridge with Turing to see the Disney film in 1938, recalled Turing repeating the couplet with relish: 'Dip the apple in the brew, Let the sleeping death seep through.'

Alan Garner's story thus adds to these nuggets and confirms that in the period before the dénouement, Alan Turing thought of the apple as significant, and specifically in terms of its imagery of death. It is notable that when Turing sought a form of therapy for the shock of events in 1952 – his arrest, trial and punishment by injection of female hormones – it was to a Jungian psychoanalyst that he turned. His interaction with Alan Garner seems to have anticipated these sessions (of which, of course, there is no record).

Turing never spoke to Garner of those traumatic 1952 events, and Garner only heard the news later that year, when he was warned by the police not to associate with Turing. Garner was very angry at this advice, and at what he then learnt had happened, and he never had the least sense of having been approached in any predatory way. The young Garner seems quite instinctively to have sided with Turing as an existentialist hero, a man road-running to freedom, and made a point of writing a sixth form essay on Greek sexuality.

And yet, perhaps inevitably, the training partnership ended dismally and without authenticity, in an incident redolent of the fiction and film of late teenage years. Alan Garner painfully recalls seeing Turing for the last time in 1953, as a fellow passenger on the bus from Manchester to Wilmslow. Being with his girlfriend, Garner found it too difficult to say anything appropriate and so he pretended not to have noticed his presence. This was soon followed by Garner's departure to National Service, during which he heard of Turing's death.

Alan Garner told me this story in 2012 as if it were yesterday. The 60-year time-shift was accentuated by the towering presence of the Jodrell Bank radio telescope, adjacent to the ancient building that Alan and Griselda Garner have made their home and archaeological base. The telescope was itself an outpost of dynamic Manchester University science, and just like the computer, the outcome of Second World War technology turned to science after 1945. The scene emphasised the would-have-been that was cut off in 1954, the great scope of new discoveries a living Turing might have made in such a creative period. Instead, he left the haunting icon of the poisoned apple, on that Whit Monday night just 10 years after D-Day. It is quite amazing that the one person he entrusted with the iconography in his mind should be Alan Garner. The writer who so distinctively bridged time and modernised ancient icons in his post-1960 writing, had been a privileged party to the real-life iconography of this central figure of the Second World War.

Even so, it is an image of the year 1938 that stares out of this story, rather than 1951. When Turing formulated his suicide plan in 1937, it was as a very isolated young gay man away in the United States, lacking his protective Cambridge friendship network. But by the time he saw *Snow White* in 1938, his life had changed. He had decided on a loss of innocence and had left the paradise of pure mathematics. He had turned down an academic career in the United

States, returned to Britain, and signed up with the Government Code and Cypher School, forerunner of today's GCHQ. It was this moral choice, defining his 'security' status in 1953, that must have haunted him. None of this, of course, was visible to anyone for decades afterwards.

For a final word, appropriate for a book devoted to appreciation of Alan Garner, we can see that Alan Turing must have sensed something special in the seventeen-year-old sixth form classicist. He would have looked forward to every training run, delighted to be accepted as an equal by a vibrant young lad. Such acceptance would have helped him through the trial of 1952 more than any words could have done. There is no call for guilt, but for open-ended wonder at the magic of time and life.

Andrew Hodges's biography Alan Turing: The Enigma *(1983) has been published in a new 2014 edition including Alan Garner's story in an additional preface.*

ALAN TO AN ACADEMIC: HISTORY AND MYTHOLOGY IN ALAN GARNER'S NOVELS

Ronald Hutton

Mercifully, I did not encounter Alan's work as an academic historian. Instead, I read the first significant piece of it, *The Weirdstone of Brisingamen*, soon after it was published, when I was ten years old. That was enough to get me hooked, and I have followed his books ever since, relishing the personal signatures on those that have appeared in the past dozen years. One and a half decades after that first encounter, I established myself as a professional historian with a special interest in myth. It may therefore be interesting – even while missing much of what I find most wonderful in Alan and his writing – to trace the themes of myth and history through his novels from the point of view of an academic scholar, and see what pattern emerges. Alan's own knowledge of history, especially that of his heartland of East Cheshire, is of course excellent, and he has made genuine contributions to the knowledge of its prehistory. Still, it is for his fictional work that he will be forever best known; and so my concern should be with that.

Even as a child and young teenager, I instantly spotted what was remarkable about Alan's novels as works of fantasy: that they stayed at home. Most such works – a genre for which I had a particular juvenile hunger – transported me to imagined realms such as Middle-earth or Narnia. Kipling did invest his Sussex countryside with magic, but his main point was to turn it into a living history book rather than to fill it with myth. *The Weirdstone* made the Cheshire countryside between Alderley and the Pennines throng with supernatural creatures, and the more vividly in that they all had antecedents in medieval northern mythologies. The core of the story, the pre-existing Legend of Alderley, was derived from high medieval chivalric romance (armoured and mounted knights), but the non-human creatures that featured in the action came out of older and more primeval tradition, mostly Scandinavian and Germanic. Even the elves are those of the Icelander Snorri Sturluson, and not of later medieval English romance. As the Scandinavian-Germanic myth continuum could serve well (with some stretching) for the early English, it may be argued that this was indeed a native mythology for Cheshire: symbolically, the tale's tragic hero dies belted to an Anglo-Saxon cross-shaft. With Alan, however, things are never that simple, and even in that first book he also gleefully raided medieval Irish and Welsh mythology and modern Manx folklore for characters and names. The sheer richness of all this, combined with the detailed action of the story in real locations, gave a compelling sense of actuality to it, of the sort which a certain kind of reader (let alone a certain kind of child) craves.

The Moon of Gomrath was of course its successor, and the only time that Alan has succumbed to writing a direct sequel to any of his books. Characters and setting remain the same, therefore, but the scope of the mythology is even broader, raiding early medieval literatures all over the British Isles to add to the existing stock. Furthermore, for the first and last time, Alan dipped into modern Druidic and Pagan lore for a framework of ideas. The cosmology of different worlds to which reference is made is that of the eighteenth-century Welsh poet, scholar and trickster Iolo Morganwg, who represented it as that of the ancient Druids. The framework of divinity that is employed is that of the modern pagan witch religion of Wicca, which had been public for only just over a decade before the book appeared. The main superhuman male figure is the horned (or antlered) god of Wicca, lord of the Wild Hunt – though being Alan's creation he has Odin's retinue, filtered through Irish imagery.

The counterpoising female figure is associated with the waning moon, and balanced and opposed by a teenage priestess – in effect – who is empowered by the waxing one. The triple Wiccan moon goddess, Maiden, Mother and Crone, is here represented by the first and last, while the central, motherly, figure is supplied by Celemon, who acts as patroness to the teenager.

Probably, and leaving aside Alan's own feelings about getting bogged down with the same characters and settings, the mixture was getting too rich to be digestible, and the next book abandoned it with a slam. *Elidor* had new people, a new and grimily urban setting, and a sparer style. Moreover, it drew much more tightly on Irish material, using the medieval myths of that land to provide its framework and in one sequence setting the action in a nightmarish version of Ireland's most famous prehistoric monument, the Neolithic passage grave at Newgrange, that nation's equivalent to Stonehenge. Still, he would not be Alan if he made it all culturally neat, and so he throws a beast from high medieval chivalric fantasy – a singing unicorn – into the middle of this primitive Celtic brew; to perfect narrative effect. Alerted by this, those in the know will spot other echoes of high medieval literature scattered through the tale to leaven it.

This looks like a new winning formula, flexible enough to be repeated for another book or two; and yet Alan immediately discarded it. For his fourth novel, *The Owl Service*, he stripped the format down to a yet simpler level and chose a single, very well-known, medieval Welsh legend and let it play out through the lives of a set of modern teenagers in the landscape from which the original story had sprung. No longer is the magic represented by non-human characters or people from the heroic past, but is inherent in a place and a set of repeating human situations.

This was a model so powerful that it cried out for repetition; Alan, of course, ignored the cry. For *Red Shift* he stuck to the idea of staging action in a single, numinous place, moving back to East Cheshire for that – though not to Alderley. However, instead of having a continuous story in a past-saturated present, he split the action into three levels with their own cast of people, one ancient, one early modern and one contemporary. Each possesses part of the whole tale, which the sacred location – the striking hill of Mow Cop – itself holds together, manifesting both in the hill itself and in a (presumably originally consecrated) Neolithic artefact which passes through all three time zones.

The book is intended for older teenage readers and the tone is bleaker than before: it is the first to have no happy ending. It also, however, marks a deeper – excuse the expression – shift in Alan's fiction, as it is the point at which history – though in a spiritualised and partly imagined form – takes over from mythology as its mainstay. Alan has indeed explained that the idea for the story is based on a famous traditional Scottish fairy ballad – 'Tam Lin' – but the resemblance is very deeply buried. This latest style suited Alan well enough for him to reproduce it in outline with *The Stone Book Quartet*, the four sequential stories which he now published about four past generations of his own family. Like *Red Shift*, therefore, the quartet moved through different phases of history, but in a shorter and more connected time span and with a mellower tone. The reader is back in the Alderley district, from which the non-human beings have now disappeared, and with them any overt magic, leaving a lingering sense of power inhering in a long-lived landscape and craft – stonemasonry. The latter is implicitly traced back to the Old Stone Age, and here I felt that Alan was stretching the archaeological record by putting Palaeolithic art into a Cheshire cave – until, in a pattern rather typical of Alan, real Palaeolithic cave carvings were found on the far side of the Pennines, at Creswell Crags, almost 30 years later.

Then came the long hiatus until *Strandloper*, but this effectively picked up where the *Quartet* left off. The book has the same tone and covers some of the same period, but it represents Alan's first complete historical novel. It starts, of course, in East Cheshire, but in a huge geographical and imaginative leap connects that, through its hero's encounter with a doomed native people of Australia – an encounter which is based in fact. Moreover, it suggests that the indigenous folk cultures of each had profound similarities, to an extent that suggests a universality of human myth. Next came *Thursbitch*, which reverted to the split-level technique, a contemporary story linked to a historic one. The latter retreated further into the Cheshire Pennines, further in time (to the eighteenth century) and further into primeval belief. *Strandloper* had suggested an enduring, organic, folk religion of the land; *Thursbitch* manifested a full-blown surviving pagan religion among rural Cheshire people. It was not that of Wicca, or Iolo's Druidry, but one of Alan's own creation, an Indo-European bull cult based on his wide reading into comparative mythology but owing most to the ancient Greek mystery cult of Dionysius. It is enacted in a genuine landscape, which may be a Neolithic ceremonial complex, and concerns a genuine historical enigma; elements of the magical, or at least the uncanny, are creeping back.

All this sets the scene for the last book to date, *Boneland*, which repeats and develops patterns and people drawn from most of those before. Historically, it is split-level again, but across a much wider span, a story in the present intercut with one set more or less in the same land during the Old Stone Age, as the linkages between the two slowly become apparent. The place is once again Alan's home district, and the main protagonist is his original teenage hero, Colin, from the first two novels, now in adulthood; the heroine of those early books remains a ghostly presence. The ancient story is one of (honourable) death, the modern one of rebirth, and indeed of re-enchantment, because here the magic is back in Alan's fiction, almost literally with a vengeance. The hero starts it disturbed, isolated and distraught – an adult shell and parody of his young self – and gradually recovers balance, confidence and self-knowledge as he regains memory of his childhood adventures and realises that all were true; which means the wizard, dwarfs and all the other non-human beings are as well. This transformation is effected by the aid of characters who at first seem human and mundane themselves but prove – it is implied – to be anything but those things.

These suggestions do great violence to the range and subtlety of Alan's use of history and mythology, and he will probably be the person most outraged by this: my chapter will hardly seem a gift to him. However, one thing, perhaps, he may accept as a summary of how an academic may view his work. Professional historians and prehistorians commonly act as providers of raw material for imaginative writers, but I cannot say that most of us do that for Alan, even when our material is the same. Rather, his own knowledge of (apparently) real and (apparently) fantastic pasts is so profound that we work in parallel, with the single great similarity that both our enterprises express a recognition that neither history nor mythology nor literature follow single and simple tracks. No other living British writer has, I believe, used history and myth in such a remarkable range of restlessly, uninhibitedly, different and personal ways. I can neither emulate nor inspire him: I can only admire.

Ronald Hutton is Professor of History at Bristol University, and the author of 15 books and 74 essays which deal with different themes in history, mythology and folklore.

THE SPEAKING OF THE STONES: TWO THINGS I LEARNED FROM ALAN GARNER

Paul Kingsnorth

On 23rd October 1642, an army of English Royalists under the command of Prince Rupert of the Rhine was marching from Shrewsbury towards London. Their aim was to meet up with the forces of King Charles I, and to crush the rebellion against his divine authority represented by the newly raised army of Parliament.

Midway between the small towns of Warwick and Banbury, Rupert's forces were intercepted by an army of Parliamentarians under the command of Robert Devereux, Earl of Essex. Battle was joined, and 30,000 soldiers clashed in a bloody melee which left thousands dead and wounded, but gave neither side a conclusive victory. Victory or not, the day was of huge significance: the Battle of Edgehill was the first engagement in what would become the English Civil War.

Two months later, just before Christmas 1642, some shepherds were walking across the battlefield, which was still strewn with rotting bodies and rusting weapons. As they crossed the site of the struggle, the shepherds later said, they could make out the sounds of battle. They heard the cries of soldiers and musket fire and the sound of horses and clashing pikes. Then, as they watched, astonished, they saw the battle itself being replayed across the landscape on which it happened two months before. An army of ghostly soldiers was refighting Edgehill.

Naturally, the shepherds told anyone who would listen of their experience, and over the next days and weeks local people gathered on the battlefield to catch a glimpse of the ghostly re-enactment. Many claimed to have done so, and the phenomenon spiralled from a local to a national talking point. In January 1643, a pamphlet entitled *A Great Wonder in Heaven* was written about the haunting. So persistent were the reports that the King himself, even in the middle of a Civil War, found the time to send a Royal Commission to the battlefield to investigate the claims.

When the Commission visited the site, its members saw the ghostly re-enactment for themselves. Paying close attention, they were able to identify some of the soldiers whose ghosts were replaying their recent traumatic experience. The Commission noted that some of the 'ghosts' they saw were of people who were, in fact, still living.

★

In December 1972, BBC television broadcast a Christmas ghost story written by Nigel Kneale, creator of *Quatermass*. *The Stone Tape* told the story of a group of electronics researchers working on a new recording medium, who move to a new research facility in an old Victorian building. One of the oldest rooms in the building, according to local tales, may be of Saxon origin and is said to be haunted by the ghost of a screaming woman.

Working in the room, many of the team experience the sound and sometimes the sight of the screaming woman themselves. But when they leave their state-of-the-art recording equipment set up in the room it picks nothing up. Puzzling this over, the head of the team notes that every time the screaming woman is seen she moves in the same way and makes the same sound. He suspects that what his team are seeing is not the returning spirit of a dead person but a recording of a past event, which is somehow being replayed in their presence. He hypothesises that some property in the ancient stone allows it to act as a recording device. It is the presence of living humans that triggers playback.

The Stone Tape popularised a theory, recently developed by the paranormal researcher T.C. Lethbridge, that recurring ghost sightings, such as the phantom Battle of Edgehill, may be 'recordings' of traumatic events which had somehow been stored and 'replayed' by the physical environment. Paranormal investigators call this the 'theory of residual haunting', but it is more popularly known these days simply as 'Stone Tape theory'.

★

Three years before *The Stone Tape*, ITV broadcast its adaptation of Alan Garner's novel *The Owl Service*. I was forced to watch this as a teenager in school English classes in the 1980s. How we all sniggered at the haircuts and trousers and production values of the late 1960s. Still, underneath the bravado, I was spooked. The weird plates. The noises in the attic. The sound of the phantom motorbike. That figure on the hill they kept seeing. Standing there with his spear, summoned by mistake. Recorded by time and now played back, unbidden and bringing malice. History, it seemed to suggest, was not something that had once happened, but something we all still lived in, whether we liked it or not. The blood must repeat the cycle.

As a writer, I have learned two things from Alan Garner. Or, rather: there were things I was already aware of at some level, things I knew I had to do, things that were in me and which I wanted to bring out with my writing. Alan Garner showed me it was still possible to write about these things, even at a time when so much fiction writing, in tune with our wider culture, is sterile, rational-realist, playing on the surface and afraid to dive underneath. 'Good novels,' asserted George Orwell, 'are written by people who are not frightened.' Alan Garner has never been frightened by what lies beneath the surface of the stories we tell ourselves to get through the day.

Garner explained this in an interview in 1989. 'As I turned toward writing,' he said, 'which is partially intellectual in its function, but is primarily intuitive and emotional in its execution, I turned towards that which was numinous and emotional in me, and that was the legend of King Arthur Asleep Under the Hill. It stood for all that I'd had to give up in order to understand what I'd had to give up. And so my first two books, which are very poor on characterisation because I was somehow numbed in that area, are very strong on imagery and landscape, because of the landscape I had inherited along with the legend.'

This is the first thing I learned from Alan Garner: that a place can be a character in a novel. That a landscape has a soul just as a human does, that it merits investigation, that it has its own inner life and history and that it can play a role in fiction not simply as a backdrop to the travails of human actors, but as a living actor itself. Garner learned to write about the character of landscape before he learned to write about the character of people. I suspect this is what baffles many critics when they consider his work. A novel, a real proper novel, written by a grown-up 'literary' writer, is supposed to be an elegant dissection of the individual human psyche. Garner is more interested, it seems to me, in investigating the psyche of the landscape than those of the people who just happen to be passing across it at this brief moment.

The second thing I learned from Garner is that the past is not past at all. Rather, history is still living, and we are all in it. This is not simply true in the obvious sense that we ourselves will be history in the eyes of future generations. It is true in the sense that history has never ended, that the past is not dead, that like the phantom soldiers of Edgehill, it returns to draw us back and entwine us. In his work, Garner comes back again and again to that image of Arthur and his knights asleep under the hill. This old legend has it that King Arthur never died, that he still sleeps somewhere under an old hill or mountain or in some deep cave, and that in the nation's hour of greatest need he will rise again with his knights to save us. There are a dozen hills in Britain that claim to have Arthur sleeping beneath them.

But Arthur here is a metaphor for the past itself, for the history he steps out from. It never dies, it only sleeps, and sometimes it returns when you least expect it, and then it can control your fate. What does a novel look like when its creator takes that idea seriously? Garner gives us one answer to that question. Like the Stone Tape, he replays the past again and again, hauling it up from the depths of the rock, until the people of the present wake up and take notice of what has come back to speak to them.

Paul Kingsnorth is the author of two non-fiction books and a collection of poetry. His debut novel, The Wake, *won the Gordon Burn Prize and the Bookseller Book of the Year Award, and was longlisted for the 2014 Man Booker Prize. He is co-founder of the Dark Mountain Project, a network of artists and writers in search of new stories.*

Alan Garner with his father Colin, 1935.

Alan Garner on the starting block, 1952.

Alan Garner, 1960.

Alan Garner during the filming of *Red Shift*, 1977.

The Lovell Telescope, Toad Hall and the Old Medicine House.

Alan and Griselda Garner at a dig in 2007.
(Photo © Mark Roberts)

GRIPE GRIFFIN

Olivia Laing

Upon a wreath of the colours, a thresher proper, his hat and coat per pale argent and gules, his breeches and stockings of the third and second, holding in both hands a flair or, uplifted over a garb on the dexter side, and over the crest upon an escroll the Motto, 'Now thus', and below the arms the Motto 'Gripe Griffin, Hold Fast'.

Time is honey. Time has a sting in the tale. Time runs forward, and maybe back.

It was Matt who told me about Thursbitch. Just past the pendulum of the millennium, in the first flat I ever lived in on my own. It was cut into the hill, so you went in at the front down a flight of steps and came out at the back to a garden falling away on the breaking wave of the South Downs. At the bottom of the hill there was a thin, glittering stream of traffic. London Road, which was once the Wellesbourne, now piped or sewered or shunted somewhere. *You daft sods. You've buggered Spirit Hole.*

It was winter, and Matt sat in my room, glasses glinting, one great dreadlock to his waist, and told me a story about someone out walking or running in the Pennines who slipped down a bank and barked their shin against a stone. The stone was carved with letters and the letters said that a man had died there in a snowstorm, one night sometime around the middle of the eighteenth century. On the back of the stone it said that beside the man's body there was found the print of a woman's shoe. Matt told me the story and then he said the name of the place, Thursbitch, and that night I had a nightmare about it. In my nightmare I knew that if I thought about the place, it would become aware of me. That it was watching me. Last night, after I wrote this, I went to sleep and had the dream again.

That flat was a hinge. I'd gone out and I was coming back in, getting more and more civilised after years living outdoors or half-outdoors, in caravans and tree houses, in woods and fields and scraps of waste ground at the margins of the towns. Places that were about to be cut down, bulldozed, removed from the map, buried beneath roads.

The last one I'd lived in was out on the Weald, on the far side of the Downs, in a bender built from stolen hazel in a field out the back of an abandoned pig farm. On full moon, I'd bike in the dark to the big hill, Wolstonbury, and lie in the bowl of the barrows. For years I'd been backing and forthing along the whole chain of them. St Catherine's Hill, up with the Dongas on winter solstice, with tarts we'd baked in the shape of *sheela-na-gigs*. Walking the maze in the half-light, wood smoke rising through the trees. Always bringing something for the moon, knocking up Winchester Hill, waiting for a door to open. Just before harvest on the rise above Moulsecombe, walking to Lewes amid a shower of larks.

Good places: Kingley Vale, where we breathed all day a haze of yew pollen, a hallucinogenic golden scurf that hung on the air. Cissbury Ring, the cornerstone, scrub oaks and cropped ground ivy. Bad places: Chanctonbury Ring, where a tree once snapped beneath me and broke my leg, the whole hillside shrugging me off. Firle Beacon, Glynde Reach, the patch of greensand between them, where commuter villages were built over battlegrounds. A place of great evil, Julian said.

★

I didn't read *Thursbitch* immediately. I read *Strandloper* first. It's about William Buckley, a Cheshire man who is transported to Australia for the twin crimes of learning to write and keeping up country customs – which is to say for not knowing his place in time, for aspiring to both the freedoms of the future and the past. It's the story of a man who learns how to inhabit a place: by tending to it, by attending it on foot, like a country doctor. *By, this here wants some walking*. Off he goes, singing the bees' song, singing even when what he finds is more of the same: more injustice, more people driven off the land or killed when they won't go, their bodies hanging from the trees, stuffed with grass that spills obscenely from eyes and ears and mouths.

That book was full of a grief I recognised instantly, a grief that was still fresh and aching when I first read it. *The dead men say that they must have the land*, and then they fence it and drain it and evict the people and cut down the forests and drench the land in poison or seal it in tarmac. No oaks, no bees. *Strandloper* records the opening sallies in man's great vanishing act, his eradication of variety.

I came to *Thursbitch* later. It tells another side of the story, which is the resisting land, the magic of deep time, geological time, the land that outlives everything that is done to it. *Snake and stone. They live forever . . . and what are we but blood and soot*? John Turner, the packman who died in the snow, is redeemed by the confluence of place and time, the way they interact and interweave.

You might not live in the valley of the demon, but everyone has one foot in deep time. The flat where Matt first told me about Thursbitch was itself a few hundred yards shy of a Neolithic burial ground, skirted by allotments and golf courses. We were sitting in Wihta's Valley, between the drove road, the dykes and the denes. The council estate on the flank of the hill was rising out of a solid geology of pure white chalk limestone. Time compacted, a centimetre each thousand years.

Say you dug down into it. Say you got beneath the tarmac, the basal layer for tarmac, the made ground, the mid grey, the compact, sandy silt. What would you find? Relics of the gone, whose place is here but not now. Two pieces of worked flint, a polished axe, fire-cracked flint, a gold armlet. A silver penny of Offa, found May 1932 on Surrenden Crescent when levelling for a lawn in the garden of 'Flodigarry', home perhaps to some homesick Scot. Time compacted, time gumming up.

You put your roots down, or you don't. You protect what you

love, or you don't. Either way you're living on live ground, on top of the dead. Time runs in ribbons, interlayered. And somewhere there's a dance of rewind and renewal, and when it's done everything is set to rights. Jack Turner does it, out under the stars on Thursbitch, and so does William Buckley, back in Cheshire at last, dancing a meadow out of the church. *Hollin, coraminga, cuckoo bread; torumba, nardoo, galligaskins; devilberry, jackanapes, goborro, mulkathandra; vervey, bolwarra, popple, marara; karagata, dargan, Robin-run-in-th'hedge. Gripe Griffin*, he tells himself: *hold fast*. Time's a long game. Time is turning and time is honey and all the bees are back.

Olivia Laing's first book, To the River, *was shortlisted for the 2012 Ondaatje Prize and the Dolman Travel Book of the Year.* The Trip to Echo Spring *was shortlisted for the 2013 Costa Biography Award and the Gordon Burn Prize. Her latest book,* The Lonely City: Adventures in the Art of Being Alone, *was published in spring 2016. She lives in Cambridge.*

THE WEIRDSTONE OF TALYBONT

Katherine Langrish

One Sunday in spring, walking a mountain track in the Brecon Beacons, I sat down on a grassy bank high above the Talybont reservoir and gazed across the valley towards the massive scalloped slopes of Cribyn and Pen y Fan. Then I looked down at the track at my feet, and a stone looked back at me. A triangular piece of sandstone with an eye-shaped lozenge traced on it, glowing. I picked it up. A shimmering blue line ran between two darker lines, enclosing a smooth-grained reddish oval. Perhaps it was more of a teardrop than an eye. It looked intentional. A sign, a sigil.

Had the mark been painted on? But why would anyone do that and then leave it on the hillside miles from anywhere? And it was the same kind of rock as all the others lying around – plain red sandstone, fracturing and weathering out of the hill in wedges, triangles and lopsided diamonds. In the sunshine the blue oval line shone with a quartzy, crystalline glitter, and a dark shadow lay around it that didn't look painted. I licked a finger and rubbed the mark. It didn't smudge. Still, I wasn't sure – till I glanced another way and saw a second eye shining in the sun, the mirror image of the first. The two pieces of stone fitted perfectly together. It must have dropped out of the bank as a single block and cracked in half.

It was clearly a Weirdstone: the 'Weirdstone of Talybont'. The thought was there at once, immediate and handy. I was in South Wales, standing on a real hill with a real stone in my hand, imaginatively inhabiting a children's book I read for the first time in 1965, and which has stayed with me ever since.

A few days later I would be at Jodrell Bank in Cheshire, listening to Alan Garner deliver a lecture on human culture and creativity. He showed his audience a black pebble, worked and chipped – a 500,000-year-old hand-axe – and told of sitting in his ancient farmhouse, holding the axe and looking across the fields at the vast dish of the Lovell Radio Telescope as it, in turn, looked at quasars far away in time and space.

The hand-axe – this was his thought – is the forerunner of the telescope. Both are products of the human impulse to explore, shape and interpret the world. Both evoke an authentic numinous shiver as we peer over our own shoulders into the dark backward and abysm of time. We can't have the telescope without the hand-axe. We can't have a landscape without the geological ages that formed it. We can't be human without owning our past.

Alan Garner's first four books changed my imagination, and imagination is a lens we use to look at the world. I'm reminded of folklore about stones with holes in them. If you peek through the hole you can see the fairies walking among us in an extra, invisible dimension that exists alongside our own.

Or a human midwife is taken under the hill to deliver a fairy woman's child. Rubbing the newborn infant with strange ointment from a green jar, she accidentally touches the sticky stuff to one of her own eyes. Some time later, having been restored to the workaday world, she sees the fairy in the local marketplace and greets her. The fairy returns the greeting and asks, 'With which eye do you see me?' 'With this one,' the midwife replies, and the fairy thrusts a finger into it and blinds her.

Some writers touch the mind's eye. Luckily for us, they don't begrudge the gift.

Under the seeing eye, landscapes reveal layers – strata – of history, prehistory, geology and legend. Places are founded in time, time becomes a dimension of place. Errwood Hall is a ruin in daylight, but whole when the moon shines on it. A half-demolished Manchester church is gateway to a fairy world, and a crazed, wounded unicorn careers through a wasteland of cleared slums, a place which appears dead but (like Elidor) will come to life again, a liminal place poised between endings and beginnings. Characters themselves are rooted in time. They re-enact old tragedies, repeat the same words. 'I'm the Governor of this gang,' says Mary's father in *The Stone Book*, echoing the fourteenth-century poem *Gawain and the Green Knight*. 'I'm the governor of this gang,' says the man painting the windows of the empty house in *Boneland*. 'Wher is,' demands the Green Knight as he rides into Arthur's hall at Christmastime, 'the gouernour of this gyng?' The ancient language is still alive, still spoken. With its evocation of the wild, mysterious landscape of the northwest midlands – Cheshire, Lancashire and the Wirral – the Gawain poem is one of Garner's touchstones.

So there I was, nine years old, lost in a book. 'On, on, on, on, faster, faster the track drew him, flowed through him, filled his heart and his lungs and his mind with fire, sparked from his eyes, streamed from his hair, and the bells and the music and the voices were all of him, and the Old Magic sang to him from the depths of the earth and the caverns of the night-blue sky.' Incantatory, intoxicating! It swept me away. No one had written for children like this before. 'Ride, Einheriar of the Herlathing!' 'And the Old Magic was free for ever, and the moon was new.'

Drunk on language and legends I pored over the notes at the end of *The Moon of Gomrath*, hoping to read the magical-sounding books cited there, *The Red Book of Hergest* and *The Black Book of Caernarvon*. They were never going to be available from my small local library, but a few years later I read the *Mabinogion*, and Robert Graves's fascinating and unreliable *The White Goddess*, and Alfred Watkins's *The Old Straight Track* (which I found disappointingly unmagical). I mopped up as much folklore as I could, and aged sixteen wrote an Alan Garner-inspired story of my own. Of course it was derivative, but at sixteen imitation can be more than flattery. It was a way to learn the craft, a writing apprenticeship, part of the buried strata of my own work. I don't remember the plot, but there was a mysterious fugitive, a moon goddess, a Wild Hunter, and a race of golden-faced, indifferent elves who wove slow, intricate dances around stone circles as the sun went down. I put in as much as I could of the moon-magic and fairy-legends in the books I'd been reading, and set it in a real landscape – the rich, physical beauty of the Herefordshire countryside which was then my home, its woods and hills.

The handwritten pages have lain in a drawer ever since, stuffed in a big brown envelope. I pulled them out the other day and braced myself for a critical flick through. But it was oddly moving. She's still there, the teenage me: ambitious, embarrassing, clumsy, passionate, hopeful. Here's one of the better passages.

> It was still early morning. Edric looked about and then jumped a hedge and ditch and rode the horse straight up the village street. Curtains were drawn at every window and the road was deserted. A dog began barking at the gate of one house, but it was chained and the horse unshod: they passed quietly by and no one woke. Martins sat on the telegraph wires and chirped; sparrows chattered. Edric slowed to a walk, and now they were nearly at the church.
>
> It seemed the only building yet awake, watching them from the corners of its high belfry windows. In the graveyard was a tall high stone. Edric leaned to brush it with his fingertips and then sent the horse forward to leap the low wall, shed the last cottages with a flick of its heels and cross into meadow and wheatfields again. They passed by Dancing Green and by scattered houses among trees, high hedges, orchards and fields. Then they struck on towards the blunt end of the Penyard Hill, covered with forestry commission trees. They jumped the wire fence into the wood and went crashing up through the undergrowth. The trees closed in behind them.

The place names are real, places I knew. I'd understood that landscape was at least as important as magic in Alan Garner's work. What I remember best about writing this untitled, unpublishable story is how happy it made me. It seemed to me then (it still does) that the job of a writer, at any rate the sort of writer I admire, is to gather up as much as possible of what Robert Graves calls the 'greatness, rareness, muchness' of our 'endless world'. Alan Garner is one such.

After I'd found my Weirdstone I put the two halves in my pockets and walked back to where we'd left our car in a lonely parking spot at the top of a terrifyingly twisty single track road. Another car was just arriving. A man and woman got out with their dogs, and I showed them the stone – it needed sharing – and for a few moments we marvelled over it together. As we were departing, the woman called out to me. 'It's a key stone! You just need to find the key!'

'But where is the door?' I called back.

They were setting their faces to climb the steep dun flank of Tor y Foel, the dogs running on ahead. 'I'll look for it!' she cried.

At home, I tried to find out what my Weirdstone might be. The place where I picked it up is called Pen Bwlch Glasgwm, where the track runs uphill towards the Bryniau Gleision, the Blue Mountains. I don't know why 'blue', but we'd seen fragile greeny-blue lines of shale eroding out of the red and brown sandstones and mudstones. All that rock was deposited by vast river systems 400 million years ago, when the area lay in the middle of the gigantic continent of Pangaea. When I knew that – when I saw it in my mind's eye – my skin prickled.

And three days later, sitting in the lecture hall at Jodrell Bank listening to Alan Garner talk about rocks and stars and deep time, and the connection between the intuitive mind and the intellect, and how we need both to get anything worthwhile done, I wondered if I should have brought my blue-eyed Weirdstone to show him. I hadn't, but perhaps I should have. Instead I'd brought my battered copy of *The Weirdstone of Brisingamen* in which, with more truth than I guessed at the time, my nine-year-old self had written 'this book belongs to Katherine Langrish' in spiky red letters. 'You can see how much it's been loved,' I said while he signed his own name in it. 'These are the ones I like best,' he replied.

In *The Stone Book*, Father breaks a stone in half for Mary. 'When you cut stone, you see more than the parson does, Church or Chapel.' Then, echoing Job 38:4 ('Where wast thou when I laid the foundations of the earth? Declare, if thou hast understanding') he sets her a challenge.

> 'Tell me how those flakes were put together, and what they are,' he said. 'And who made them into pebbles on a hill, and where that was a rock, and when.'

I still don't know what made the blue eye in the stone I found. I don't know what kind of fossil it is, or even if it's a fossil at all. But it reminds me of the power and magic of stones and hills, the long stretches of deep time that made such a thing, and the serendipitous moment that tumbled it out of the hill at my feet.

Mary, in *The Stone Book*, wants a prayer book to carry to church, though she cannot read. In the Book of Job (which is a poem) God responds to Job's suffering not with answers, but with page after page of relentless questions hammered home like nails. What are the dimensions of the earth? How are its foundations fastened? Who set the cornerstone, 'when the morning stars sang together'? Who stretched his measuring line over it? Have you descended to the springs of the sea? Can you draw up Leviathan with a hook? 'He makes the deep water boil like a cauldron, he leaves a shining trail behind him, and the great river is like white hair in his wake.' On, on it goes, a paean to the pitiless beauty of creation, the wonder and the ungraspable mystery. 'Read the book of the world,' God seems to be saying to Job – as Father says to Mary, as Alan Garner says to us. 'For the world is my only answer.'

> 'And Mary sat by the fire and read the stone book that had in it all the stories of the world and the flowers of the flood.'

Katherine Langrish is a critically acclaimed British author of several historical fantasies for children. Her titles include the trilogy West of the Moon, *and* Dark Angels *(US title* The Shadow Hunt*), a tale of ghosts, elves and hobgoblins set in the Welsh Marches. You can find Katherine at her blog 'Seven Miles of Steel Thistles' [http://steelthistles.blogspot.co.uk/] where she writes on folklore, fairy tales and fantasy.*

THE JOINING OF THE SONG

Hugh Lupton

'All in!' shouted Ozzie Leah.

The three men took their scythes and a whetstone each and sharpened the blades, two strokes below, one above. The metal rang like swords and bells.[1]

The craft is held in the sharp edge of that fine honed blade where the written and the uttered word meet, where the eye meets the ear. On the one side we have 'grammar and syntax', on the other 'pitch and cadence and the colour of the word'[2].

Born into the first generation to reap the benefits of the 1944 Education Act, educated at The Manchester Grammar School and then Oxford University, it would have been easy for Alan Garner (like most of his generation) to leave his origins behind him and step into the bold new post-war world that promised to shake away the old class-ridden consensus.

But instead he returned. He went back to Alderley Edge, his birthplace, the place his ancestors had inhabited for as long as any one of them could remember. And he set about finding – with all the discipline of the western academic intellectual tradition at his disposal – a language and a narrative form that could be true to the deep culture of his place.

Grammar began to meet song, thought began to meet dream,

1 *The Aimer Gate* p.15
2 *Introduction to Book of British Fairy Tales* p.7

on that path (familiar to Lancelot) 'difficult to tread, narrow as the edge of a razor'[3].

And it is a sharp path, beset with thorns and briars. The 'deep narrow' culture of Alderley, as he had discovered during his school years, fought shy of 'education'. Even now, as I try to make a list of what seem to me to be the consuming questions that lie 'aback of behind'[4] in Garner's books I can hear those voices, withering and canny in equal measure, cutting me down to size. They are voices that must have haunted him from the outset.

Question: How does an oral culture apply the breadth and depth of its knowledge to its own locality?

Answer: That's for thee to see and me to know.

Question: Given that an oral culture is unbroken and bound to place, what ancient traces might it still carry?

Answer: What indeed, quoth Kettle to his mare.

Question: Given that exceptional individuals can be born anywhere, how might they have been accommodated and understood in a small community?

Answer: Ay, there's always one . . . that has his arse hanging out of his britches.

Question: How might traditional narrative: myth, legend and folk tale, be made to speak to us today?

Answer: You're a right 'un, soft as me pocket. You've flewen high and let in a cow clap at the last.

Question: In what ways does the memory – the 'dreaming' – of a landscape make itself present?

Answer: What! Hark at you! Now you're after swallowing the whole beggaring cheese![5]

Garner's heroic endeavour, the work of a lifetime, has been to locate the fine line that brings these voices together, that makes

3 *Katha Upanishad* 3-14

4 *The Voice that Thunders*, 'Aback of Beyond' p.25

5 All 'answers' quotes from Alan Garner, from *The Stone Book Quartet*, *Strandloper*, *Thursbitch* and *The Voice that Thunders*.

an accommodation 'between Manchester Grammar School and Alderley Edge'[6] – not as thesis but as living language, as story.

The project, beginning with *The Weirdstone of Brisingamen*, achieves its fruition with his two interlocking masterpieces – spanning eight generations of one family's history – *The Stone Book Quartet* and *Strandloper.*

These two (or rather five) books were 23 years in the making; and they could be comfortably read, from start to finish, over a couple of evenings. They are of such a distilled precision, they are so layered, so finely observed, so pregnant with what lies under their surfaces, that to say so might be the equivalent of suggesting that *Four Quartets* could be read in 40 minutes. But it's true and it's a compliment. They are first and foremost stories, constructed to hold the reader to the page, baited and barbed with their own inner compulsion, their demand that we keep on turning the pages.

But they are also books that we never finish. The reader returns and returns, and every return offers fresh riches, new insights.

Most recently (rereading them again) it has been the way they explore the negotiation between eye and ear, between what is 'read' and what is 'spoken', between 'grammar' and 'song', that has most moved me.

In *The Stone Book*, Mary, who wants to learn to read but is not allowed ('Lord Stanley doesn't like his maids to read') is led into another kind of reading by her father. She is led into the reading of her landscape. First she's lifted onto the back of the weathercock at the top of the steeple he's been building and spun so that the outer perimeter of her world spreads out below her. She reads her horizon. Then he splits the stones she has been picking from the fields and reads her the paradox of their interiors. Finally he shows her the way down into Glaze Hill where she reads for herself the mystery of a painted bull that has been struck by the arrow that is also her father's mason mark. In one day she has read the breadth and depth of her place, its geography and its hidden histories. Mary

6 *The Voice that Thunders*, 'Achilles in Altjira' p.57

asks him for a prayer book to carry to chapel and at the end of the book he makes her one:

> ... he took the one pebble and worked quickly with candle and firelight, turning, tapping, knapping, shaping, twisting, rubbing and making, quickly as though the stone would set hard if he stopped. He had to take the picture from his eye to his hand before it left him.
>
> 'There,' said Father. 'That'll do.'
>
> He gave Mary a prayer book bound in blue-black calf skin, tooled, stitched and decorated. It was only by the weight that she could tell it was stone and not leather.
>
> 'It's better than a book you can open,' said Father. 'A book has only one story ...'[7]

This is a classic Alan Garner moment. It is the hands that are fluent. The spoken words are blunt. But behind the agile hands and the terse speech is a profoundly poetic idea – that the stone book is an embodiment of the landscape Mary has just entered and read, and that it contains both story and prayer.

Throughout *The Stone Book Quartet* there is a deep respect for the skills of craft, whether stonemason or smith, whether building a wall, adjusting a clock mechanism or fashioning a sledge. And at a certain moment the reader begins to understand that this is the 'grammar and syntax' of Alderley Edge. The disciplines are in the 'mysteries' of making, and they are as hard-won as any academic training. A man or woman's worth is measured by the facilities of eye, arm and hand. It is where the eloquence lies. Here's the stone mason again, in *Granny Reardun*:

> Then he was splendid.
>
> He took the new stone, the square dimension, and he built. He smoothed and combed the blocks, and they fitted together with hardly a knife-space between them. Their weight was nothing for him ...[8]

7 *The Stone Book*, p.58
8 *Granny Reardun* p.38

And we see his grandson, Joseph, 'playing wag' from school. It's a day of revelation. It's the day on which he understands that he wants to be a smith, not a mason like his grandfather:

> That great steeple, that great work. It was a pattern left on sand and air. The glint of the sun from the weathercock shimmered his gaze, and the gleam was about the stone right to the earth. He saw golden brushes, the track of combing chisels, every mark. The stone was only the finish of the blow. The church was the print of chisels in the sky.[9]

But the spoken words, when Joseph confronts his grandfather, struggle to communicate the strength of the revelation.

> 'You don't want stone,' said Grandfather.
> 'No.'
> 'And why don't you want stone?'
> 'Because,' said Joseph.
> 'Because?' said Grandfather, 'Because of what?'
> The words blurted out. 'Because of you!'
> 'Oh.' Grandfather was still.
> 'You're all over!' said Joseph. 'I must get somewhere: somewhere aback of you. I must. It's my time. Else I'll never.'[10]

It's in *The Stone Book Quartet* that Garner aligns himself with his ancestry. He too has served his time. He has his indentures and certificates. If his great-grandfather's work was with stone and his grandfather's was with iron then his is with a material as obdurate and hard to manage – language. He is a generous and ingenious wordsmith 'learned in the art, craft and mystery . . .'[11] all too aware of those canny ancestors peering over his shoulder sizing up his creations.

Not for him his grandfather's raised eyebrow and narrowed eye: 'Who made that codge?'[12] If *The Weirdstone of Brisingamen* was

9 *Granny Reardun* p.27
10 *Granny Reardun* p.49
11 *Granny Reardun* P.32
12 *The Voice that Thunders*, 'Aback of Beyond' p.25

an apprentice-piece, then *The Stone Book Quartet* is the work of a master craftsman.

In *Strandloper* he takes the argument a stage further. The book begins in the late eighteenth century, a generation earlier than *The Stone Book*. William Buckley is learning to write, his teacher is Edward, the radicalised son of Sir John Stanley. William is on the brink of literacy in an oral world. He is to play Shick-Shack, 'the man of leaf and golden hood', in the village May ceremony. His sweetheart Het is to be Teaser. Edward Stanley, with his notebook, is a constant presence, recording the ritual.

From the outset Garner sets up the tension between the educated outsider who can only look on, and the deep culture of the village.

As the ritual unfolds we hear an English folk poetry that carries echoes of what must once have been a complete and complex spiritual system, with men's and women's mysteries played out side by side.

> . . . The vicar dipped the green twig in the font and shook the water over William and said:
>
> 'Gently dip,
> But not too deep,
> For fear you make the golden bird to weep.'
>
> He put the twig back on the rim and faced the altar. The men formed a file, a flail handle on each shoulder. The vicar headed the procession up the aisle, singing.
>
> 'Fair maiden, white and red –'
>
> '– Comb me smooth and stroke my head,' the people responded.
>
> '– And thou shalt have some cockle bread,' sang the vicar.
>
> 'And every hair a sheaf shall be –'
>
> '– And every sheaf a golden tree.'[13]

The ritual is cut short by Sir John. He has printed posters that forbid the cutting of branches from his oak trees (the branches that Shick-Shack carries). They are posters that none of the unlettered

13 *Strandloper* p.46

villagers can read. In fact it is William's education that Sir John really wants to curtail. His intervention marks the last time the Shick-Shack ritual will be observed. The threat of literacy has brought an end to ancient custom. Garner presents us with the sharp edge of the wedge that will eventually divide us from ourselves. Only Edward Stanley's scribbled notes will survive.

As William is arrested Sir John shouts: 'They shall not write.'[14] He is wrong. It is Edward's radical vision that will win the day and destroy the old culture. And Garner, grammar school scholarship boy, knows that with the privilege of education comes the pain of that separation. It is one of the 'sweet sorrows' that pervade the book.

William is tried and transported to Australia.

It is at this point that the story becomes a work of genius. William escapes his prison camp and is on the point of death when he is found on the mound of Murrangurk, and restored to life as a returned ancestor. As Garner reveals the complexity and beauty of the Aboriginal belief system, we see that William has entered a culture where the land truly is both story and prayer. Where place is sacred text. And we see in the English folk rituals he has left behind, the echoes and traces of a Palaeolithic spirituality.

And at the same time Garner's meditations on the tension between the spoken and the written word continue. When Murrangurk (William) writes 'Het' in the sand he is challenged:

> 'Why cut sand?'
> . . . 'It will make the word stay.'
> Nullamboin breathed through his nose and looked at Murrangurk.
> 'If you cut sand?'
> 'Yes.'
> 'If you cut bark?'
> 'Yes.'
> 'Wood?'
> 'Yes.'

14 *Strandloper* p.55

'Rock?'

'Yes.'

'Can it be drawn?'

'Yes.'

'Show me 'Mami-ngata'.'

Murrangurk scratched the sand.

'That is 'Mami-ngata?' said Nullamboin.

'Yes.'

'Show me his big name.'

Murrangurk scratched 'Bunjil'.

'That is Bunjil?'

'Yes.'

Nullamboin shouted, and rubbed out the mark with his foot.

'Is it still there?'

'No,' said Murrangurk.

'But you could cut it, in another place, and it could stay? In wood or rock?'

'Yes. It is how to make words.'

'And it would be for those to see, if they came, or it could be carried far off and seen by strangers.'

'It could.'

'. . . Then all will see without knowledge, without teaching, without dying into life! Weak men will sing! Boys will have eagles! All shall be mad! Why have I danced this thing?'[15]

It is immediately after this exchange that Tirrawal, a man from another tribe, appears. There is a new dream. The sky is about to fall on the heads of the people. It is the dream that presages the coming of the white man. With hindsight the reader knows that the whole, beautiful structure of Aboriginal culture is about to be destroyed and the land and its dreaming desecrated.

Murrangurk goes to meet the newcomers to try to make an understanding between his two worlds. And as William Buckley, after 32 years 'in the bush', now a revered Aboriginal elder, he finds himself pardoned and returned to Cheshire.

15 *Strandloper* p.139

On arriving home he hears the chanting of children. His house has become a school. A teacher ('the man could not have led warriors') is leading his pupils in a rote learned reading and handwriting exercise. Edward Stanley's radical vision has taken hold. A catechism of the letters of the alphabet ('D. Determination overcomes great difficulties. K. Kindly excuse the shortcomings of others . . .') has replaced the old folk poetry. The people are destined to 'see without knowledge'[16].

This is the first impoverishment of language in William's return, but Garner gives us a second to match it. William has returned to his birthplace as a fully initiated Aborigine. All he has at his disposal to communicate what he knows is the blunt Cheshire dialect of his young adulthood. He doesn't have the words that can speak his knowledge.

We are returned again to the tensions between physical eloquence and verbal terseness that *The Stone Book Quartet* explores. But this time, because we've shared William's epic journey, we understand the depths that are carried by the short exchanges. When he finds that the mere has been drained for potatoes he utters the immortal line: 'You daft sods! You've buggered Spirit Hole!'[17] And we know the anguish behind what he's saying, even if it's a mystery to Niggy Bower. When William finds Het, she's about to destroy a bee skep to take the honey. It is William's actions, not his words, that tell her who he has become:

> . . . 'Hold still,' William said to Esther, and he started to dance the Bee. Esther dropped the pail and ran to the door. He danced Thuroongarong.
>
> 'Will?'
>
> He danced.
>
> 'Is that what they learn you?'
>
> He danced. And stopped. He lifted the skep from the stone and turned it. Esther slammed the door shut, then opened it a crack.

16 *Strandloper* p.186
17 *Strandloper* p.185

> 'Will! You're daft! They'll have you!'
>
> William began to sing. And the bees left the skep and settled on him, over him, his clothes and face and skin, until no part of him could be seen but the burs of their hair and wings. And he sang.
>
> When the skep was empty he took out a comb of honey. The comb was a Dreaming, but the flat at the tip where it had been fixed to the skep. There was no silence for a greater Dream. Yet the net of the comb was the Six Points of Time, the Joining of the Song.
>
> He took out all the combs and laid them on the slab. The bees left him and flew back into the skep. He put it down, and picked up the combs. Esther opened the door.
>
> 'Well, they do learn you summat,' she said.
>
> 'Ay, they do,' said William.[18]

William Buckley, who has been both Shick-Shack and Murrangurk, who has borne witness to the destruction of two cultures by the same spiritually impoverished vision of advancement, carries the possibility of a healing. He is able to dance the 'Joining of the Song'. Like smith and mason his eloquence is the other side of language. Somewhere beyond words he is able to bring together the Dreamings of his two lost worlds and mend them. It is how the story ends and it is the dance of his own death.

> ... the hollow logs beneath the chancel and the nave boomed as he stamped. He danced the Morning Star. The windows flared hollin, coraminga, cuckoo bread; torumba, nardoo, galligaskins; devilberry, jackanapes, goborro, mulkathandra ... he danced at the font for the Man in the Oak and the Crown of Glory ...[19]

And Garner, with a language that dances on that knife-edge between grammar and song, the native who has been away and has returned, achieves in *Strandloper* the proper function of his 'art,

18 *Strandloper* p.193
19 *Strandloper* p.200

craft and mystery' – which is to heal. At the back of our battered landscapes and our tattered shreds of folklore he gives us story and prayer, the deep culture of England. Where words run out he gives us image. Nothing is gone. William is still dancing. His story is 'how the sweet sorrow is sung'.[20]

Thank you, Alan.

Hugh Lupton's interest in traditional music, street theatre, poetry and myth, led to him becoming a professional storyteller in 1981. For 12 years he toured Britain with the 'Company of Storytellers'. Their work was instrumental in stimulating a nationwide revival of interest in storytelling. Since the mid-nineties he has worked as a writer, solo performer and collaborator. He tells stories from many cultures, but his particular passion is for the hidden layers of the English landscape and the stories and ballads that give voice to them. His first novel The Ballad of John Clare *was published in 2010.*

20 *Strandloper* p.200

BUT STILL WE WALK

Helen Macdonald

How many minds do sweetness cause
To catch suggestion, evening hours? The air
Full for falters, spills quarry
Bells on songs that split to silhouette
Our single plaints. Plaits to. Combine brow.
Spilt aspect, the hop and tilt, a ladder
Ship's-deck artifact poised in the gloom
Marbled whites and moiled stones of
Uncomfortable softness, steeping
This primary world in pepper, thick
Pewter, shredded clouds, clean
Architectural hints pinched at its corners
To ruins and all their fervour run.
But still we walk; of course we do.
Here is a cup with flowers about the rim
A singing spray of petals & a hitch of glass.
A woollen glove half-buried in quartz
All mute points shadow outward thrown
On cuttle-soft ground the patch of grass
Hands dropped and miniature. Some paths
Are visible like ribbon handing the old
Hansel and Gretel, the find-your-way-home deep
Scratch in the ground and you'll find light there—
Tiny fiercenesses in belligerent trefoil
Speaking of fixed attention, pinnate

Hearts & must. There might be owls
Or flowers stacked, the brittleness
Of happenstance, the shapes of stories
In curves of hills, in keratin, in wings as thick
And curled as white card sculptures. Coincidences
Of solidity and air, words that speak of us, for us,
Of paler eyes, of old wounds, of the turning worlds
And the small made vast in song.

For Alan Garner, with deepest thanks for those books that carried me to other places.

Helen Macdonald is a writer, poet, illustrator, historian, naturalist, and affiliated research scholar at the Department of History and Philosophy of Science at the University of Cambridge. She has also worked as a professional falconer and on raptor research and conservation projects across Eurasia. She is a contributing writer for The New York Times Magazine. *Her books include* Shaler's Fish *(2001),* Falcon *(2006), and* H is for Hawk, *which won the 2014 Samuel Johnson Prize and was 2014 Costa Book of the Year.*

THE EDGE: A NAME-MAP

Robert Macfarlane

Shuttlingslow, Shining Tor, Wildboarclough, Wizard's Well, Adder's Moss – when I think of Alan Garner's fiction, I think of – *no*, I think in – place names. His prose bristles with them. He relishes the ways that place names hold story tight within themselves, curled and sprung, ready to flicke r forth into the imagination. Place names have a poetry in his work – but they also possess power. They record history – but they also force the future into form.

Alderley Edge itself is a landscape of such ancient acculturation that almost no part of it has gone unnamed – from the shafts and adits that riddle its interior, to the outcrops and escarpments of its surface. So when thinking of how to celebrate Garner's novels, and their influence upon my own sense of place, I decided to abandon narrative. Instead I tried to find a visual means of representing the clasp between place and place-words in his prose.

The result is the map you will see on the following pages. It is a name-map of Alderley Edge and its surroundings, in which the contour lines are made of all the toponyms to be found in the *Weirdstone* trilogy, including those in the titles of the three books: *The Weirdstone of Brisingamen*, *The Moon of Gomrath* and *Boneland*.

To make the map, I first had to abstract the Edge into pure contour, and then I had to abstract the novels into pure place name. So I took the 1:50,000 Ordnance Survey map of Alderley Edge, then I picked out the main contours in black ink, then I followed those in pencil on tracing paper, then I reversed the tracing paper and re-traced the lines so as to avoid inversion when I then transferred the pencil lines back onto a clean sheet of white paper. This left me with faint pencil tracks of the Edge's contours, stripped of all other topographical information. Those tracks – which bunch together in the north-west of the page, indicating the escarpment itself – became the guidelines for the place names.

To gather the toponyms themselves, I read the trilogy through in a single sitting in the course of an afternoon and long evening, noting every place name mentioned. I realised as I read that Garner's place names mix the actual, the fantastical and the celestial: from Sinadon (an 'old name', as Garner calls it, for Snowdon), through the invented Earldelving, to the Pleiades, the constellation that Colin studies through the astro telescopes of Jodrell Bank in *Boneland*, seeking the resting place of his sister.

Then I inked the place names along the pencil lines of the contours – and at last rubbed out the pencil to leave a name-map.

What follows here, by way of postscript, is a full list of the place names mentioned in the *Weirdstone* trilogy. Even when arranged in columns and alphabetically, if spoken aloud and in number they have the air of an incantation.

Robert Macfarlane is the author of a series of award-winning books on landscape, walking and language, including Mountains of the Mind *(2003),* The Wild Places *(2007),* The Old Ways *(2012) and* Landmarks *(2015). He is a Fellow of Emmanuel College, Cambridge.*

Place names of the Weirdstone Trilogy

Abyss of Ragnarok
Adder's Moss
Armstrong Farm
Artists Lane
Atlendor
Bag Brook
Bearstone
Bent's Wood
Big Tidnock
Black Fernbrake
Black Peaks
Boneland
Bosley Cloud
Brindlow Wood
Brisingamen
Broad Hill
Brook Lane
Buxton
Caer Rigor
Capesthorne
Castle Rock
Cat's Tor
Cave of the Svartmoot
Chatsworth
Chelford
Church Quarry
Clinton Hill
Clockhouse Wood
Clulow Cross
Dale of Goyt
Danes Moss
Daniel Hill
Dark Lane
Dingle Bank
Dinsel
Dogger
Druid Stones
Dumville's Plantation
Earldelving
Eelstream
Elthan
England
Errwood Hall
Ethel
Fern Hill
Flatlands
Forties
Front Baguley
Front Hill
Fundindelve
Gawsworth
Golden Stone
Gomrath
Great Rock
Hare Hill
Hayman's Quarry
Heligoland
Higher House
Highmost Redmanhey
Hill of Dawn
Hill of Death and Life
Hill of Night
Hocker Lane
Holy Well
Holy Well Bog
Hoo Moor

Hulme Hill
Isle of Iwerddon
Jenkins Hey
Jodrell Bank
Kerridge
Lamaload
Lamda Herculis
Lindow Common
Llyn-dhu
London Road
Lower Lands
Ludcruck
Macclesfield
Marlheath
Minith Bannawg
Mobberley
Moel Fammau
Monks' Heath
Moss Lane
Mottram St Andrew
Nab End
Northland
Nut Tree
Old Gate
Old Man of Mow
Painter's Eye
Piggford Moor
Point of Moel
Prydein
Pyethorne Wood
Radnor Mere
Radnor Wood
Redesmere
Rift Valley
River Goyt
Rivington Pike
Rockside
Row-of-Trees
Saddle Bole
Seven Firs
Seven Sisters Lane
Shining Tor
Shuttlingslow
Sinadon
Sodger's Hump
Soss Moss
Squirrel's Jump
St Mary's Clyffe
Stormy Point
Sugarwell
Sutton Common
Svart Warren
Swanscoe
Talebolion
Tunsted
The Beacon
The Bollin
The Hough
The Mother
The Parkhouse
The Pleiades
The Riddings
The Roaches
The Taurids
The Wood of Radnor
Thieves' Hole
Thornycroft Pools
Threshold of the Summer Stars
Thursbitch
Toft
Tor of Ghosts
Tytherington

Valley of Life
Welltrough
Welsh Row
West Mine
Westwater
Whins Brow
Whisterfield
White Rocks
Wildboarclough
Wilmslow
Windgather Rocks
Windmill Wood
Windy Harbour
Withenlee
Withington
Wornish Nook

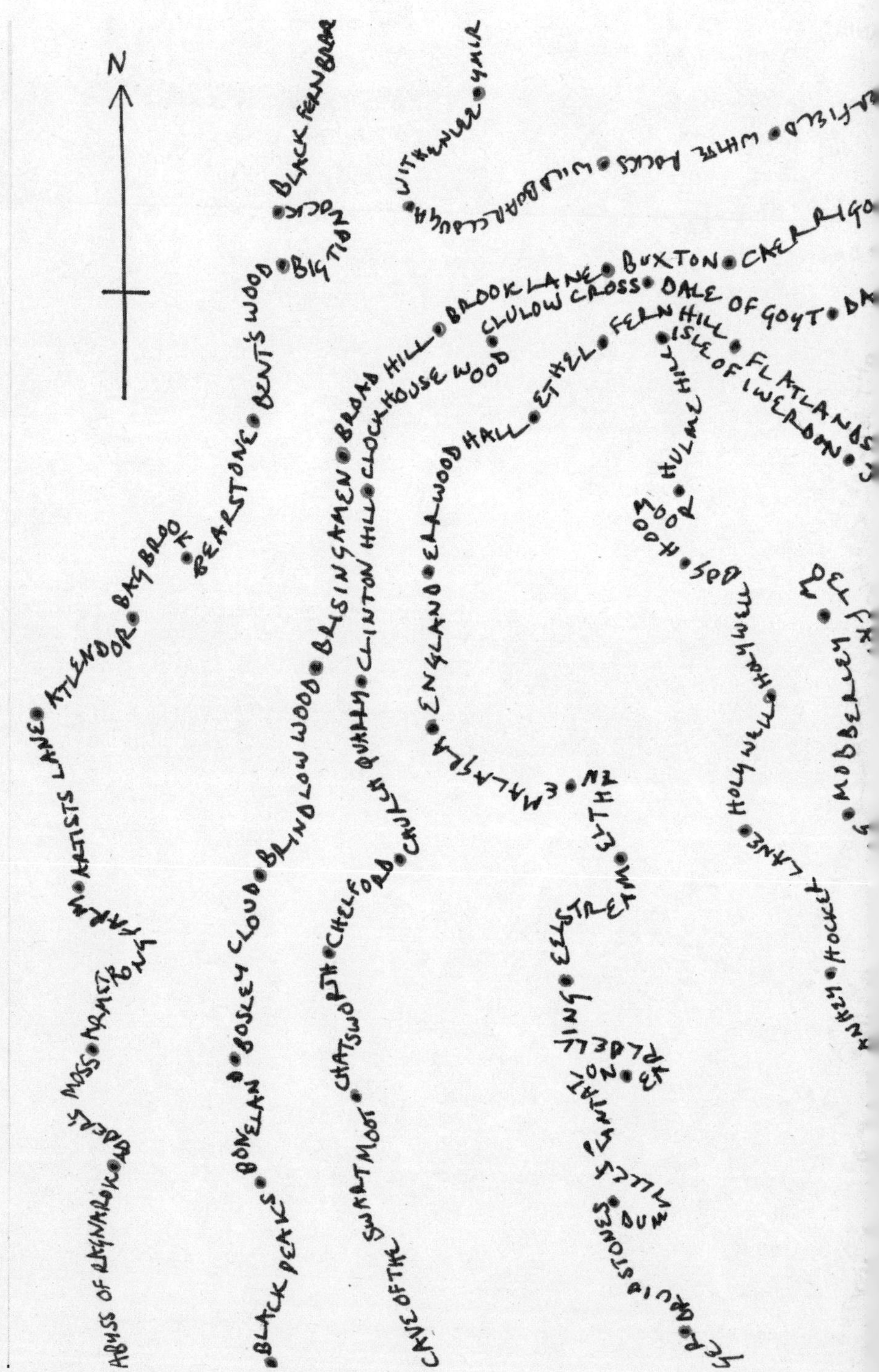
N
ABYSS OF RAGNAROK
ADDER'S MOSS
ARMSTRONG
ARTISTS LANE
ATLENDOR
BAG BROOK
BEARSTONE
BENT'S WOOD
BLACK PEAKS
BONELAND
BOSLEY CLOUD
BRINDLOW WOOD
BRISINGAMEN
BROAD HILL
BROOK LANE
BUXTON
CAVE OF THE SWART MOOT
CHATSWORTH
CHELFORD
CLINTON HILL
CLOCKHOUSE WOOD
CLULOW CROSS
DALE OF GOYT
ENGLAND
ETHEL
FERN HILL
ISLE OF IWERDON
FLATLANDS
HULME HILL
HOLYWELL
HOLYWELL LANE
HOCKET
MOBBERLEY
WHITE ROCKS
DRUID STONES

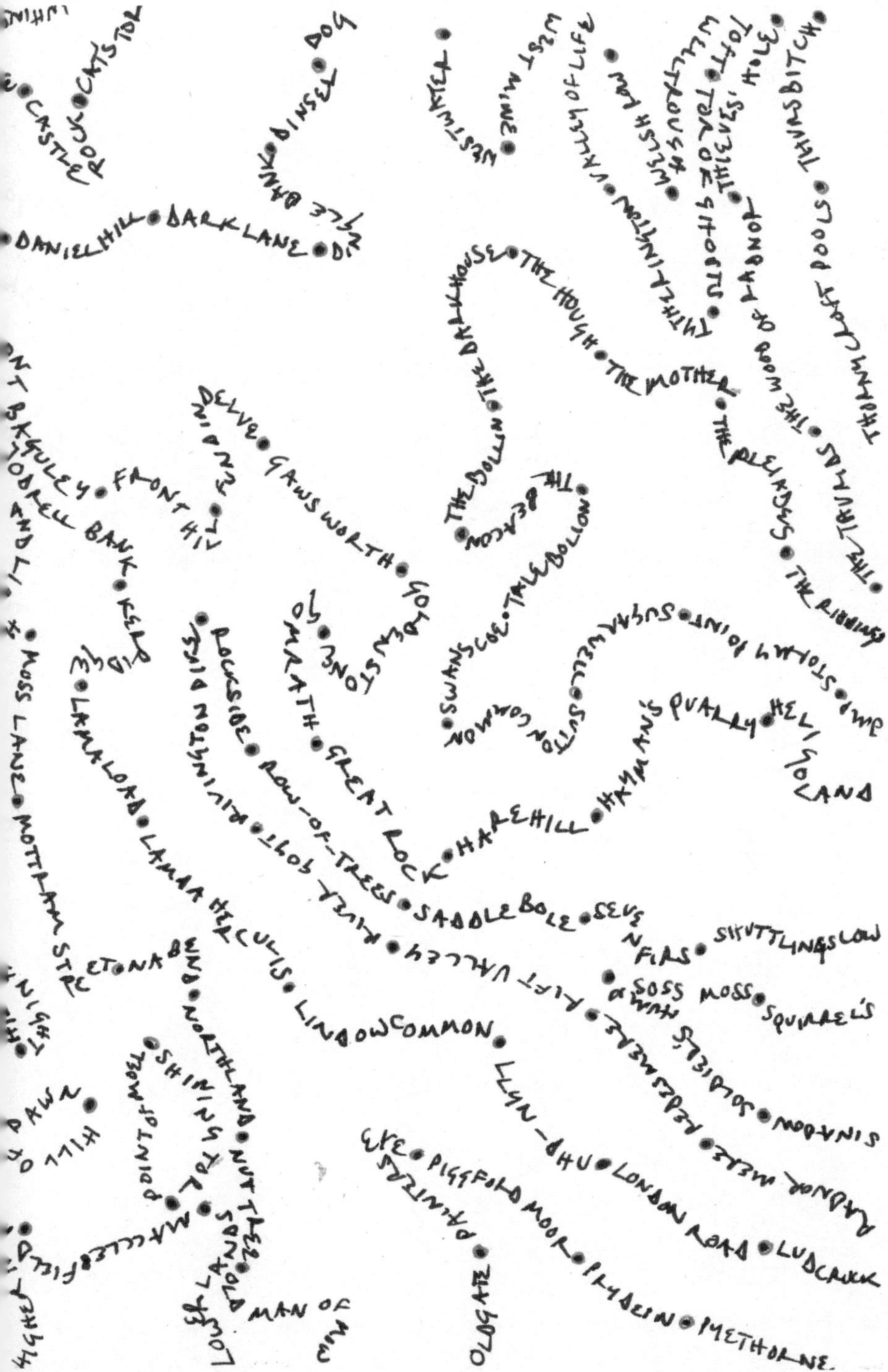
CASTLE
ROCK
CATSTOR
DINSEL
DOG
DANIEL HILL
DARK LANE
WEST MINE
VALLEY OF LIFE
THIEVES' HOLE
THE HOUGH
THE MOTHER
THE PLEIADES
THE RIDDINGS
THE BEACON
THE BOLLIN
SWANSCOE
SUTTON COMMON
HARE HILL
GREAT ROCK
GAWSWORTH
DELVE
FRONT HILL
BANK
ROW-OF-TREES
SADDLE BOLE
SEVEN FIRS
SHUTTLINGSLOW
SOSS MOSS
SQUIRREL'S
LINDOW COMMON
RIFT VALLEY
LLYN-DHU
LONDON ROAD
PIGGFORD MOOR
METHORNE
OLDGATE
PAINTERS EYE
MAN OF
LOWER LANDS
NORTHLAND
NUT TREE
SHINING TOR
HILL OF DAWN
MOSS LANE
LAMALOAD

THE BULL-ROARER

Gregory Maguire

After decades of enjoying Alan Garner's steady collegiality and distant friendship, and his genius, I approach my apprehensions of the man as if over a flattened landscape of riverbed stones, a plenitude stretched to the horizons on all sides. I have to leave to others the summation of his achievements. I'm too often blinded by magnificence, so I lower my shades against the glare of accomplishment. I fit my eyes to peripheral agitations and satisfactions. I think, I hope, he and his admirers will accept this wisp-o'-the-will emanation from a dream-horde of mine as it is meant: given in homage. It's the best I can offer. A Brownian cloud of impressions, naturally less accurate than criticism, but I hope not less true.

So what is this landscape of stone? Why am I alone here when I'm looking for Alan Garner? I sense moisture in the air. It has a character. Not the clean iron aroma of sea-washed rain but the more randy reek of peaty, mouldy soil. The light from the sky is flat and sourceless, but the grey stones, the size of the thumb-pads and the palms and soles of giants, are laid out in gravity's scatter, not on their parabolic edges but mostly flat side up. As if spilled in stone storm, splashed and finished in the act of capture upon the world.

Other lights; other airs. This is a field of making. Hence it is a field of time, a field of all possibility without apparent verdure or ordure or even grandeur. It is the place where someone with that untoward power will cup his hands and say a few words – perhaps over and over for a decade – to find that when his hands are unclasped, something new has come from nothing.

From nothing? Perhaps not from nothing – but from where it comes, that's beyond the scope of my ability to know. Even though, from time to time, I try to crawl to this same plain and, self-mocking and embarrassed at my hubris, I whisper or chortle some words, too, as if some enchantment might actually, by accident, blurt from between my fingers. Usually all I get is a foul puff of air, nothing alive.

How has Alan Garner done it? Not just once, but time and again? How does he do it?

★

The challenge to think about language and landscape – this time with a Garner focus – is timely. (Though, as it happens, what is not timely as it happens?) I am on a flight between Boston and London. I have just finished page proofs of a novel set in nineteenth-century Oxford, and although I intend nothing but to rest, I can't help sensing around the parenthetic blur of the visible globe another narrative territory I might choose. Is it Bavaria, does it have German romantic roots, is it inflected Grimm? Behind what I can see – drawing rooms with Biedermeier gentility and plaster pilasters cast in shades of bone, of pale blues and rose – loiters, lurks, huddles a small, lost forest. Something hides in the forest. It is too indistinct to make out yet. Finding it – finding it in its own forest, finding it in my mind – is what writing is for.

Making it something of value, something others might want to find, or be grateful that I found – oh, sure, I'll try, but maybe that's asking too much of writing, I've come to think. A writer as hired spelunker? As merchant marine, with a manifest? No. I'm an independent ferret. A garner. I'm a one-fellow salvage unit. I haul what attracts my eye to the market square mostly to get rid of it. Someone else can weigh it, credit it, crate it up or cart it to the tip.

But this business of landscape – the inchoate landscape of unwritten story, this landscape as yet unidentified that draws the rogue writer – it intrigues me the more as I get older.

The things that landscapes mean! The things they evoke just by their names!

Golgotha
Runnymede
Kitty Hawk
Camelot

Easter Island
Appomattox
Yoknapatawpha
Troy
Oxford

★

While pawing about Oxford two summers ago, doing research for my novel, I hauled my two younger kids along. They were then new-fledged teens, or nearly: kids of today, and kids of mine. That means they grow twisted by opposing influences: the intense book reverence of their two dads on the one hand, and on the other, the hedonistic allure promised by their cyberspatial overlord, speaking to them (seducing them) through the 'video mesmorama' called the internet. *Google, Google über alles*. I was surprised, therefore, that my children condescended, and affably, to join me at a small and vivid exhibit mounted at the Bodleian. That exhibit. 'Magical Books – From the Middle Ages to Middle-earth'. Cooper, *The Perilous Gard*, Pullman, Garner, Narnia, Mordor et cetera.

My own Oxford writing efforts that year had involved two landscapes – the town-and-gown environs of Charles Lutwidge Dodgson and his fellow Oxfordians, on the one hand; and the anarchy of Wonderland, which because of its genius has spawned relatively few successful imitators. Perhaps the cabinet meetings under President George W. Bush can be considered the nearest approximation of Wonderland's devotion to inconsequence. What Carroll did, it seems to me, was glance out of his stone casements at Christ Church and apprehend, somehow, a landscape of dream. Perhaps the Liddell girls were to him as Beatrice to Dante. Or Eurydice to Orpheus. But it doesn't really matter. What matters is that Dodgson leaned so far out his college casements that he was able to get to that hitherto uncharted territory, and to return. No one else has done it as fully. He brought back for us a vivid, startling, genuine, authentic map of the landscape of dream. This happened a century and a half ago as I write. I am still in awe.

At the Bodleian, two or three small rooms showed contemporary pantocrators at their own works. (In Byzantine iconography, Christ Pantocrator most often holds a book, but sometimes he holds a world, and once in a while – charmingly! – he also wields a ruler and a compass over his world.) It is hard for me to imagine contemporary life, let alone my own childhood, without the literary experience of Narnia, Middle-earth, and Camelot. (Also Oz, though Oz wasn't represented in Oxford.) Here in these hallowed English rooms, approached through a quiet quad across sunny cobbles, my two beloved young barbarians pored over vitrines for the first time in their lives. C.S. Lewis, Tolkien, something of T.H. White. And a select few of their heirs and assigns: Philip Pullman, Susan Cooper, and Alan Garner.

I fear I'm taking too long to get to my point. I and my younger kids drifted apart from one another, choosing our own inchoate strategies of preference in the viewing of notebooks, manuscripts, totems and tokens, pinned as reverentially to cards as Melanesian love charms and the Amazonian shrunken heads are displayed in the Pitt Rivers Museum. The writers' notes, drawings. Amulets. Maps. The spindrift of creativity. It looked like evidence of impossible journeys.

I recognise these are items of a different category. The actual thing – the Dodo's withered claw, for argument's sake – is a specimen of history. It proves history. The simulacrum – let's say an out-take of a stitched unicorn fetlock from one of the 'Unicorn Tapestries', removed because the artisan had had too much mead and put the hoof on backward – doesn't prove history, only proves devotion.

And yet I now feel, perhaps from intellectual laziness or from the sloppiness of ageing, that the two sorts of evidence are closer in nature than I had used to believe. And certainly that they are equally thrilling.

★

Bletchley Park
My Lai
Atlantis
Nineveh

★

I'm looking for the name of a concept. Which one? I had thought I meant the objective correlative, but I looked it up – the internet isn't all poison – and once again I have misremembered what o-c means. I'm looking for synecdoche, where one scrap stands for a whole. A mere floating em-dash in an Emily Dickinson poem stands for her brave apprehensions about experience and eternity. A bullet-hole in a doorsill near the Old North Bridge in my home town of Concord, Massachusetts, an aperture in which one can hardly wiggle a forefinger, proposes the entire history of the founding of our nation. A small drawing by my oldest child done when he was only five, featuring an amoeba-headed TV announcer in a TV box speech-ballooning: 'I hate the guvmint,' is a holy ikon to me. It arrests that year for me, holds it from final decay as long as my eyes and my memory can regard the gummy paper he worked upon.

What forces are conjured up and released by verbal synecdoche.

Roswell
Los Alamos
Elsinore
Tiananmen Square
Alderley Edge

So, for a moment, to turn to what I myself have tried to do, ineffectually, with story; and this is still (if discursively) in pursuit of the notion of what I think Alan Garner has tried to do, and succeeded.

Over the decades, interviewers and graduate students have asked me, 'Why Oz? Why did you borrow Oz for four huge novels, roughly five hundred thousand words? What does Oz stand for?'

Well. I think what they mean is this: 'Of what is Oz a symbol, as in John Bunyan the Celestial City is for poor Pilgrim his salvation, his heaven?'

In order to answer this, I've had to look at the other landscapes of magic that have appealed to me. Seamus Heaney, who harvested peat on his family's farm, once described the bogs of Ireland as 'a landscape that remembered everything that had happened in and to it'. Recently I've asked a question of landscapes: what they remember, what they evoke. Wonderland and the Looking Glass world seem to me the identikit examples of dreamscape. Narnia, which I discovered upon a library shelf – I was in fifth grade, trembling like stout Cortez silent upon a peak in Darien – was not only England, but also a kind of England-that-would-yield Shakespeare, Dickens, and Noel Coward. The 100 Aker Wood provokes in me the sweet solipsism of preschool – very little remembered, but that doesn't mean very little happened. LeGuin's *Earthsea* is, perhaps, Homeric, Cycladic ('Aye on the shores of darkness there is light / And precipices show untrodden green'), though I got Homer later in my life than some, having been stirred up instead at the age of 10 by the *Lives of the Saints*, the American Catholic parochial school's hedge against the paganism of antiquity.

As a child, I had not met Pullman, Cooper, or Garner in their books, for I am too old and unlucky to have found them during my childhood – though later, my charmed life managed to proffer friendships with those living honorees represented at the Bodleian Library that summer.

But then there is Oz. And at the risk of capsizing my slender thesis with too much example, let me merely say that I've come around, in interviews, to saying 'I chose to write about Oz because it seems to me Oz has exactly the width, depth, complexity, inanity, amnesiacal approach to its own history and culture that the United States has.' In other words, Oz is like the map in the Borges story, 'On Exactitude in Science', a map that unfolds to be the exact dimensions of the thing it is mapping. I wanted to use Oz as a simulacrum of the United States I knew and know. For me, Oz is a map of today. In stories about political nerve, betrayal, intellectual ambition, power and its aphrodisiacal allure, Oz works perfectly. John Updike once titled a *New Yorker* piece on L. Frank Baum's work 'Oz Is Us'. Us, meaning perhaps us Americans. Or perhaps U.S. You can decide.

Neverland
Sherwood Forest
The Forest of Arden
The forest primeval

★

And so to Philip Pullman, Susan Cooper, and Alan Garner. There are others worthy of worthy inclusion in this company – Salman Rushdie, Maurice Sendak, Neil Gaiman, to name only a few. But the Bodleian exhibit focused on Oxford associations, and celebrated Pullman, Cooper, and Garner. It's toward my sense of Alan Garner's signal accomplishment that I have been leaning through these pages.

Not allegory; hardly analogy. Something else. Less like a map, and more like a haunting suggestion of something unmappable.

What inspires Pullman's vision of the universe – the multiverse – is it Einstein, Escher, Hawking? And Susan Cooper – does her vast, compelling *Dark is Rising* sequence suggest as much about the power of myth that still wreaths Glastonbury, Avebury, Cader Idris, as anything else?

And Alan Garner? Eliot's *Four Quartets*? The 'dark backward and abysm of time'?

Here at last I come to how the thought of Alan Garner's work sits in my system. For the work is so various, yet so of a piece that in aggregate it stands for something of grave significance. I chose the word 'grave' as a placeholder and I've tried to revise it, but it won't go. I mean it in an ancient sense of heavy, full of portent: the Gothic is kaurus, or so winks a sexy reference from an online etymology saloon.

I first came to know Alan's work through Betty Levin's course syllabus for Fantasy, which she taught at Simmons College's Center for the Study of Children's Literature, in Boston. My fellow students and I tore through *The Owl Service*, *Red Shift*, and *The Stone Book*

Quartet, and then everything that followed the week it was published. Only, however, with the arrival of *Boneland* did I finally go back and fill in with the first two of Alan's novels, *The Weirdstone of Brisingamen* and *The Moon of Gomrath*. Though they'd both been published in time for me to read them as a child, my small branch library hadn't carried the pair, or I'd have snatched them up for their compelling titles. (50 years ago I might only have understood the words Colin and Susan and virtually nothing else in the novel; I'd likely not have known where I was; but hasn't that been one of Alan Garner's central ambitions: both to place and to unsettle his readers?)

Surveying the landscape of Garner's oeuvre as I survey the landscapes, in my mind, of Earthsea and Oz, of Brocéliande and Perelandra, of the Inferno and of vast Russia and of Olympus and of Macondo, I return to the notion with which I began. What does the *corpus vivendi*, in aggregate, suggest to me? And what am I trying to celebrate here?

Brisingamen
Gomrath
Wales
Illiers-Combray

I've been saving that one for last. Illiers-Combray! There's the highway sign on the side of the A-11 in the department of Eure-et-Loire. Proust's invented Combray has risen from the pages and spoken itself so urgently that it has merged, municipally speaking, with the actual French village that inspired it, Illiers.

This is what invented landscapes do, if they are invented with genius. They reinvent the world. Proust Pantocrator.

⋆

The work of Alan Garner means to me nothing less than the landscape of thinking itself. By its strength, its nerve (its particularity, its brave parochialism) it defies analogy, it shucks off easy objective correlatives. When I consider, from a wary and respectful distance, those books on my case of most honoured books (there is such a real bookcase at the top of the stairs; the IRS auditor refused to consider it a professional library, so I happily pay full taxes upon it, rendering unto Caesar), what the Garner books evoke in me is a kind of talismanic awe if not even dread: not *Hic sunt dracones* but here is what the landscape of thinking looks like.

I've been writing this for some days now. It seems I have overshot London and I am in the Peloponnese, nearly to Nafplion. I am drunk at the edge of the wine-dark sea, and the watery terrain in the dusk holds promise and terror. I'm still thinking of Alan Garner and (because this is how I work), at almost the same moment, that other possible unwritten novel, that next novel, which lurks, its outlines inchoate, hidden by the bulk of everything I've ever thought of or read before. No Gandalf or Tiresias can help me now. The compelling example of Alan Garner's work just might, though. With his example as my werelight, I shall have to push on and see what I can learn, while there is time, while there's hope that learning is still possible. Philhellenism in Bavaria; laurel and pan-pipe: their parts in German romanticism. But how to begin this universe? How to call it into being?

Some decades ago, as I recall it, the first time we met, Alan Garner delivered a lecture at Simmons College called 'Achilles in Altjira'. He began by recalling the words spoken to him by Eric James, High Master of Manchester Grammar School. 'For each generation, the *Iliad* must be told anew.' Alan went on to discuss the peculiar process of rationality and intuition, as distorted and distilled through language, that characterises creativity in storytelling. The effect of listening to this talk, given passionately and heard passionately – has remained a touchstone for me my whole writing life. Sure, other benisons emerge from memory's cloaking fogs. Years later, a charming visit to Blackden; lunch with Griselda and Alan after a trek across a boggy meadow where the gate stuck on black hussocky ruts; various dubious vintages, late-night ceremonious plonk splashed into plastic cups and shared with colleagues and students in college dorm rooms on either side of the Atlantic. But none of these cherished memories means as much to me as the implication of Alan's collected achievement on my shelves. That achievement is both challenge and encouragement to me.

And a final moment to share. A Children's Literature New England conference I helped direct, called 'Let the Wild Rumpus Start: Play in Children's Books'. Year? 1998. Alan joined Philip Pullman and Susan Cooper – and, among others, Russell Hoban, Margaret Mahy, Sylvia Waugh, Jill Paton Walsh – to address the international audience assembled at Newnham College, Cambridge. He began wordlessly, by bringing forth a string and a button. He threaded the string through the button and wound the cord tightly. The intensity of his expression, the tautness of the string. We were in a dark cave. A world of stone. Light had not been captured yet. 'The bull-roarer,' he whispered. 'Rhombus. Thunder-spell.' Then he pulled hard on both ends of the string. The button spun. The air thrilled. *Homo tympanus*. Pantocrator. The universe began.

Gregory Maguire, an American writer and educator, was living in London in the 1990s when he wrote his first novel for adults, Wicked, *which inspired the Broadway and West End musical of the same name. Other novels for adults include* Confessions of an Ugly Stepsister, Mirror, Mirror, *and* After Alice, *each a meditation on childhood lore. His novels for children include* Egg & Spoon, a Tale of Old Russia; What-the-Dickens: the Story of a Rogue Tooth Fairy; *and* Matchless, *a recandescence of Andersen's* The Little Match Girl. *He now lives in New England and in France.*

Quotation from Seamus Heaney taken from *The New Yorker*, March 16, 2015

IT WASN'T MEANT TO BE LIKE THIS

Bel Mooney

The beginning of this story was a notion rooted in fond family memory, which led me astray. Never trust a simple narrative.

'At some time or other, but not long since' (as Garner begins a folk tale) I emailed Erica Wagner with a positive thought: '. . . there is a piece to be written on how Garner's work has the capacity to heal.' For 10 years I have been writing a newspaper advice column (among other things), therefore the quest for healing is always to the forefront of my mind. And did I not clearly remember discussing *The Owl Service*, *Elidor* and *Red Shift* and the pain of adolescence with my teenage son? Those books were a portal to sharing and solving. This is the story I would tell here.

Yet it came to pass that my son, now 41 and a father, had no recollection of such conversations. Had I imagined them – and if so, why did I cling to the certainty which betrayed me?

For writers there is usually a gulf between a commission and the deadline approaching; it was much later when I checked the rest of that email to the editor of this volume. It said, 'Never too sure about the definition "fantasy" (although it's accurate) because it implies an "otherness", whereas I see Garner's worlds as aspects of the bruised soul within. And therefore all too real. But light in the darkness.'

Yet (unsettled by my false memory – or was it my son's failure to recall? His wish to forget vulnerability?) I had no idea where that thought came from either. After all, I had not read Alan Garner for many, many years. Sometimes words spark from your fingertips with no aforethought – then burn. So it was then – and the real beginning of this story is pain. It wasn't meant to be like this – but when I came back to Alan Garner, fond memories forcibly abandoned, I'm afraid I found no healing. The books were blows which did indeed bruise the soul. They drove me (a magical, punishing beating-stick) into the dark hill. 'Afraid' is the correct word for what was to come.

I began rereading with *The Weirdstone of Brisingamen.*' Then a twenty-seven-year-old co-pilot called Andreas Lubitz deliberately crashed Germanwings A320 Airbus Flight 4U9525 into the French Alps, murdering all 150 people on board. Shape-shifting: within the locked chamber the ordinary man became a monster. My nightmares heard the desperate blows on the cockpit door as the pilot (the Good One) tried to enter; was transfixed by screams of terror; saw the debris of lives spread over the rocky mountainside. At this point I felt at one with Colin and Susan as 'they journeyed into despair. For no way led upwards for long.' I began to feel uneasy in my world and strangely at home in theirs: 'Down, down, always down!' cried Susan bitterly, 'Are we never going to see daylight again?'

It continued. Something was triggered. The creatures that swarmed from Garner's pages into my mind reminded me of my unease when I first read Christina Rossetti's 'Goblin Market' as a child – the obscene little men 'clucking and gobbling,/ Mopping and mowing,' and offering addictive, evil fruits. They were the hybrid monsters in great wall paintings of the Last Judgment, inflicting unspeakable cruelties upon the pitiful damned. *The Weirdstone* and then *The Moon of Gomrath* (closely followed by all the other books) became my Pandora's box. When your mind unexpectedly tumbles on a dizzy, downward gyre, how can you not tremble, knowing 'they' are always among us? The nameless ones in the treeline? The watcher in the pub who will flee into the darkness when rumbled? Listen! The teeming bodachs and palugs and svart alfar and lyblacs are just there . . . outside on the porch. You know it because you hear them rattling the letter box and sparking a short-circuit in the heart.

It wasn't meant to be like this. Living a blessed life, excited at the thought of writing an essay about the work of a deeply admired writer, why was I so afflicted? Lowness in spirit and health dragged me down. So many things combined: Garner's unsettling 'stories', relentless headlines about the psychopaths who call themselves Islamic State, the endless uncovering of sexual abuse (on and on), the permanent pollution of the Dark Web, the fact that ten-year-old children can easily access the most loathsome, violent pornography, the anarchy of desperate displaced people – hatred, envy, conflict, need. Intolerable havoc spills from page and screen. Violence and cruelty ooze and seep, the lowest common denominator is exalted, the charnel house in the hillside gapes, 'And the crack in the teacup opens / A lane to the land of the dead.' We are (in Garner's phrase) 'blind to the light and call on darkness'. I felt newly poisoned – and, like Roland in *Elidor* that 'It's my fault.'

My teetering pile of Garner's books seemed a distillation of the darkness of the outer world. Old Master of the Word, how can you so terrify? Having studied Grendel and the Green Giant (as you did) I now sit frozen in horror at your snowstorm, *Thursbitch*. You have smashed the glass I thought half-full – and how thirstily the endless desert spreads, beyond the horizon to the stars. Poor Susan and Colin have this sense of abandonment at the start of *The Moon of Gomrath*: 'Almost they wished they had never discovered enchantment; they found it unbearable that the woods for them should be empty of anything but loveliness . . .' Yet it was fantasy and fairy tale and the consolation of beauty I had sought, forgetting that here is no happy ending.

During the time of rereading I had to assemble (for publication) an anthology of my advice column – reading the oeuvre celebrated in this volume at the same time as a mountain of 'real' stories. Forced to confront the proofs of emotional damage that are the stock-in-trade of a column like mine and simmer within the pages of *Red Shift* and *The Owl Service* I felt despair. In his article 'A Bit More Practice' (1968), Garner wrote, 'Myth is not entertainment, but rather the crystallization of experience and, far from being escapist, fantasy is an intensification of reality. When I first read *Math vab Mathonwy* it struck me as being such a modern story of the damage people do to each other, not through evil but through the unhappy combination of circumstance that throws otherwise harmless personalities together.'

Yes indeed: and reading that was a relief, because I realised that the author, the shaman, was bestowing permission not to like, not to be entertained. Not to expect ease. Each week, sad, angry and tragic readers' letters enter my quiet room and there is no escaping. Significantly, in one of the epigraphs to *The Owl Service* Garner quotes an article in *Radio Times*: 'Possessive parents rarely live long enough to see the fruits of their selfishness'. Of this I know the truth.

It is not so much the patterns of owls or flowers that bothers me – in Garner and in life – but the patterns within families. Alan Garner knows this; what else is the theme of the beautiful, melancholy *Stone Book Quartet*? Larkin's famous dictum, 'Man hands on misery to man', is enacted, again and again (although not always overtly) in Garner's work. Parents are absent (like Colin and Susan's) or are uncomprehending (*Elidor*) or act with malice through stupidity (Tom's in *Red Shift*) or cause potential catastrophe, like the *deus ex machina* (Alison's mother, in *The Owl Service*, whom we never actually meet but whose pernicious legacy is made clear). How many of us love our parents (still, still . . .) yet have longed to be orphan? Perhaps this, the ultimate betrayal, is inevitable; thus we deal with what Cadellin sees (at the death of his estranged brother) as 'the gulf of their lives'.

(There I was, desperate for 'a new story'. A sprained ankle surely no accident, because I felt unsupported. A virus; what Garner calls 'nervous fatigue' and also 'the knowledge that is sad to know'; terror of headlines yet compulsion to read them; inability to breathe, to rise, to smile. I no longer recognised the sad, tense face in the mirror. The new GP, younger than my daughter, asked me earnestly, 'Have you ever wanted to harm yourself?' No, I said. How can you confess your rage? That it is others you wish to harm: both the svarts and the stupid ones who open the door to them?)

Those of us who were terrified by Disney's *Snow White*; who heard voices in the traffic along Queen's Drive in Liverpool; who saw faces as well as clouds in the cracks in the ceiling and knew that as soon as Mum put out the light the creatures of darkness would crawl out from under the bed . . . Those who know we do not belong anywhere yet understand the necessity of seeming brave … Yes, we recognise Alan Garner's divided self. The noble Cadellin and his wicked brother Grimnir are like Siamese twins; Alison asks her reflection, 'Which is me?' and knows she is doomed to be 'one person with mummy, one with you'; the different boys in *Red Shift* are fissiparous; twins Colin and Susan are one, yet split forever. Knowing such truths, acknowledging your estrangement, results in what Garner describes (speaking of his own life) as 'a shocking alienation' – a self forever divided, forever lost, forever seeking to be whole. These are the contradictions the inner adolescent understands only too well. To the question 'owls or flowers?' the answer, of course, is both. As Alan Garner has written: 'I live, at all times, for imaginative fiction, for ambivalence, not instruction.' He will not supply answers.

Reading that, I come up from sleep at last and accept that if my dreaming had died, it was surely the wrong sort of dream. I whirl back through starlight to Garner's work and revel in contradictions: 'the cold thrill and burn of the spray', the 'pain and gladness', the 'thick light' and 'cold fire', and so on. He knows that Death is the electric current that animates all things. Nothing is as it was meant to be – and at this very point we learn to accommodate the pain. We stand still in the midst of havoc and let the lightning strike. Referring to life during the Second World War Garner recalls, '. . . the need to endure, to survive . . . to be tempered in whatever furnace was required'.

The smith (black and white, working hard and soft) is, the author knows, 'aback of everything': without the metalworking skills of the craftsman we cannot survive. Thus Alan Garner's books burn, but they shape too – and if their shapes shift, that is because such changes are an essential part of our myths and our lives. Nowadays happiness is seen as a right, to be studied, taught in schools, achieved through the panacea of counselling – which seeks even to draw the sting of death. Desperately people turn away from the soft, charcoal mists that gather at the edges of consciousness, like blackened, crumbling edges of charred paper. But it can't be done.

How foolish I was to imagine that Alan Garner could be read for comfort. Instead, he offers a confirmation of all the darkness you ever imagined and tells you to deal with it. Not how to – just that there is no choice. He warns you that the magical, indescribably beautiful unicorn will appear, will sing, will save and then be destroyed. That is how it is. That is how it was meant to be, since the planet was formed by creatures of earth, air, fire and water, laying down their patterns on land, sea and soul. And will be, until earth is destroyed, leaving behind only our myths, our spirits in old haunts.

Such thoughts, as Robert and Joseph in *The Stone Book Quartet* say, 'put a quietness on you'. That moment of cessation is, paradoxically, an expression of Picasso's '*l'inquiétude*' – meaning restless anxiety, a haunting sense of emptiness. This (expressed in the splintering of Cubism, in dissonance and in the limits of narrative) manifests the quest of the perpetually divided self for completion. How wrong I was to use that glib phrase (to Erica Wagner), 'light in the darkness'. For it is the absolute acceptance that there is no illumination which starts, slowly, to allow the darkness to soften, to assuage, even to heal.

After all, it has to be good for something . . .

And that – the first glimmer of light – is as good a place to end as any.

Bel Mooney has been a journalist for 45 years, contributing to almost every national newspaper and many magazines. She is the author of six novels, over 30 children's books, and a variety of non-fiction works. Her career as a broadcaster spanned radio and television; she is a Fellow of University College, London and also holds an honorary doctorate from Bath University. In 2005 she joined The Times *as an advice columnist, but since 2007 her highly-regarded column has appeared in the* Daily Mail, *for which she also writes articles and book reviews. She is currently working on her second memoir.*

UNFINISHED BUSINESS

Richard Morris

The telephone rang a lot at the Council for British Archaeology. Calls came from people who wanted advice on how to go on a dig, journalists, government agencies, campaigners. Our receptionist buzzed my extension one summer morning in 1995: 'There's someone wants to talk to you.' She put him through. 'It's Alan Garner.'

I had last heard Alan's voice 16 years before. Hearing it again now it might have been 16 minutes. In one way this was not a surprise. Our relationship had been adjourned, not broken. Back in 1970, before I turned to archaeology, we had been collaborating on a piece of music theatre which it was down to me to finish. I had imagined that sooner or later it would be me ringing him. But this was not what Alan wanted to talk about. Something odd had turned up in the garden of Toad Hall.

Jane, my wife, and I went back to Blackden. Our first visit 25 years before had been up a puddled track to an isolated, dilapidated house set in an acre of tussock and willowherb dotted with a few elderly fruit trees. This time we drove up an all-weather lane into managed grounds coloured by herbaceous borders, and Toad Hall was adjoined by the Old Medicine House that might always have been there. Bordering both was the railway atop an embankment. Today this seems like a piece of Cheshire's solid geology but it dates only from 1841, when it changed Toad Hall from a place with wide views into somewhere secluded. And as you notice in Alan's 1980 television play *To Kill a King*, conversations in the Old Medicine

House are often punctuated by passing trains.

The thing we had been invited to look at was indeed odd. Gardening had opened a small hole beside a flight of steps that led down to the Old Medicine House in front of Toad Hall. Peering blankly out of it was a skull. At first sight it looked real. On closer view it was not quite the right shape and made of gypsum plaster. Even so . . . Was this some quirky foundation ritual? A joke? There was more to discuss. Since we were last there Alan and Griselda had married; two children had been born and grown; *The Stone Book Quartet* had been published; *Strandloper* had been written. Meanwhile I had turned to archaeology.

I thought back to the first meeting. In hindsight it was crazy. I had written to Alan in March 1970, about 10 weeks before my final examinations at Oxford. I had been studying English and should have been revising. But Keats's Latinate diction and Old English irregular verbs did not quicken my pulse and for three years I had done little academic work. Instead I had been writing music. By early 1970 I had come to suppose that student performances of a few of my pieces provided sufficient foundation for collaboration on some original music drama. I was looking for a mythological subject rooted in Britain. Most of the writers I knew had other preoccupations. The spark, when it landed, arrived from outside. Jane, then my girlfriend, taught at a village school near Oxford. One of her colleagues had been reading *The Owl Service*. Here was the man. I wrote to him. On the Friday after Easter, Alan replied. 'Your letter . . . has made my spine creep. I've been brooding over just the type of thing you suggest for two or three years now . . . obviously we must talk.' He would ring to discuss a visit. The telephone call came before the letter.

'It's Alan Garner.'

Jane and I drove to Blackden the next day. Alan's directions had sounded a bit like the boundary clause of a medieval charter: from the M6 to Holmes Chapel, thence towards Chelford, beside the railway viaduct over the river Dane, up the hill to Twemlow Green, then left and immediately right towards Goostrey, where he would meet us in the car park of the Red Lion. And there he was, tall, a little hawk-like, leaning against the side of a long wheelbase Land Rover. Toad Hall is a distance from public roads and I assumed that the car park rendezvous was to enable Alan to guide us on the final stretch. Alan later explained that it was a precaution in case we turned out to be time-wasters.

There are several ways to reach Toad Hall. One begins near the Red Lion along a private track which gives glimpses of Bosley Cloud and the Pennine flank – *Weirdstone* and *Thursbitch* country – before descending into a tree-canopied hollow that brings you to Blackden Hall and then into the valley of the Blackden Brook. A second approach, the one we took that Saturday, strikes off alongside some interwar semis next to a triangular sandy field fringed by Scots pines. This is a remnant of Blackden Heath, once a distinctive kind of Cheshire landscape where relict heath, meres and mosses mingled. From here a sunken lane leads to a causeway across the flood-plain of the Blackden Brook, where it meets the track coming down from Blackden Hall.

Strangers who have got this far need nerve, for until you know better there is a strong sense of being in the wrong place. However, a gate opens north-eastward under trees. If you turn in you find yourself looking up a track to Toad Hall. Beyond it, the dish of the Lovell Telescope listens for pulsars, nebulae, and the birth of stars. Lost at one moment, in the next the visitor is in a place where past, future, local and universal meet.

Yet more absorbing is the journey from the north. Today you do this on foot, although when Toad Hall was new it seems to have been the main approach. Alan came this way in 1957, as he recalls on The Blackden Trust's website:

> There was a torn piece of hardboard lodged in the hedge. On it was daubed in whitewash: 17th. CENTURY COTTAGE FOR SALE. I opened the wicket gate and pushed my bicycle down the overgrown path, across the brook and up the field.
>
> The line of the roof appeared and, with each step, the house stood up from the land. I began to shake. This was no seventeenth-century cottage. I was looking at a timber-

frame medieval hall. I lifted the doorknocker at 7.20pm, 19th April 1957. Good Friday.

The price was £510, and I had 8s.3d. and no prospects. I rode back to Alderley.

'And what's up with you, then?' said my father.

'I've seen the only place I can ever live.'

'And where's that?'

'Blackden.'

Toad Hall in 1957 had no electricity; 13 years on it still lacked mains water, drainage, and a lavatory. The floors rested on earth. For some years it had been the policy of successive governments to demolish buildings like this as hazards to public health. Happily, attempts by the local authority to condemn the house had been parried, first by Alan, more recently by the then Ministry of Public Buildings and Works which in 1967 had listed the house as a late sixteenth-century cottage with walls of brick 'and brick-nogged timber framing, formerly thatched now with corrugated sheet roof'. The man from the ministry was right about the roof but wrong on some other things. Around 1880 the house had been divided into two cottages. Before that it had been a farmhouse. In origin, however, as Alan recognised, it had been a hall. There were original casements and evidence of a gallery. Much of the timber-framed north side was still filled by panels formed of woven hazel rods daubed with clay, dung, straw and sand.

Alan had moved in by stages. When he arrived the western part was still occupied by Betty Carter, whose father had worked nearby as a railway signalman in the 1880s. When Betty departed Alan bought the other cottage (the rooms of which to this day are known as 'Mrs Carter's') and began to re-unite the two. In 1970 this was still work in progress: Mrs Carter's parlour had been temporarily colonised by Alan's first three children as a place to play, while the upstairs room, as yet without electricity, housed the Elsan.

So began a remarkable period. In my memory it seems to have stretched across several years; Jane's diary shows it to have been a few months. One focus during this time was Alan's workplace in the former service room at the east end of the house. The room was the width of the house. It had a fireplace beside which talk ran into the night, a tiled floor upon which you slept on a camp bed when the talk was done, a working counter for Alan's papers and typewriter, and shelf upon shelf of books. The books dealt with vivid subjects like Celtic iconography, star-craft, children's games, vernacular building, Anglo-Saxon magic and the powers of plants. A striking thing was Alan's ability to put a photocopy of a given page into my hand while we were talking. Photocopiers were then rare, or at least they seemed so to me, and this was the first I had met in a house. Such forward-looking technology seemed all the more arresting in a house where water came from a well and non-compostable rubbish was buried in pits ('boggart holes').

Looking back, there was another aspect. In 1970 Alan Garner was on fire. *The Owl Service* had been televised a few months before. *Red Shift* was in progress; he was revising shooting scripts for *Elidor*; the libretto of 'The Green Mist' was taking shape within a month of our meeting and finished by early July – the month in which Griselda and Alan saw the Old Medicine House for the first time and decided to save it. More on this later: the point here is that Alan was living a creed. As he put it in a letter at the end of April: 'act first, ask later . . . bypass the lot, and get on with it.' The photocopier and electric typewriter were simply aids to the getting-on.

The other focus was a long, scrubbed table in the kitchen. Evening meals in Toad Hall were a kind of long drawn-out ceremony which might begin with discussion led by Griselda about the day's events and what the meal would be. A trip into the garden to select vegetables, herbs or gather raspberries would follow. Griselda had been pioneering a vegetable plot in one corner of the site (Figure 1, again), and years of living on the breadline had led her to experiment with wild as well as cultivated plants. Weed salad, with delicacies like dandelion leaves, was one of her specialities; steamed young nettles another. While the meal was being cooked more talk would ensue – sometimes serious, sometimes uproarious, often both. The arrival of the food, often long after nightfall, invariably delicious, came as an apotheosis. After this, a ritual grinding of coffee beans by Alan in

Toad Hall from the air, 1970. (Photo © The Blackden Trust)

a hand-turned cast-iron mill screwed to a doorpost, and a return to the fireside.

The fireplace and its chimney had been introduced when the eastern gable was rebuilt in brick in the seventeenth century. Above Alan's work room is an upper chamber, and above that a sleeping loft under the base coat of thatch that still survives beneath the corrugated iron. It was up here that early in his occupancy Alan had made a discovery. Next to the chimney was a carapace formed of clay into which twigs of gorse had been stuck when the clay was wet. Within it were seven shoes that had been put there in the seventeenth century. One morning during our second or third visit Alan brought them into the kitchen. They were in two old Start-rite shoe boxes, which out of prudence were normally kept close to the place that the shoes had originally been deposited to protect. Alan put the boxes on the long table and lifted the lids. One shoe was a wooden-soled clog – apparently the earliest of its kind yet found in Britain. Four had been worn by children. I picked one up and

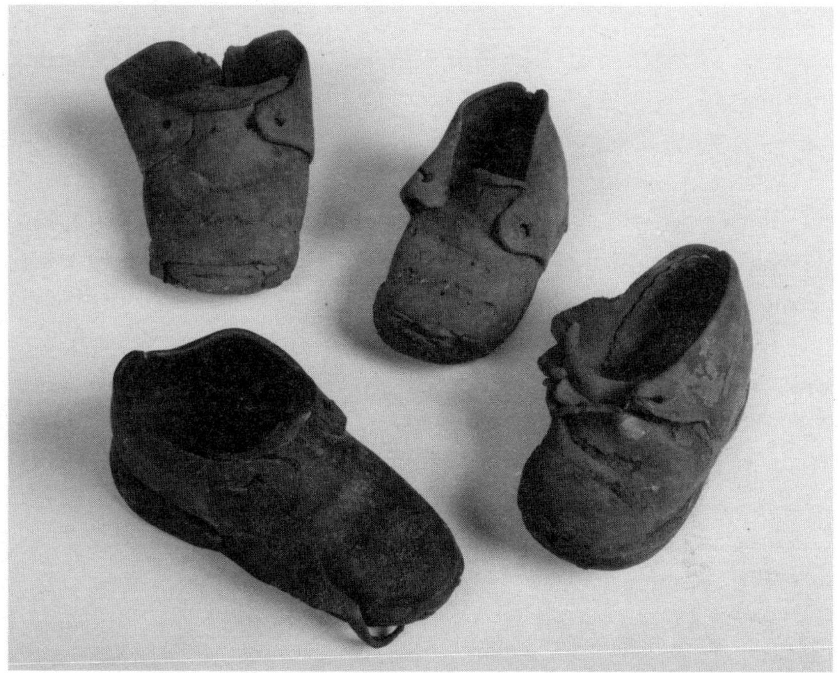

Four children's shoes found at Toad Hall. (Photo © David Heke)

looked at it sideways. Between the leather sole and the upper was a smear of cow dung, a vestige of the last day that the shoe had been worn. For a few seconds I was so close to the youngster sloshing around in the farmyard outside that I cried to meet him.

Such moments led me to think of Blackden as a place of heightened reality – a kind of supercharged environment in which strange and powerful things would happen. The same feeling extended to surrounding places to which Alan took us. One of them was Ludchurch, a chasm in the rocks of Staffordshire Moorland where at some point since the last glacial period a mass of Roaches Grit had split away from the side of the Dane valley leaving a rift about 110 yards long and up to 50 feet deep. In 1958 Ralph Elliott, a scholar of medieval language at University College, Keele, had used toponymy, textual evidence and historical sources to pinpoint Ludchurch as the model for the Green Chapel in the fourteenth-century romance *Sir Gawain and the Green Knight*. Ludchurch is open to the sky yet unseen until you step into it. It is exactly the 'creuisse of an olde cragge' described in the poem, and on the Saturday following our first visit, text in hand, we re-traced Gawain's journey on New Year's Day to the place 'with a hole on Þe end & on ayÞer syde,/& ouergrowen with gresse in glodes ay-where'.

Elliott's own life was hardly less eventful than that of Gawain, and links with Blackden. He had been born in Berlin in 1921 as Rudolf Wolfgang Viktor Ehrenberg, into a family of illustrious academic traditions. (As a child – Elliott later told Alan – he had often met Einstein at the house of his uncle, the physicist Max Born, 'and was witness to many discussions between the two men, which he thought was how all grown-ups talked'.) In 1931 his father moved them to Karlsruhe. Five years on, increasing anti-Semitism caused Rudolf and his younger sister to be sent to live in Edinburgh with Uncle Max, who had already left Germany following the Nazi purge of Jewish physicists in 1933. In 1939 Rudolf enrolled to read English at the University of St Andrews. His studies were interrupted in 1940 when he and his father (who escaped just before the outbreak of war) found themselves among the 30,000 aliens who were interned by the UK government. Rudolf was sent to Canada. Here, the cases of German Jewish refugees were individually examined. As a result he was soon back in Britain, now a member of the Pioneer Corps, a unit of the British army that undertook support tasks like laying roads and handling stores. From here, while still a German national (a 'kilted Kraut' as he referred to himself), he was selected for officer training at Sandhurst. As a Lieutenant in the Manchester Regiment he was badly wounded during fighting in the Teutoburg Forest in 1945. After the war he returned to St Andrews, became a British citizen (confirming the name Ralph Warren Victor Elliott that he had taken in the army), and progressed to a lectureship at Keele. In 1959 Elliott emigrated to Australia, where a succession of academic appointments and achievements culminated in the award of the Centenary Medal for service to Australian society 'and the humanities in the history of the English language'.

In 2003 Alan reviewed a new translation of *Gawain* in which he reflected: 'I was fortunate in that I did not read *Sir Gawain* until I wanted to. And, as a native of Cheshire, I was puzzled at so many footnotes. I did not need them . . . neither did my father when I read extracts to him aloud. He could not have known that I was quoting Middle English.' It was Ralph Elliott who 30 years before had written 'out of the Antipodean blue' to suggest to Alan that he 'was the first person since the Gawain Poet to draw on the same language and landscape'. His perception had a wider context. Just as Nikolaus Pevsner – another German Jewish exile – brought the eye of an outsider to his 1955 Reith Lectures on 'The Englishness of English Art', so Elliott's books on *Chaucer's English* (1974), *Thomas Hardy's English* (1984) and *The Gawain Country* (1984) draw on detachment to define what is native. Elliott became a visitor to Blackden. Alan recalls him declaiming *The Battle of Maldon* in the Medicine House chimney. 'The chimney became central to Ralph's English identity, and he often wrote about his need to be back there, his yearning for the place. He called it the Blackden megaron . . .'

After Ludchurch came trips to places in *Red Shift*. Alan talked about the emerging book – the reliance on dialogue, the idiolect of GIs in Vietnam as a proxy for the speech of Roman legionaries, its landscapes, the graffito that gives the aching last line. We examined the parish church at Barthomley, tramped Mow Cop, admired Crewe station and wandered the sandy woods of Rudheath. Occasionally, I later realised, we were straying inside the book itself, as on page 10 where one evening we foreshadowed Tom's thirty-foot flying jumps down a conical heap of sand. Later still I came to appreciate the extent to which 'The Green Mist' and *Red Shift* are related. In each there is a troubled family – invasive mother, father, son – and a girl. In both, too, there is a 'real and special thing' which becomes a pivot of betrayal, and splintered syntax is used to build a charge of feeling and understanding, so that 'single words become universes of meaning'. On the other hand, one ends in desolation, the other in joy. Moreover, the experience behind this English rite of spring in which a teenage girl dances herself to death, threw up an arresting cross-reference: to the violin concerto' of Alban Berg, composed in 1935 'To the memory of an angel', following the death of Manon Gropius, the eighteen-year-old daughter of Alma Mahler and Walter Gropius. Whether such allusion was to be slight or large, structural, thematic or through direct quotation I could not then tell, but the discovery of a link between 1930s Vienna and ancient Cheshire vernacular only quickened my sense that Blackden was at the heart of everything.

From late May to early July letters from Alan arrived at the rate of two or three a week. In them he discussed sources, offered advice ('Only excellence will do' … 'Don't be afraid of arrogance: it is achieved only through humility.'), tried his hand at composing ('Could we not, at one cataclysmic moment, do something really violent? I thought of breaking glass'), and talked about the weather. Cheshire was experiencing its hottest June in nearly a century. On the 10th: 'I have to do all the letters in the morning, before the sun moves to the window; thereafter it's a case of typing with the blinds down and no air.' On the 13th: 'I cast runes here and produce six hours of thunderstorms, but couldn't be certain of pushing them as far south as Oxford.' He added: 'Aren't you taking some exams round about now?' I was, and it was difficult to concentrate.

In July came gooseberries. Competitive gooseberry growing remains a living pursuit in mid-Cheshire. Alan's father was a grower, and Betty Carter's son Frank had found Toad Hall's soil and climate to be ideal for the propagation of new varieties. Nurturing gooseberry cultivars is not a pastime for anyone with a short attention span: it takes years to introduce a new one, and some years more to find out whether it will bear champion berries. The 16 new varieties bred at Blackden by Frank Carter have thus acquired a legendary reputation, not least because several of them continue to win prizes. The names given to types of gooseberry at different times bear their own messages. Some nineteenth-century varieties like Wellington's Glory, Hero of the Nile, or Lord Kitchener suggest preoccupations with campaigns and empire. By contrast, Frank Carter's berry names quietly extolled his place: Just Betty, his mum; Blackden Firs, his home; Jodrell, his horizon; Blackden Gem, Blackden. On the last Saturday in July we were taken to the gooseberry show in Goostrey, a drama where yellow, white, green and red fruits the size of hens' eggs were weighed against each other in apothecary's scales, the weights of potential champions being loudly and tensely incanted in pennyweights and grains.

Yet more excursions were made to rescue things. In the garden stood the shaft of an Anglo-Saxon cross that had been saved from break-up. From Barthomley came the page of a medieval gospel of St Luke that had been re-used as a leaf in a post-Reformation account book and was about to be thrown out when Alan intervened. Two seventeenth-century gravestones had been salvaged from a clearance in Knutsford. An early visit saw us rattling down a lane in Alan's Land Rover to retrieve a boundary marker that had become displaced and was at risk. For a demonstration of Alan's axiom 'act first, ask later', however, none of these missions came close to the saving of the Old Medicine House.

The televising of *The Owl Service* had provided the means to improve Toad Hall's slender amenities. One immediate effect of this was to throw new light on Toad Hall. Alan had been put in touch with Michael Peach, a young architect who specialised in vernacular buildings. Peach arrived in mid-July to survey Toad Hall, the better to understand how it might be extended. Three days later Alan wrote to me to apologise for a delay in copying the libretto. 'But,' he continued in what may be the longest sentence of his career,

> if you had recognised something at the age of twenty-one and clung on to it for thirteen years without being able to do more, and then had discovered the man who really knows about these buildings; and if that man had, before your eyes, gone into a coma of wonder, and said that he was going to spend a week 'getting to know every timber', and you had been able to stand by him as he did his professional survey, and you had seen him make discoveries of such beauty, and others of such interest, that our very reins did melt, and if, after three days of unbroken work, this man, close on midnight, had straightened his back from his drawing board and said, 'This must be the longest surviving house of its kind; it's the biggest in the country; it's very, very exciting and very, very important,' I think you would find it hard to sit down at a typewriter, and you would also feel a warmth for

the justification of that twenty-one-year-old's recognition and tenacity all those years ago.

The words stood up off the page. At the time I did not appreciate the extent of the struggle, the scepticism, and – now – vindication that lay behind them.

One way to add to Toad Hall was to use comparable materials recovered from elsewhere. Michael Peach was aware of a timber-framed building which was about to be demolished. It was said to date from the sixteenth century and stood about 18 miles away in the Staffordshire hamlet of Wrinehill. It was known as the Old Medicine House and all efforts to save it had failed. Peach suggested that timbers from two of its rooms might be used to extend Toad Hall. Alan and Griselda went to look. The day after the Goostrey gooseberry show Jane and I went with them to look again.

Wrinehill lies in gently undulating countryside a few miles west of Stoke-on-Trent. In the later sixteenth century it was a scatter of households on 'the Wrine Hill', and the seat of Sir Ralph Egerton (d.1596), whose vast Egerton estate lay astride the Staffordshire/ Cheshire border. Indeed, the house stood in Staffordshire only by the narrowest of margins. On this quiet, sunny Sunday afternoon we took stock of it. To the rear it was overgrown. Walls were bowed and bulged. Window frames sagged. The feet of some timbers had perished or no longer connected with their neighbours.

Within, on the floor, under floorboards, were bottles, jars and boxes bearing the labels of Johnson's Patent Medicines. Samuel Johnson (1838-1921) was a local draper who acquired the building in the 1880s and used it for making medicinal pills and oils. In 1891 he lost a libel action brought by a doctor who had denounced him for quackery. The damages tipped him into bankruptcy, but he recovered and the business survived. So the building became known as the Old Medicine House, and when the manufacture of remedies ceased it was remembered as the Old Medicine House. Before Johnson it had been a public house. One of its innkeepers was William Cooper, whose contested will tells us that in 1755 his house 'at the sign of the Red Lion' contained 60 gallons of ale, three gallons of cherry brandy, one gallon of gin and a gallon of wormwood. Who lived there first we did not then know, but out of the shadows, behind the brickwork, flaking plaster, bodged repairs and superficial additions we saw an original timber frame with a vast timber chimney at its heart. Such completeness implied a use history akin to that of Toad Hall – a drift down the social scale that left original things as they were. Among them (it was later found) were panels of Tudor wall painting, which when combined with cloths of painted linen had brightened the interior when it was new. Dearth is the friend of authenticity.

Alan and Griselda had already made up their minds to save the building by bringing it to Blackden. In following days there was talk about ways and means. Maybe help could be sought from Collins, Alan's publisher. Indeed, might the story of the move be the subject of a book. Or a film? 'It's tycoon day today,' wrote Alan on 23rd September. 'We've decided to finance the film ourselves, taking all the risk (and the profits).' But there were to be no profits.

The decision was ethically as well as financially brave. I have wondered since whether at the time they knew how brave it was. The Manifesto of the Society for the Protection of Ancient Buildings (SPAB), written by William Morris and others, issued in 1877, urges owners and architects 'to resist all tampering with either the fabric or ornament of the building as it stands'. In their eyes the removal was not rescue but annihilation. 'As good buildings age,' says the Society, 'the bond with their sites strengthens.' (Could anyone now contemplate moving Toad Hall to Wrinehill?) 'A beautiful, interesting or simply ancient building still belongs where it stands however corrupted that place may have become.' Yes. But for all its rhetoric the conservation establishment failed to defend the Old Medicine House where it stood, while original timbers that were never given a second glance at the old site are now telling remarkable new stories. In the process, Blackden itself has been changed. In the balance of things, we are the richer for 'act first, ask later'.

The cumulative events of that summer were akin to a great wave that knocked me over as it broke. When I touched bottom again things had begun to change. Alan and Griselda were fixed on the Old Medicine House while I went to York to begin a year of postgraduate study in composition. Naively, I had hoped that this would polish my skills. In the event, in the company of accomplished musicians and composer teachers it did not take me long to realise how few skills I had, and how far I would have to travel to acquire them. At the end of the year, deflated, not rejecting composition but knowing that I had to do something properly, I turned to an earlier calling – archaeology. And since only excellence would do, I had to concentrate.

It was archaeology that occasioned our last face-to-face meeting before the long pause. In late summer 1972 *Red Shift* was approaching completion. Alan works through real things, and telephoned to say that he needed something connected with the Ninth Legion of the Imperial Roman army. Coincidentally I was by then with the team excavating under York Minster, which stands upon the remains of a Roman legionary fortress that had been built by the Ninth Legion in the first century. Roof and hypocaust tiles bearing the legion's stamp – LEG[IO]IX HISP[ANA] (the Ninth was nicknamed the Spanish Legion) – were quite common. It was not possible to divert an archaeologically excavated example into Alan's hand, but a search of the contractor's spoil dump soon produced a stamped tile that had been thrown away. We drove over to give it to him. Back at Blackden, we stood in the newly re-erected Old Medicine House for the first time.

About a year later a parcel arrived containing a copy of the newly-published *Red Shift*. On the flyleaf Alan had inscribed IN MEM LEG IX HISP. On page 148 the song 'I'll dye, I'll dye my petticoat red' brought me up short. Alan later sang the traditional tune. It was brisk and jaunty. I had not heard it like that at all. What I did hear reminded me, with a jolt, that there were skills to be acquired for unfinished business.

Speaking of which, what of the plaster skull? To this day we do not know who put it there or why, and it belongs to no genre that anyone has yet recognised. It is another Blackden mystery. All we can say is that is more recent than the small deposit of charcoal and calcined bone that was found by builders during construction of the link between Toad Hall and the Old Medicine House in 1972. The find was boxed and put to one side. When Alan showed it to me years later it looked like a cremation, and it was. In 2012 a sample of the charcoal was submitted for radiocarbon dating. The calibrated date, at 95% probability, is in the range 1879–1687 BC.

Richard Morris is Emeritus Professor of Archaeology at the University of Huddersfield. He has been a trustee of the National Heritage Memorial Fund, director of the Leeds Institute for Medieval Studies, and Council for British Archaeology. His book Time's Anvil: England, Archaeology and the Imagination *was longlisted for the Samuel Johnson Prize and shortlisted for the 2015 Archaeological Book of the Year. He chairs The Blackden Trust.*

FROM CALCUTTA TO CHESHIRE

Neel Mukherjee

Baggin. Gondering. Thrutch. Swarf. Weisening. Dollytub. Bant. Swedgel. Skrike. Pobs. Brogged. Mithering. Bazzil-arsed. I understood none of them – worse, I couldn't find them in any dictionary I had access to – nor make sense of, to me, the clearly ungrammatical locutions such as 'Doesn't it fear you up here' and 'I want no feathers in me baggin, nor in the clock, neither'. To a boy of twelve, growing up in Calcutta, whose English reading consisted overwhelmingly of Enid Blyton, Jennings, and P.G. Wodehouse, and whose education involved strict instructions in English grammar, the volumes in *The Stone Book Quartet* – I can't remember how I stumbled upon them – were baffling and incomprehensible. They did not depict the England that I was beginning to form a picture of from my reading, nor were they written in a language that I identified as proper English. I put the books aside.

It took me over a decade to return to them. The reason for going back? An impassioned and incandescent plea by a friend during an animated discussion of children's literature in which I had let slip that I hadn't got on very well with the work of Alan Garner. Sometimes books make time for you and not the other way round; often the first acquaintance with an author is made at the wrong time – Kafka, Camus and Dostoevsky all occupy this niche of wrong, or mistimed, beginnings in my life. 'How many things by season season'd are/To their right place and true perfection!' I should have that carved and displayed in a very prominent place.

It was serendipitous that I was, at the time, immersed in secondary reading that made me look closely at what kind of social work genres perform. I was reading Raymond Williams and Louis Adrian Montrose on the Elizabethan and seventeenth-century pastoral and how that mode was complicit in the erasure of labour, so labour and work were uppermost in my mind when I began again on *The Stone Book Quartet*. What a difference time and a little bit of learning make: that theoretical thinking on work in literature was like a secret key given me to unlock this cabinet of wonders.

Labour moors and defines and makes the world of the *Quartet*. It begins with Robert, the stonemason, through Joseph, his grandson, who becomes a smith, deliberately choosing not to follow in his grandfather's footsteps – a daring decision, this – because he wants to 'get aback of' the older generation, to William, poised on the threshold of possibility. The last-published book of the quartet, *The Aimer Gate*, which, incidentally, is not, chronologically, the final book of the series (that is *Tom Fobble's Day*), came out first in 1978. It would be nearly 20 years before an essay, originally a lecture first given in 1991 and then extended to an address in 1996, examined more explicitly this notion of 'getting aback'. In 'Aback of Beyond' published in his astonishing collection *The Voice that Thunders*, Garner writes: 'There is a particular pride amongst the Houghites. Each generation feels obliged to better, or do other than, the one before. It is called "getting aback of".' I shall come back to the Houghites later but for now, it's enough to note how this essay reveals the beating autobiographical/familial heart of the *Quartet*. The series is really a family history: Robert, the stonemason who plays the ophicleide, is Garner's great-great-grandfather.

But the history arrives aslant, with great leaps in time and the attendant lacunae, the information and links sometimes scalloped, sometimes staggered. Reading it teaches attentiveness, demands the ability to pick up clues, echoes and distant reverberations, and piece them together into a unity. Only the later essay will make clear why Joseph is a 'granny reardun' (reared by his granny), a partial explanation why these books are about fathers and sons and not, as the first book, *The Stone Book*, may have led you to believe, about fathers and daughters, and how Joseph's 'getting aback of' his grandfather by choosing to become a smith will resound, this time outside the text, in Garner choosing to read Classics at Oxford, followed by a lifelong career in writing.

Central to this idea of 'getting aback of' lies work: the way it defines our identity, our very being. True to this, the *Quartet* pays exquisite attention to both the craft and the art of work, and, crucially, to the nature of someone 'reading' or experiencing that work (Mary on the church spire made by her father; Robert inside another spire more than half a century later). Stonemasonry, smithing, corn harvesting, how escapement makes a pendulum clock work, the making of a sledge, even the playful, artful business of cornet and ophicleide playing – here are detailed, luminous pages on each of these. They are written with passion and pride and love – very much the love and pride craftsmen and artists take in their work – and in the reader they generate something approaching euphoria. Read the pages on the corn harvest on Leah's Hill in *The Aimer Gate*, or Joseph's last day at work in his smithy (witnessed by his grandson, William) in *Tom Fobble's Day*, or the brief passage at the beginning of *The Stone Book* where Robert works on a pebble, transforms it and gives it to his daughter, and you will see what I mean.

Work/craft is one of the ties that binds the successive generations in an unbroken yet variant rhythm of continuity. The Houghite Garners belong to these generations, both in the *Quartet* and in 'real life'. In the four books, this transmission of craft is effected through a series of internal correspondences and assonances which are musical, dizzying in their cumulative effects, repaying attentiveness with such immense rewards, chief of which is joy. A clay pipe (a 'Macclesfield dandy') falls to the ground in the first book and, miraculously, does not break; it will be disinterred by chance, in the final book, by the great-great-grandson of the man from whose hands the pipe had dropped. That same pipe smoker in *The Stone Book* notices his daughter's wonder at the geological marvel that is Tough Tom and remarks, 'That's put a quietness on you.' The identical words are spoken by the pipe smoker's grandson, Joseph, the smith, to his son, Robert, as the boy discovers something wondrous and magical, too: in this case, the dawning of the knowledge that work, or art, can be independent of its audience/viewer/reader.

What is being passed down is a lesson of the sanctity of work, how we make it and how, in turn, it makes us. The characters' response of wonder to the miracle of craft in each of these books – that important experiencing of someone else's work I mentioned earlier – awakens a similar response in the reader, resulting in an enfolding of the two, work and wonder, each generating the other. If the *Quartet* has one meaning, it is this: it is our work that is magical, and it is our work that, if well-made, will survive.

Here is the moment when Robert revisits his discovery of his great-grandfather's self-carved name and his signature rune Tyr in a spot where he knew it would never be seen:

> In the dark his hands could read. And in the dark his hands could hear. There was a long sound in the stone. It was no sound unless Robert heard it, and meant nothing unless he gave it meaning. His chosen place had chosen him. Its end was the beginning.

The enfolding we have just seen shifts and becomes something else: it is now augmented by bringing in the perceiver (or reader) in a way that does not nullify or make incomplete that earlier totality of the relationship between the maker and the made; the two aspects of art (or work, or craft, or skill, call it what you will) sit next to each other in perfect balance and harmony. It is not unusual for children's books to feature wonder, either as their theme or as part of the arsenal of their effects, and Garner is nothing if not consummately aware of the role of wonder in literature – good classicist that he is, he quotes both Plato ('Wonder is only the first glimpse of the start of philosophy.') and Aristotle ('The lover of myths, which are a compound of wonders, is, by being in that very state, a lover of wisdom.') on the subject – but what is extraordinary about *The Stone Book Quartet* is the way the marvellous and the marvelling are embedded in, and inseparable from, work.

The northern working-class roots of this glorification of work are legible on almost every page. That rich local vocabulary, examples of which appear at the beginning of the piece, those 'non-standard' local locutions, all anchor the book to place; the anchoring is both intense and intensely particular. Again, an essay, 'Achilles in Altjira', in *The Voice that Thunders*, shines a light on the language that my twelve-year-old self, reared entirely on Standard English, had found so baffling. In it, Garner talks of his 'primary tongue' as 'North-West Mercian'. He quotes a (beautiful) passage about harvesting from *The Aimer Gate*, and provides a self-commentary: 'Standard English and North-West Mercian are there combined in syntax, vocabulary and cadence. They speak for me, as the head to the heart; as the consonant to the vowel; as Romance to Germanic; as the stem to the root.' The ancients had a term for the guiding spirit of a place, its soul, if you will: genius loci. Alderley Edge, 'a wooded scarp in Cheshire', has found such a witness, chronicler, and animating spirit in him.

Here is an example of how the local informs his work. A reader may speculate about why Mary, Robert's daughter, disappears from the following book (*Granny Reardun*); why her son, Joseph, is brought up by his grandmother; why there is some unexplained animosity that the grown-up Joseph harbours against Faddock Allman in *The Aimer Gate* . . . but there are no answers, no explicatory lessons. Only when Garner writes about the 'ferocious caste system' of the area in 'Aback of Beyond' do all the pieces fall into place. It's worth quoting in full:

> There are four farming families [in the Hough], who interbreed without any apparent harm. Then there are the craft families, the Houghites, who service the community. Below the Hough stretches Lifeless Moss, bad land, fit only for the hovels of the unskilled families, the Mossaggots, and now the houses of Manchester's stockbrokers. The Houghites have a terrible fear of being polluted by the Mossaggots. I was not allowed to play with their children. Yet Robert Garner's favourite daughter Mary fell in love with Joseph Clewes, Mossaggot, and had a son by him. Robert forbade the marriage, expelled his daughter, and he and his wife brought up the boy, my grandfather Joseph, themselves.

> He was thus a 'grannyreardun'; and the shame of his birth affected the rest of her life. In the words of my grandfather, 'She never put her bonnet on again.' That is, she never left the confines of the garden. She felt the taint of Mossaggotry till death.

To read this is to appreciate how profoundly a book can render a place, its people, their micro-customs. It's as if such things comprise the air that one breathes in while both writing and reading: there's no need to remark on something as omnipresent, as pervasive, as vital as air; it's only when it's absent that you notice it.

Reading his work it becomes clear that Garner effortlessly knows every square centimetre of that Cheshire landscape, every gradient, every stone, every blade of grass. Here is something that I would come to recognise retrospectively as one of the great lessons of writing: there is nothing more universal than the particular, that the local is the world. At a time when meaningless chatter about 'globalisation' and 'global lit' has seen the rise of books that seem to depict places which have all the distinctiveness of an airport lounge, this lesson is one to hold to one's heart ever more fiercely.

At the end of the first book, Robert gives his daughter, Mary, a prayer book that he has carved out of stone. 'It's better than a book you can open,' he says. '. . . A book has only one story.' No: Garner's own books have legions of them, each reading shedding a new and different light on the landscape of his language and his work.

Neel Mukherjee's first novel, A Life Apart *(2010), won the Writers' Guild of Great Britain Award for best novel and was shortlisted for the inaugural DSC Prize for South Asian Literature. His second novel,* The Lives of Others *(2014), was shortlisted for the Man Booker Prize, the Costa Novel Award, and won the Encore Award for best second novel. His third novel,* A State of Freedom, *is out in 2017. He lives in London.*

A GHOST BOOK: THE 'STONE BOOK'

Richard Ovenden

In 1979, Issue 82 of the influential photography magazine *Aperture* featured a short biography of one of that issue's contributors, Alan Garner. It also included an announcement of a forthcoming publication, a collaboration between Garner and the American photographer Paul Caponigro:

> Alan Garner is an innovative contemporary writer. A bookworm during his childhood, he adored Victorian literature, and won a scholarship to Oxford University, where he studied the Greek and Latin classics. In 1957 he left Oxford to become a writer. His children's books have won numerous awards in this country and England. He is at work on a major text for Paul Caponigro's book on the megalithic stones to be published by *Aperture* in 1980.

Issue 82 of *Aperture* also included a portfolio of images by Caponigro of Stonehenge and another group of images of prehistoric stone monuments which were accompanied by a poem by Garner, entitled 'The Island of the Strong Door'. Garner's poem evokes the atmosphere of the stones documented in Caponigro's photographs with considerable power: his own response to ancient landscapes and their connections with the people who erected them and have lived in and around them since their creation is a significant feature of his writing, especially in his novels *Elidor* and *Thursbitch*. Garner's own interest in ancient monuments and their early archaeology is almost at a professional level. The poem draws on Celtic myths for inspiration and quotes *The Song of Amergin* and *The Book of Taliesin*, and has been described as a 'hymn to the numinous essence of the British landscape'[1]. Garner's poem has not been published in its entirety elsewhere, and deserves a wider exposure:

THE ISLAND OF THE STRONG DOOR

Stone-rise to man-set is a moment.
Not enough to enter
The bone of the Mother,
The rope of blood.
It is not enough to enter
By hewn birth
The island of the strong door.

I shall not be older, I shall not be younger
Than I was in the beginning.
There will not come from my design
Fear or death.
I see not, and I am not seen.
Where twilight and the black night
Move together I gather all given
And give back.
In the island of the strong door.
In the four cornered castle.
In the spinning circle.
In the garth of glass.
Hill weight to horizon.

Higgar Tor and Wet Withens behind us

1 Neil Philip, *A fine anger: a critical introduction to the work of Alan Garner* (London: Collins, 1981), pp. 147-8.

We climbed among harebells and larks
Above land.
A long sound
In the flint answered the field
And the wood. Beyond the crest
Pools cupped water in sarsen,
Below were stones:
Stone lugged on stone
Upheaven over the crop.
We poured a libation,
The last from the bottle.
Flat glass about the dolmen. The wine
Gleam spilt.
High at the lee of the wind
We sheltered by slates in a valley.
Aching, aching,
The hill hung.

Hinged on the sky
It is lonely, it is lonely,
And the miles between.

Yet I am the willow
The heather the willow
The fir and the ash,
And, clockway as the year
Among grey wethers
Flintshard and skull
Cromlech to pebble,
Over again shall catch
The exploding blood:
And sleep
On the bones of the moon.

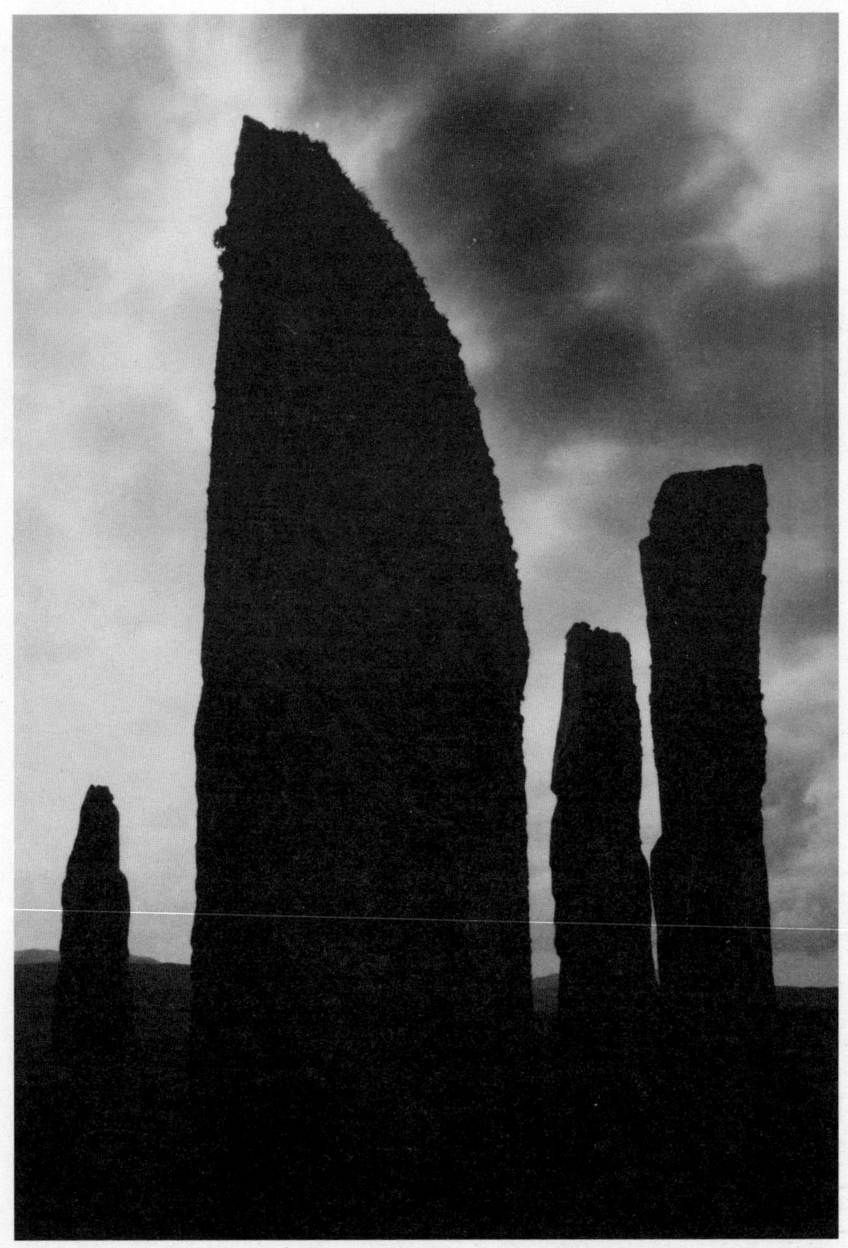

(Photo © Paul Caponigro)

In 1985 the American publishing house of Little, Brown (based in Boston) published a book of photographs, with accompanying text by Paul Caponigro (the publication was made simultaneously with the New York Graphic Society). The book contained 119 images of Caponigro's photographs, beautifully reproduced in duotone by the celebrated graphic printing establishment, Meriden-Stinehour of Lunenberg, Vermont. The images are accompanied in the book by text written by Caponigro himself, Alan Garner's name does not feature in the publication, which was entitled *Megaliths*.

The published volume, however, did not represent the original intentions of the photographer. The original intention of Caponigro, encouraged by Michael E. Hoffman at *Aperture*, was to have the images accompanied by text provided by Alan Garner, as a collaboration between text and image that would unite the sensibilities toward ancient stones and their relevant landscapes that both artists displayed and shared between one another.

The Alan Garner papers, held in the Bodleian Library, Oxford, hold material that sheds tantalising light on this ghost production, leaving us with glimpses of a book that never was.

Alan Garner first met Paul Caponigro in 1977. Caponigro himself had been photographing the ancient stones of northern Europe since 1966 thanks to a Guggenheim Fellowship that was awarded to fund his travel to Ireland. Over the following 20 years he visited 50 sites in England, Scotland, Ireland and France, on numerous visits, partially funded by the National Endowment for the Arts, and the Arts Council of England.[2] By 1977 Michael E. Hoffman, then Director of the Aperture Foundation, was attempting to bring Caponigro and Garner's work together and to get firm commitments on what Caponigro was already calling 'the stone book'.[3] Caponigro viewed the project with enthusiasm: 'You do your thing with words and I'll take responsibility for the visuals.' At this stage the photographer did

2 Jennifer A Watts and Scott Wilcox, *Bruce Davidson / Paul Caponigro: Two American Photographers in Britain and Ireland* (New Haven, Conn.: Yale University Press, 2014), pp. 34-43.
3 Bodleian Library, Alan Garner Papers, Letter from Paul Caponigro to Alan Garner, 18 September 1977.

not want to 'explain' things but felt, 'Rather, to let the poetic force of the material shine through.'

In the same letter he sketched in words what he wanted the book to convey:

> Stones are brought up and out of the earth to be placed throughout the land. Through this action, prehistoric man expresses, for me, his need to keep a contact with the Eternal One. The different configurations of stones at various sites express one or another aspect of a process or journey the soul must pass through to free itself from the fall into physical matter and move on to greater heights.
>
> I see the primary attitudes of the stones, as they have been placed by man, to be that of endurance and aspiration. The stones seem to murmur steadily and confer amongst themselves about the task ahead, of returning to the source. Callanish Circle in the Hebrides and Arbor Low are both particularly intense and lofty in their silent conference about the upward acsent [sic].'
>
> Constant, organic, timeless sentinels to eternity, these mysterious stones abide and silence men with wonder. In this wonder and silence one could hear the unspoken word.

Caponigro concluded with the hope:

> . . . that there is enough in these words to convey something of my involvement with the Megaliths . . . I will of course be anticipating a response from you as to where we meet in our separate thoughts about the Stones.

Alan Garner responded in a letter of 27th September 1977, giving some indication of his 'thoughts about the Stones':

> Meanwhile I keep filtering the stones. Something big is there, and I have to keep going again and again to listen. It's a rhythm and a flow, from the grain to the sky, and it helps that in Cheshire the rocks are still called clouds. I have a note scribbled beside one of your prints – 'It is not enough

> to enter.' (i.e. 'To enter is not enough.') The stone leads into the earth leads out to the sky. And beyond that. Your 'source-ward'. The 'task ahead' – and the end is the beginning.[4]

(Photo © Paul Caponigro)

By May 1979, Garner's ideas for the literary accompaniment to the images had developed sufficiently for him to provide a synopsis of his approach:

> SYNOPSIS OF ESSAY. (Not for publication.)
> The quest for the Self through the medium of land and stones.
>
> Life has two channels of force: 'zoe' and 'bios'. They are Greek words, because the Greeks differentiated between the forces in a way that English does not. Zoe is life unqualified, unquantified, limitless and, therefore, without direction or

4 Bodleian, Garner Papers, Letter from AG to PC, 27 September 1977.

self-knowledge. 'Bios' is the life of an individual, historical, bounded in space and in time, but specified and directed. Zoe knows nothing of Bios, but Bios is formed of the stuff of Zoe and returns to Zoe through the experience we call death.

The land is Zoe. The stones are the Bios of land. My Bios tries to comprehend Zoe through the transcendental experiencing of a land. The way in is through the stones, from the man-formed to the weather-formed to the time-formed: architecture to geology.

Of the megaliths, a Zoe-bias is shown by dolmens and circles and unshaped stone: Bios of stones is reached through angularity and isolation; the single stone reaches for a singularity, the infinity of a point. For the stone, that point is the equivalent of my own unique moment, and through the moment and the point both stone and man reach the infinite, which lies around us as land, which the unshaped stone exemplifies. In the counterpoint of stones, in the transcendental experience of land by man, Bios is integrated with Zoe but not yet reabsorbed. Self-knowledge and the infinite are in balance, as the stones are to the land.' (N.B. The terms 'zoe' and 'bios' are a shorthand. The essay will be written in longhand, and may not need to use this jargon.'[5]

From the correspondence up to this point it is clear that the two men had a firm intention to collaborate on the book, but between 1979 and 1983 both artists experienced health problems and were involved in other projects that together caused significant delays to the project. Eventually Alan Garner withdrew his involvement, as his own career had taken him in other directions, including a major lecture tour to Canada and Australia. Throughout this period, and beyond, the two men remained on excellent terms with one another, with Caponigro sending prints to Garner as they were completed ('The prints of the stones coming out of the darkroom are beautiful

5 Bodleian, Garner Papers, Letter from AG to PC, 16 May 1979.

and I expect the final book (arriving Sept, 86) will be equally so'),[6] and asking for information and advice. Both men had experienced frustrations with Michael E. Hoffman's famously combative style, and Caponigro eventually took the project away from *Aperture* and negotiated a new publishing arrangement with Little, Brown/ New York Graphic Society, with a new contract eventually signed in January 1986.[7] Garner and Caponigro were still corresponding in 1984–86, as the publication was nearing completion regarding the details of the volume, Garner even citing in one letter the opening lines of the poem printed in Aperture, 'Stone-rise to man-set is a moment', perhaps forgetting that it had featured in their earlier collaboration.[8] All through the correspondence between the two during this period, they refer to the publication as 'The Stone Book', but eventually that title would disappear. Garner at one point suggests a title for the book: 'Megaliths of Western Europe', perhaps providing the inspiration, in truncated form, for the eventual title.

The version of *Megaliths* that was eventually published in 1986 was a beautifully conceived and carefully designed production. The publishing records do not survive for the volume, but Caponigro clearly took exquisite care in the layout and production values. Some records for Caponigro's book *Sunflower,* also published by Little, Brown/New York Graphic Society and printed by Meriden-Stinehour, do survive, and they demonstrate a close attention to the detail of the book-making which both Paul and Eleanor Caponigro, by then his ex-wife, were intent upon: being insistent about details of the reproduction of the images, the accompanying letterpress, and even the binding.[9] The same paper was chosen for both books: Mohawk Superfine, which allowed the duotone images to be reproduced to a remarkably high quality. *Megaliths* is one of the great photographically-illustrated books of the 1980s.

During his visits to Ireland in the 1960s and 70s Caponigro consulted the Board of Works in Ireland which maintained a library

6 Bodleian, Garner Papers, Letter from PC to AG 18 January 1986.

7 Bodleian, Garner Papers, Letter from PC to AG, 18 January 1986.

8 Bodleian, Garner Papers, Letter from AG to PC, 29 January 1986.

9 Dartmouth College Library, Department of Special Collection, MS. 959-57. I am grateful to Morgan Swan for help in investigating the Meriden-Stinehour papers.

of photographs and documents related to the monuments in their care, and drew on the information he found there, in support of his photographic journeys.[10] Caponigro provided explanatory texts to precede each section of images, with the combination of texts and images being laid out as portfolios (neither the text pages or the photographic plates are paginated, heightening this sense of the volume being a series of portfolios). More detailed, descriptive text on the sites was provided at the back of the volume in the form of a Gazetteer, with information supplied by an editorial assistant, Ann Mason. This Caponigro referred to as the 'back matter to give the readers some orientation to the place . . . geographically and historically'.[11]

On 14th September 1986 Caponigro sent a postcard to the Garners revealing that he was 'sitting here stunned, looking at 1st sheets off the press of the *Megaliths* book. Beautifully printed and bound copies ready Nov. 1st. A great release and I am ready for my post-partum. Will send a copy when I get some.'[12]

Caponigro's explanatory texts evoke his own artistic and psychological response to the photographs, but we are left wondering at the lost collaboration between Caponigro and Garner. How powerful and striking would that production have been! It was an inspired notion to attempt to bring these two artists together, bringing Caponigro's spiritual response to landscape and ancient stones together with Alan Garner's own unique understanding of landscape and man's continuing, additive relationship over thousands of years, expressed in some of the most powerful literature on the subject in the English language. In one letter early in their relationship Alan Garner wrote to Caponigro in a style that gives us a tantalising glimpse at what could have been the powerful literary foil to his magisterial images:

10 Oral History Interview for the Archives of American Art, July 30–August 12 1999. http://www.aaa.si.edu/collections/interviews/oral-history-interview-paul-caponigro-11968
11 Bodleian, Garner Papers, Letter from PC to AG, 18 January 1986.
12 Bodleian, Garner Papers, Postcard from PC to AG, 14 September 1986.

(Photo © Paul Caponigro)

> You know that, while you create a relationship between a stone and its land, the relationship does not depend on you for its existence, only for its expression. Without using the terms, you know about geological and cosmic time, the enormity of land and stone. What has phased you is something quite other. It is this. The megaliths are not benign. They are not malignant, but they were established for ends that a rational Western mind would find dark. I can't work at your sequence of pictures for more than half an hour at a time . . . with the megaliths, you are in the grip of the subject. Its all the more unsettling because we don't expect to be made unwell by clumps of rock. You can't back off. You've seen them. The only way around is straight through. Don't fight the megaliths: but don't surrender before them. They are elementals, and they are not benign. That's all. (Like hell it is.)[13]

Richard Ovenden is Bodley's Librarian of the Bodleian Libraries, University of Oxford. At the Bodleian he is also Director of the Centre for the Study of the Book, and holds a Professorial Fellowship at Balliol College. Richard is author of numerous works on photographic history and book history including John Thomson (1837–1921): Photographer *(1997),* A Radical's Books *(1999) and contributions to the* Cambridge History of Libraries *(2010) and the* History of Oxford University Press *(2013). He is a Fellow of the Royal Society of Arts and of the Society of Antiquaries, and was elected to the American Philosophical Society in 2015.*

13 Bodleian, Garner Papers, Letter from AG to PC, 19th June 1979.

BEYOND THE SINGULARITY

Neil Philip

There is a telling moment in *Boneland* when Colin is urged not to resign his post as a professor of astrophysics at Jodrell Bank, because 'you have it in you to go beyond the Singularity.'

This urge to go 'beyond the Singularity' is one peculiar to Alan Garner. The way his books layer time and space is not simply a narrative technique, but indicative of a deep-seated vision in which the narrator, like Tom in *Red Shift,* sees 'everything at once'. Garner's understanding of time is rooted in astrophysics. Whatever you perceive as happening in the transient 'now' depends on where you are observing it from. But it is rooted too in the eternal Now of the Aboriginal Dreaming. For Garner, dreamtime and spacetime are the same thing.

Garner cherishes puns for their quality of palimpsest, the overlapping of one perception over another, as when 'memento' becomes 'momentum' in a crucial scene in *Red Shift*. His work depicts a collapsible universe, in which everything folds in and in on itself to achieve the required density of meaning.

We all carry our own archaeology with us, but Alan's is more many-layered than most. He's managed to incorporate into his own mental world a historical perspective that enfolds the nineteenth-century convict-turned-Aboriginal man of high degree William Buckley, the eighteenth-century packman John Turner, the fourteenth-century Gawain poet, and the Iron Age sacrificial victim Lindow Man as living presences.

It is perfectly feasible that Garner may be biologically related to any or all of these individuals, such is the extremely local nature of his universal vision. In *Strandloper*, Garner, Buckley and the Gawain poet all inhabit the same space in the text – in a sense share the same soul. The overlap is never perfect, for as the Hasidic master Rabbi Nachman said, 'G-d does not do the same thing twice. Even when a soul is reborn, it is not completely the same.'

The personalities of individuals in Garner's work are often blurred into each other in this way – the modern actors in *The Owl Service* and their models in Welsh myth; Macey, Thomas, and Tom in *Red Shift*; most recently Colin in *Boneland*, whose consciousness is fused with that of an Ice Age shaman who seems to be the last survivor of a group of archaic humans (possibly *Homo erectus*, but maybe Neanderthals) on Alderley Edge. And that unnamed shaman's centre of being is none other than the Gawain poet's Green Chapel, the natural chasm in the millstone grit at Ludchurch.

So complex is this mental layering that by the time *Red Shift* appeared the initial categorization of Garner as a children's writer was becoming inadequate. After the publication of that echo chamber of perfection *The Stone Book Quartet*, it was evident that in Alan Garner, England had a major writer on its hands, one whose perception of language, landscape and legacy was as vigorous and as subtle as that of Ted Hughes or George Mackay Brown.

The three major works of fiction Garner has published since then – *Strandloper, Thursbitch*, *Boneland* – have all been aimed at an adult audience. The preoccupations remain the same, and themes, ideas, and even images and phrases from the earlier work are constantly hovering in and around these newer texts, like recurrent musical motifs. At the end of *Boneland*, for instance, elements of Garner's libretto for the 1975 opera *Potter Thompson,* whose psychodrama of thwarted development haunts the entire novel, rise to a crescendo. Colin, like Potter Thompson, tells the sleeping knights not to wake, his head 'no more rampicked by the stars, no more agate with dreams'.

The fact that *Boneland* is as much a re-imagining of *Potter Thompson* as it is a conclusion to *The Weirdstone of Brisingamen* and

The Moon of Gomrath shows how involuted Alan Garner's work is; in it, each part stands for the whole. To divide it into work for children and work for adults is futile. Nevertheless the novels published for adults are an important extension of the earlier work I discussed in my critical study *A Fine Anger*, 34 years ago.

In his 1983 essay 'Achilles in Altjira', Garner wrote, 'My concern, in writing and in life, is that, by developing our greatness, the intellect, we should not lose the other greatness, our capacity to Dream.' This statement is key to all three of the late novels, but very obviously to *Strandloper*, which traces the fate of a Cheshire man, William Buckley who, transported to Australia on trumped-up charges, escapes the penal colony and is rescued in the outback by a band of Wathaurung Aborigines, who regard him as the reincarnation of the shaman Murrangurk. This is a true story, still remembered in the Aussie slang term 'Buckley's chance' or 'Buckley's' which means 'cat in hell's chance'.

The passages delineating Buckley's life among the Wathaurung are an astonishing feat of imaginative recreation, for Garner enters as deeply and completely into Aboriginal culture as Buckley himself did. He told Michele Field, when she interviewed him for the *Sydney Morning Herald* in 1996, 'Everything William Buckley experienced – even the "Aboriginal Dreaming" and the trans-hallucination – I have experienced myself. I am a Western European trained to be a classics professor and I had to let go of all that. The Aborigines say that Europeans have "one skin more and one sense less". I had to pray for one sense more, I had to jump, and there was somebody there to catch me.'

The other sections of the book are equally striking. In the first, set in Buckley's home village of Marton, Garner invents a plausible folk fertility ritual out of scraps of English folklore, and enacts it within a brilliant evocation of the class stratifications of a Cheshire village of 1802, with the shockwaves of the French Revolution still buffeting the old social certainties. And when Buckley is arrested on the orders of the vindictive Sir John – ostensibly for his part in the Shick-Shack ritual but really because Stanley disapproves of his wish to learn to read and write – there follows a nightmarish season in hell, crossing the ocean on a convict ship, HMS *Calcutta*. This section of *Strandloper*, with its magnificent babel of voices and pungent use of thieves' cant, is one of the most compelling passages of writing Alan Garner has published. Luckily for him, and us, this particular voyage of HMS *Calcutta*, and the lives of its officers, crew, and the convicts transported on it, formed the lifetime study of the historian Marjorie Tipping, published as *Convicts Unbound* in 1988. From this work, Garner deftly winnows out the details he needs to sustain his narrative, such as the presence among the convicts of an fourteen-year-old Jewish boy from Newcastle upon Tyne, or the character of the sozzled sporting chaplain, Rev. Robert Knopwood.

At the end, the book roots itself back in the Cheshire landscape, re-envisaged in terms of Aboriginal Dreaming tracks and waterholes. It also folds itself into Garner's masterpiece, *The Stone Book Quartet*. For Buckley's lost love, to whom he returns in one of the novel's most moving passages, is the mother of Robert Garner the stonemason, father of Mary in *The Stone Book*. This is just one of many connections between *Strandloper* and Garner's preceding work; there are many links to *Red Shift*, and lurking behind the whole book is Garner's poem 'The Island of the Strong Door'.

The whole of Alan Garner's life and work is a study in what the Australian anthropologists Alan Rumsey and James F. Weiner call 'emplaced myth'. Nowhere is that more true than in *Thursbitch*, a novel in which the haunted valley of Thursbitch is almost more vital a character than any of the human beings. I can't think of a novel other than *Wuthering Heights* in which the story is so deeply embedded in the living landscape. Anyone who has heard Alan give his lecture 'The Valley of the Demon', about the research for this novel, can't help but be transfixed by the extraordinarily vivid sense he conveys of this valley as a reservoir of unpredictable power. That sense is equally present in the electrically-charged text of the novel.

Once again, themes from earlier novels, especially *Red Shift* and *Strandloper*, are revisited and tied satisfyingly together. Here there are two time frames, one in the mid-eighteenth century, one in the present day. The eighteenth-century story, with the packman Jack Turner as the shaman of an age-old bull cult, is rich and rewarding, and on its own would have made a deep and lasting novel. But the present-day story, in which the ailing geologist Sal (suffering from a neuro-degenerative disease) and her physician and ex-boyfriend Ian (who also appears to be a Jesuit priest) walk the valley and slowly discover its secrets – much as Alan and his wife Griselda did in real life – is drained of vitality. The energy that is generated in the story of Jack and Nan Sarah, and expressed in salty, resonant dialect, is dissipated in the brittle bickering of this spiky pair. Garner's constant attempt to reconcile intellect and instinct is played out in Sal's growing emotional response to the valley, but the two strands of story only truly come together in the last, masterly few pages. When Sal resolves to die in Thursbitch, she tells Ian, 'I shall dance till I swarm.' The novel's persistent images of bees, bulls, and snakes, so essential to the religions of Neolithic and Bronze Age Europe, coalesce, as Sal transforms into a melissa, a bee-priestess.

Boneland returns to this theme of the sentient landscape. In his 1998 pamphlet 'Approach to the Edge', Garner asks the questions, Is the Edge alive? Is it sentient? Does it, too, know? and answers, 'My human reaction is "Yes" to all.'

Although *Boneland* is a sequel to Garner's first two novels, it will confound anyone who reads it for a simple continuation and conclusion to them. For the clear implication is that the events of the first two books were what one might call 'true hallucinations', emanating from the landscape. Garner has hinted at this idea of stories being dreamed by the characters in them before, notably in *Red Shift*. In an undated letter to his friend Peter Plummer about the film version of *Red Shift* (quoted by Rupert Loydell in his review of the DVD release in *Stride* magazine), Garner writes, 'in the final episode it becomes clear to the dumbest that the reality is Macey's visions. We, history, and the TV set are being dreamt along with the story.'

This idea of 'being dreamt' pervades *Boneland*. The whole idea of objective truth is as irrelevant to the book as the idea of linear time. Quite possibly not just this book but the entirety of Alan Garner's life's work is actually being dreamt by the Ice Age shaman in Ludchurch, whose rituals are essential to preserve and renew the world.

In this book the astro-archaeology that underpins *Thursbitch* takes an even more prominent role, alongside rather overdetailed real astrophysics. The precession of the equinoxes, the gradual shift in the Earth's axis of rotation by means of which the world moves from one astrological age to another, has been an obsession of Garner's since *Red Shift*. Whereas the rituals in *Thursbitch* enact the end of the age of Taurus, those in *Boneland* lament its beginning: 'Once, when the world was full, the Hunter walked the sky. Above him was the Bull, and through the nights of winter it went before him with lowered horns. But when the world grew empty the Hunter left to follow the herds; yet the Bull stayed.'

Boneland is a very complex book. In it, Garner's ancestral landscape is evoked with the passion of a lover describing his beloved. And once again themes and images that date right back to *The Weirdstone of Brisingamen* are interwoven in new patterns. For me, the prehistoric scenes, with their resonance of William Golding's 1955 novel *The Inheritors*, work more powerfully than the modern-day ones, in which much of the dialogue is stiff and expository. While I recognise that the modern scenes are deliberately non-naturalistic, the self-conscious references to *Sir Gawain and the Green Knight* (Colin's beard, his axe, some direct quotation) still sit awkwardly. But Colin as a character is well-drawn in his tormented eccentricity, the latest in Garner's long line of reluctant shamanic initiates and socially awkward visionaries. His depiction owes something, I think, to Garner's friendship as a young man with the computer scientist Alan Turing; significantly, Garner revealed in an interview with Steve Paulsen that what connected them, apart from a shared love of running and fear of the Wicked Queen in Disney's *Snow White*, was that Turing 'would make very good puns'.

All three of these late novels have a rare poetic intensity. They burn with a white heat. The language is sharp as flint. They have their faults, of course. What some readers see as a challenge to their intellectual curiosity, others may find annoyingly obscure. And the writing is weakest where the novel itself is traditionally strongest, in its depiction of social relationships and human truths. Garner's idea of the human drama is all about inner space and inner time, and his cosmos-eye view of humanity can seem reductive. His elliptical style can be heartbreaking, but it can also be exasperating.

And yet, and yet, how thrilling these books can be, especially in their closing pages. Garner has, at least since *The Owl Service*, produced a series of breathtaking endings to his novels, weaving together themes and images and emotions in moments of transcendent illumination in which the illusion of time disappears. At the end of *Strandloper* it is not clear to the reader whether Buckley has physically returned home or is in a visionary trance, not even if he is alive or dead – and it doesn't matter. In the triumphant and celebratory scene in which Buckley dances his Dreaming in Marton Church, words and images reverberate like rolling thunder.

'Strandloper entered into his bone country. The wave bore his right foot, and the earth his left.'

William Buckley, at least, has got aback of the Singularity.

The writer and folklorist Neil Philip is the author of A Fine Anger: A Critical Introduction to the Work of Alan Garner *(Collins, 1981) and of two essays on Garner's work, 'Alan Garner and Shamanism' (*Labrys *7, 1981), and 'England's Dreaming' (*Signal *82, 1997). Neil's other books include* The Cinderella Story, The Penguin Book of English Folktales, Mythology *(with Philip Wilkinson), the novel* The Tale of Sir Gawain, *and three collections of poetry. He is married to the artist Emma Bradford, and lives in the Cotswolds.*

'AN OAK SHOVEL . . . ROUGHLY USED'

John Prag

It was the shovel that started it.

One day in 1991 the phone on my desk in the Manchester Museum rang. 'There's a Mr Alan Garner here who would like a word with you,' said the porter on the reception desk, 'I'll pass the phone to him.' 'Not *the* Alan Garner?' I asked – for not long before my son had come home from school in great excitement because the famous Alan Garner had come to address his English class at Manchester Grammar School. The visitor admitted to being *the* Alan Garner, and said he had a couple of stone heads at his house out in Cheshire that he would like to show me for the museum, but no, he did not want to come up to my office to talk about them now. So I duly found my way out to Toad Hall (Alan's idea of giving directions consisted in providing a map reference and leaving you to it – but then I had been in the Boy Scouts): here *the* Alan Garner produced not only two stone heads but many other Beauty Things too, the prize among them being an old oak shovel. The shovel came with a story, of course, and from the shovel and its story grew a friendship that has lasted a quarter of a century. Almost coincidentally it also set off a research project, The Alderley Edge Landscape Project, that has lasted nearly as long, has inspired many, many other people with a larger story – the story of Alderley Edge – that began about 250 million years ago, and has still not finished. Like having a new child in your family, it changed my life (not for the worse), and I think it changed Alan's too.

The story of the shovel has often been told but it is such a good one that it bears a retelling here.

In 1874 the copper miners on Alderley Edge were clearing round an old surface working ahead of new work when they came across a number of grooved stone hammers. Such hammers were common finds on the Edge. Professor William Boyd Dawkins from the University of Manchester visited the site later in the year and again in 1875, when not only more stone implements came up, some of them broken, but also 'an oak shovel that had been very roughly used'. Boyd Dawkins tentatively attributed the whole group to the Bronze Age, although his arguments had to be based simply on their crude workmanship. The finding was described and illustrated in 1878 by Dr J.D. Sainter on page 47 of his splendidly titled *The Jottings of some Geological, Archaeological, Botanical, Ornithological and Zoological Rambles round Macclesfield*. Then it disappeared from sight. Or at least from most people's sight.

In 1953 a bored Manchester Grammar School boy was slogging through Aeschylus' *Agamemnon* in the Manchester Central Reference Library when his eye was caught by Sainter's book on the shelf behind him. For this lad from East Cheshire *Jottings round Macclesfield* held much more intriguing prospects than matricide and mayhem at Mycenae. On page 47 he found drawings of a shovel that he knew he knew – but from where? A while later he remembered where: it had hung on a nail behind the door of the classroom in Alderley Edge Council School (Infants' Department) where he had been confined at the age of six. He rushed to the school, found Miss Fletcher the headmistress, and panted out his quest for 'the shovel in Miss Bratt's room'. Despite Miss Fletcher's calm reassurance (she had taught not just him but his father and uncle too, and knew the family's manic ways), the shovel was no longer on its nail. The school caretaker suggested it had gone to the tip when 'Twiggy', a previous headmaster, retired – or, that it might have been stowed under the stage. And there, with the aid of the caretaker's torch, the boy found it, behind all the clutter that accumulates under a school stage, with even its label still just attached to it.

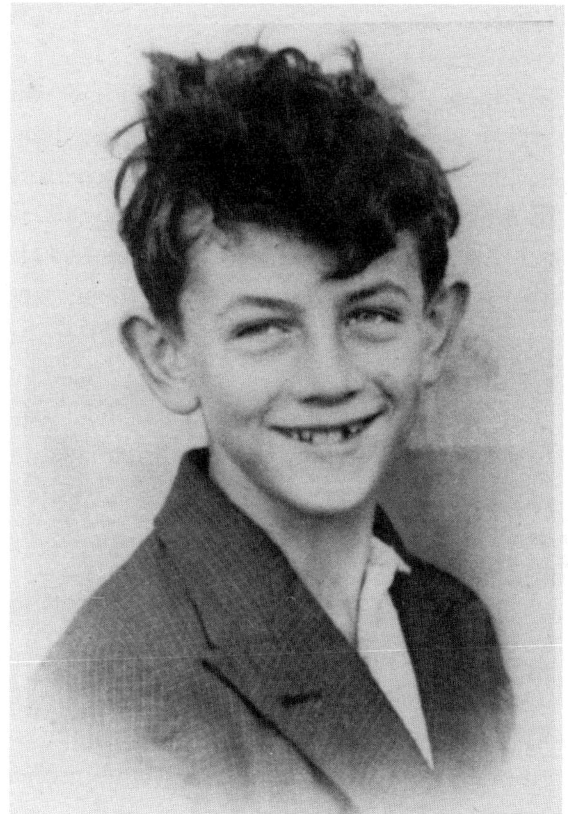

Alan Garner in Miss Bratt's class at
Alderley Edge Council School, aged six.

He was allowed to keep it. Dutifully, he took it to the Manchester Museum, where apparently no-one could be bothered to come down to see him (shame on my predecessors!). He took it to the British Museum: 'possibly a Tudor winnowing-fan'. Later the Ashmolean declared it to be a Victorian child's spade. All this despite the evidence of its discovery in Boyd Dawkins's and Sainter's publications.

So he decided to wait, and always to keep it by him in case his parents lost patience and really did consign it to the tip. During National Service it lived in his kit-bag. One day he and his shovel would meet the right person, but that day took nearly 40 years to arrive.

None of this should have happened. Why did those Bronze Age miners not simply turn their broken shovel into a useful bit of firewood (or, perhaps, use it for digging their vegetables)? Why had it survived so well when it had not been found in (for example) a waterlogged context where the lack of oxygen would have prevented decay? Why did the Victorian miners who found it bother to keep it? Why did it end up in a local infants' school? Why didn't it go to the tip? Why was a schoolboy fired up to remember it 12 years later and to retrieve it? Why was he allowed to keep it? Why was he so persistent in his conviction that it mattered, in the face of the indifference and arrogance of those who, allegedly, knew better?

And why, of all people, was that boy around whom this whole story revolves Alan Garner, dogged, persistent, some would even say bloody-minded, but always one to mine a good story for every nugget it can yield?

I might add, why me? Why was I the one who had the good fortune to be 'the right person'? Like Alan, I remain awed by the tenuousness of the thread by which the shovel survived, but where he commented on the sense of achievement which he felt when he formally placed it into my hands, I knew from the start that this item brought with it more than the usual curatorial responsibilities. My first task was to try to get a confirmed date for our new acquisition, and the donor bravely agreed that we submit the shovel to the Radiocarbon Accelerator Unit at the Research Laboratory for Archaeology in the University of Oxford for carbon-14 dating: when the answer came back, 'about 1750 BC', it set the shovel firmly in the Early to Middle Bronze Age. So Alan's (and, I have to say, my own) conviction that he had rescued not just a true antiquity but a very important piece of British prehistory was irrefutably confirmed.

Most of those 'why?' questions I cannot answer, except by linking them somewhere to the web of tales and happenstance that seems to swathe Alan wherever he goes. Yet I think I can begin to find an answer to the first question, and from that throw out some suggestions for the others. I am not a spinner of stories, only an archaeologist, but it is part of an archaeologist's trade to search for facts and then to construct their story and the story of the people behind those facts.

The shovel is not quite intact: there is a large sliver missing from one side of the blade, and the handle is broken off short. That seems not to have stopped the young and enthusiastic Alan Garner from taking it down the mines and confirming by practical experiment that its short handle made it ideal for use in such a confined space. A wise teacher at Manchester Grammar School told Alan 'always pursue the anomaly', but on this occasion his youthful enthusiasm carried him away. For in that string of 'why? why? why?' questions it is the first one that is crucial. When you look at it properly, the wood from which the shovel was made is still perfectly sound, even today; the breaks are all very neat, there is little sign of wear on the underside of the blade, and there is no reason why a slice should have parted from the side of the blade and no visible weakness in the stump of the handle that could have caused it to snap in normal use. So why did the miners apparently discard it?

When we came to look more closely at the rather sketchy notes made by Boyd Dawkins as he investigated the find-spot of the shovel in 1875 it became apparent that it had almost certainly been carefully buried, and that some of the stone hammers that accompanied it had been broken deliberately. Hammers and shovel had in fact all been 'killed' and put out of use – they had been sacrificed, perhaps as a thank-offering for the safe and successful winning of copper ore, perhaps to seek divine protection – for mining is a dangerous business. There are plenty of parallels from all over the ancient and not-so-ancient world for the sacrifice of tools and weapons as well as animals and crops as thank-offerings or to back up prayers and hopes. The miners may even have killed their precious tools in the hope that they would be rewarded with an especially rich seam.

There still remained the question of why the shovel, made of perishable wood, had survived almost intact. Copper was not the only material to have been dug at Alderley: later miners also sought for lead and even cobalt. When the Alderley Edge Landscape Project carried out surveys of the groundwaters they found that the soils of the Edge contained other minerals such as arsenic. The fact that the shovel had lain in a copper-rich environment for nearly four thousand years would on its own have ensured good preservation, especially if the copper was accompanied by arsenic as a binding agent (like modern preservatives such as Cuprinol did before health regulations banned the arsenic content). Yet other ancient timbers, such as some Roman planks, recovered from the mines had fared less well, so there was evidently something special going on here.

By now the story of the shovel had excited folk in all kinds of other disciplines (as is often the way in archaeology), and an X-ray investigation into the distribution of minerals through the shovel using portable X-ray Fluorescence (PXRF) along with synchrotron-based X-ray Absorption Spectroscopy (XAS) measurements of the copper and arsenic at the government's Daresbury Laboratory near Warrington concluded that the copper and arsenic along with a significant quantity of lead had entered the shovel during its original use in working mineral-rich deposits, and not through the burial environment. The report concluded that 'the insights gained are expected to be applicable to other wooden artefacts recovered from ancient copper mines in other places', which was just the kind of thing that we all wanted to hear. The shovel still had a great future before it in stimulating interest and excitement in unexpected places.

It has always been a mark of Alan's work that he has not confined himself to any single discipline – one need only look at the list of contributors to this volume to understand that. It must delight him that his shovel has inspired so many people in so many disciplines and so many walks of life to delve into the story of 'his' Alderley Edge: over 50 people have contributed to the two major books that report on the work of the Alderley Edge Landscape Project – *The Archaeology of Alderley Edge: Survey, Excavation and Experiment in an Ancient Mining Landscape* and the thousand pages of *The Story of Alderley: Living with the Edge* – and many, many others have become involved in many other ways. I am appending a list of some of the progeny – books, articles and websites – but to name all the people here would far exceed the word-limit set by our editor.

Instead, we must return to the questions that the shovel itself still had to answer. Just how, and where, did the copper and arsenic get into the shovel? A further examination by PXRF (this time at Birmingham Museum) showed that they were richest round the undamaged edges of the blade, as one would expect from a digging and shovelling tool, and also notably so along the unbroken parts of the handle. In other words, here we were seeing the marks of the miners' sweaty hands, dirty from handling lumps of copper ore, as they gripped the shovel 4,000 years ago.

Alan, you have always been very conscious, and very proud, of your Cheshire heritage – and this is about as hands-on as it could be. If those miners prayed for a good outcome when they sacrificed their precious shovel, they couldn't have asked for a better one.

Thank you for letting me play a part of your story. However, now that the Alderley Edge Landscape Project for which your shovel dug the foundations is about to be topped out with the publication of the enormous *Story of Alderley*, at long last, I am looking forward to going back to my first love, Aeschylus' *Agamemnon*.

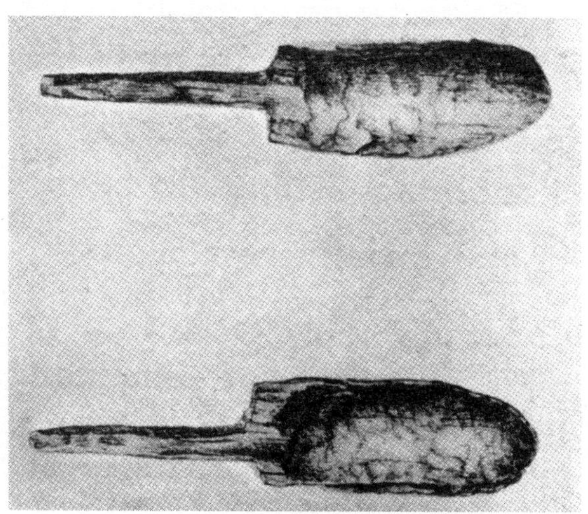

The Alderley Edge shovel. J. D. Sainter's drawing (after W. Shone, Prehistoric Man in Cheshire) (Chester: Minshull and Meeson, 1911, fig. 39).

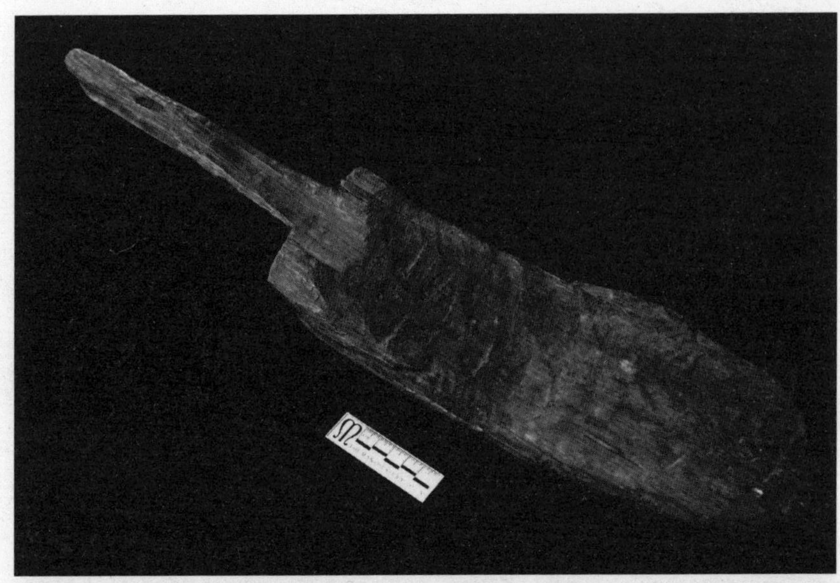

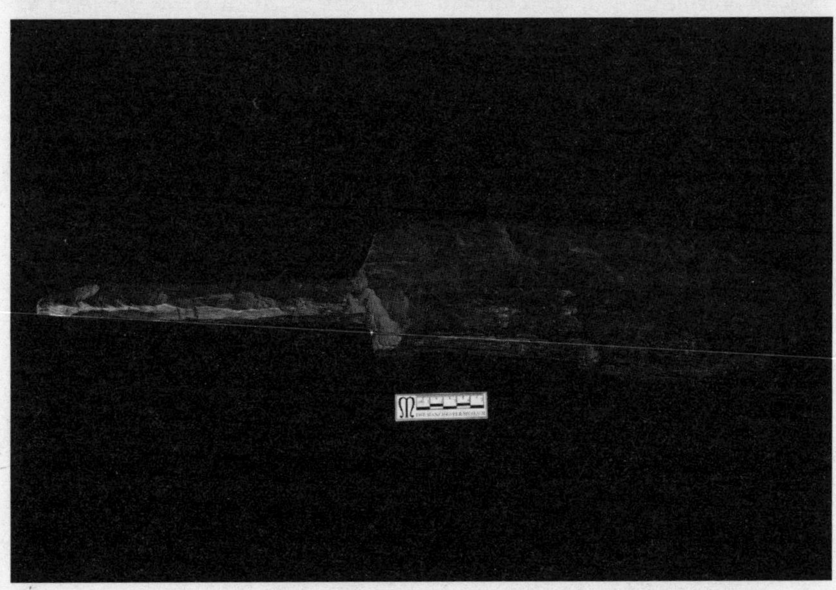

The Alderley Edge shovel, front and back: Manchester Museum acc. no. 1991.85. (Photo © Manchester Museum, University of Manchester)

John Prag is Hon. Professor in the Manchester Museum and Professor Emeritus of Classics at the University of Manchester. From 1969 until 2005 he was Keeper of Archaeology and then Professor of Archaeological Studies at the Museum. However, he remains a Greek archaeologist at heart, and 25 years later he is looking forward to returning to Aeschylus and the iconography of Greek legend.

References, progeny and further reading:

Boyd Dawkins, W. 1875. 'On the Stone Mining Tools from Alderley Edge.' *Proceedings of the Literary and Philosophical Society of Manchester,* 14: 74–9.

Casella, E.C. and Croucher, S.K. 2010. *The Alderley Sandhills Project: An Archaeology of Community Life in (Post-)industrial England.* Manchester: Manchester University Press for English Heritage.

Garner, A., Prag, J. and Housley, R. 1994. 'The Alderley Edge Shovel' *Current Archaeology*, 12 (5): 172–5. (Reprinted in Garner, A. 1997. *The Voice that Thunders*, 184–92. London: Harvill.)

Hyde, M. 1999. *The Villas of Alderley Edge.* Altrincham: Silk Press

Logunov, D.V. 2003. 'Preliminary Survey of the Spiders, Harvestmen and False-Scorpions of Alderley Edge, Cheshire'. *Newsletter of the British Arachnological Society*, 98: 4–5.

Prag, A.J.N.W. 1994. 'Note on the Bronze Age shovel from Alderley Edge in R.E.M. Hedges et al.', Radiocarbon dates from the Oxford AMS System: Archaeometry Datelist 18. *Archaeometry* 36, 355-6.

Prag, A.J.N.W. (ed.). *The story of Alderley: living with the Edge.* 2016. Manchester: Manchester University Press (includes two chapters by Alan Garner).

Pye, Clare. 2004. *Wilmslow and Alderley Edge: photographic memories.* Salisbury: Frith.

Sainter, J. D. 1878. *The Jottings of Some Geological, Archaeological, Botanical, Ornithological and Zoological Rambles Round Macclesfield.* Macclesfield: Swinnerton and Brown.

Smith, A. D., Green, D. I., Charnock, J. M., Pantos, E., Timberlake,

S. and Prag, A. J. N. W. 2011. 'Natural preservation mechanisms at play in a Bronze Age wooden shovel found in the copper mines of Alderley Edge'. *Journal of Archaeological Science*, 38(11): 3029–37.

Timberlake, Simon and Prag, A.J.N.W. (eds). 2005. *The Archaeology of Alderley Edge: Survey, Excavation and Experiment in an Ancient Mining Landscape*. Oxford: British Archaeological Reports, British Series 396 and Oxford: J. &. E Hedges (Several reprints).

A website

AELPHER, 'Alderley Edge Landscape Project: Heritage and Educational Resources' (http://www.museum.manchester.ac.uk/community/alderleyedge/ no longer extant except as a CD, but the link leads to the British Library's archived version). The brainchild of Griselda Garner, its purpose is to make the Alderley Edge Landscape Project's findings and archive available to a wider audience; and to use that archive to create a learning resource that addresses the dip suffered by many children as they move from primary to secondary school, and which could be used in tandem by secondary schools and their feeder primaries. It is based on Alan Garner's *The Stone Book Quartet*.

OF THINGS AND PEOPLE

Francis Pryor

Alan Garner makes you think. Now you might suppose that his writing has nothing whatsoever to do with the sort of archaeological non-fiction I write myself. And it's not just that our styles are different: you could say that our entire approaches – what some pompous academic might call our 'paradigms' – are so contrasting. But these things don't really matter: they're merely the icing on the cake, because deep down I suspect that we're both trying to address eternal problems of identity and meaning. And we do it through metaphor or parable. Alan's parables are born of his imagination, mine come from the ground. But they are still essentially narratives with hidden subplots and deeper meanings that their authors are grappling with. And speaking entirely for myself I'm aware that I'll never, ever get to grips with them – which does not mean that I shouldn't try, nor indeed be aware of what might be happening.

When Alan told me about the discovery of a metal bowl from a small pit near a freshwater spring a short distance from the garden of his house, I took one look at it and was convinced from its size, shape and profile that it was probably Iron Age: and if asked to hazard a date for its manufacture, I'd guess somewhere between 150BC and AD/BC. So far so good. As Alan and I both knew only too well, Iron Age Britons – some call them Celts – would often place offerings in wet places, such as rivers, springs, bogs, lakes and fens. It's a subject that has been dear to my heart since November 1982, when I discovered the tip of a large oak log on the edge of a drainage dyke in Flag Fen, just east of Peterborough. Much later I was involved with the excavation of another well-known watery site – labelled Seahenge by the press – and located just across the Fens in the marshes along the southern shores of The Wash at Holme-next-the-Sea, near King's Lynn, in Norfolk. These two sites set me thinking about the sanctity of wet places in the minds of people in the Bronze and Iron Ages. Flag Fen, at around 1300 BC, is the younger of the two sites. Seahenge has been dated with extraordinary precision, thanks to tree rings, to sometime in the months of April, May and June, in the year 2049 BC. Some may not be aware of it, but there's another buried Seahenge circle a few steps further along the beach, which dates precisely to the same time. So what on earth was going on?

And this is where my work moves closer to Alan's. In the past – for example when I was at Cambridge in the late 1960s – there was a radical movement in my subject, known as the New Archaeology. We New Archaeologists wanted to sweep away the 'subjectivity' of the old school and replace what we saw as bad, history-based interpretations with proper, science-based observations that could be backed up by facts, figures and solid statistics. With hindsight I can see that probably 80% of the New Archaeology was hogwash. But still, 20% of good stuff isn't bad for any new movement. And it was good to get away from ideas such as 'diffusionism' – whereby all innovations were thought to originate in the eastern Mediterranean and then spread – diffuse – west. Then came the radiocarbon revolution of the 1960s and 1970s, which proved beyond any doubt that many new ideas actually moved in the opposite direction – from west to east. The New Archaeology has been replaced by numerous other theoretical developments, some of which owe more to modern sociology and philosophy than to history. Lévi-Strauss and structuralism, for example, have been big for many decades. So where does that leave us?

Essentially prehistorians today try to think about the distant past through other eyes. We hope that the narratives we construct to explain the things we observe in the ground would be credible to people at the time. It would perhaps be oversimplifying to say that we try to get inside the heads of Bronze Age people, but that is more or less what we try to do – while at the same time being acutely aware that we are doing so as inhabitants of the twenty-first century. To be honest, it calls for a slightly schizophrenic attitude of mind. It also demands that we read a lot of anthropology, which I enjoy. But there are other ways, too: for example, I've found that being a farmer helps. Let me explain.

In 1971 I had the great good fortune to discover and excavate what is still the earliest surviving field system in Britain: it had been laid out along the edges of the Fens, just east of Peterborough, around 2500 BC. That's the date when communities on Salisbury Plain were hauling stones from Wales and were erecting the great uprights and lintels of Stonehenge. And nothing changes: people in the South-West still cavort and dress-up in sheets, while we in the more frugal, grounded East earn the money that allows them to indulge themselves. But I digress. When we discovered the Fengate field-system we noted that it was characterised by double-ditched drove-ways and the fields all seemed to feature corner entranceways. Now, having spent my entire childhood living on or near farms in rural Hertfordshire I was aware that this was important.

I don't know whether you have ever tried to move farm animals from A to B, but if you haven't got dogs or a group of people to help you, by far the greatest challenge is simply to drive them across an open field. As soon as they see an expanse of grass they'll decide to go in different directions. And it doesn't matter how much you shout, curse and swear at them, they'll ignore you – and quite right: they've got better things, like food, to attend to. It was this tendency for domesticated and wild animals to wander hither and thither that set the first hunter-gatherers and farmers thinking about how to channel and guide them. Mesolithic hunters, in the millennia following the last Ice Age some 10,000 years ago, burnt or cut down trees and scrub around watering-places as a way of encouraging grass growth and of providing a nice place for their prey to congregate. These open areas also gave clear fields of view for the men with bows and arrows. The first farmers, most of whom were 'converted' hunter-gatherers (real life is never a simple split between Cowboys and Indians), adopted some of these approaches to the management of the newly introduced cattle and sheep (and probably swine, too, but to a lesser extent – pigs have always been different!). So they constructed double-ditched drove-ways with a hedge, and most probably a laid one, on either side. Confined within a drove-way, animals become far more amenable, and easier to drive. Dogs, which were first domesticated from wolves in the early Mesolithic, were retrained from being helpers on the hunt. We're still not certain precisely how they were used, but they most probably ran with the sheep to protect them from wild predators. As time passed they would have helped with droving. But we know that they soon became man's best friend: we have found numerous dog skulls (mostly the about the size of my old Border Collie Twink) at Flag Fen, buried, I believe, in a sacred place. But to return to those fields.

It took the first three seasons of excavation, from 1971–73, for me to realise that the early fields at Fengate were part of a hugely sophisticated system of livestock management. And the key to that realisation was those corner entrance-ways. All the fields on the sheep farm where I am writing this, for example, feature them. In fact they are a sure sign that the farm is primarily for livestock. The same can be said for medieval town marketplaces, which are almost invariably entered at the corners. And it makes plenty of practical sense, because the two sides of the market-place or field converge, funnel-like, on the corner and livestock naturally head in that direction. As any livestock farmer knows from personal experience, had the exit been placed midway along a side, the animals (and especially flighty lambs) would have bunched and strayed all over the place. But when I first suggested my thoughts on the significance of corner entranceways to the world of archaeology, people thought me very odd. I can remember getting strange looks in bars at conferences: 'Oh dear, here comes that strange chap who thinks the world revolves around sheep . . .'

To be honest, I found this hugely frustrating, largely because the significance of those drove-ways and corner entranceways was so damn obvious to anyone with a rural background. And it was then that I realised that the world was changing, that most students of archaeology came from urban and suburban Britain. Yet they were studying an entirely rural prehistoric world. It was about then that ideas, ultimately rooted in an offshoot of the New Archaeology, about 'prestige goods economies' and the growth of ranked or hierarchical societies began to gain ground. And they then went on to dominate the thinking of prehistorians for almost 50 years. Places like Stonehenge were built by Big Men and the rich grave goods found in Bronze Age barrows were signs of 'competitive consumption'. The trouble was that those of us at the coalface could find no evidence at all of such societies. If anything, we were revealing an essentially egalitarian world, albeit organised on tribal lines, where large houses were extremely rare. Yes, there must have been chiefs and rulers, but as in most tribal societies today, they were held in check by elders and family obligations. This family-based view of prehistoric life was less sexy as a theory, but we now realise it was closer to the truth – even at Stonehenge, as Mike Parker Pearson and his team are currently demonstrating so convincingly.[1]

At this point you must surely be thinking: what about Alan's bowl? But please bear with me: this isn't one of my digressions. The point I'm trying to make is that we view the past, both very distant and most recent, through our personal experiences. So it suited many people to see Bronze Age Britain as a middle-class Conservative (with a large 'C') society, where competition ruled and Mrs Thatcher would have felt completely at home. I have to say, this made me smile, because many of the academics who supported ideas of Big Men and competitive hierarchies were firmly left-leaning, Labour supporters. So for me at least, the past was throwing light on the present, rather than the other way around. And it was then that I vowed I would never become a full-time academic; I realised that less fickle friends could be found in the real world. So I took up farming and in the process have learnt a huge amount about prehistory, which I now realise was always about the home and the family.[2]

1 Mike Parker Pearson, *Stonehenge: Exploring the Greatest Stone Age Mystery* (Simon and Schuster, London, 2012)

2 I discuss these ideas in *Home: A Time Traveller's Tales from Britain's Prehistory* (Penguin Books, London, 2014)

So was Alan's metal bowl an Iron Age offering – part of a family-based ritual near a spring? I'm increasingly convinced it was. I also suspect there will be further finds there in the future. And when they're made, we must then work with infinite care because wet sites can preserve so much information: pollen grains, seeds, leaves, twigs, hairs. Potentially that bowl offers us a route into lost worlds of infinite richness – if, that is, we are willing to step outside our ever-present concerns about daily life. So thank you for showing me the bowl, Alan. Through it, I have been able to glimpse eternity.

The Blackden bowl. This copper alloy bowl was found near a spring. The fact that it is complete and in good condition suggests that it was not thrown away, but was placed in the water, as a deliberate offering. Such offerings near water were a feature of pre-Roman, Celtic Britain. The shape of the bowl (diameter at the rim ca. 10cm) is identical to Iron Age pottery vessels of the late 1st century BC, or early 1st century AD. (Photo © David Heke)

Francis Pryor was born in 1945 and read archaeology at Cambridge. He is an archaeologist, writer and sheep-farmer. He spent 40 years researching into the prehistory of the Fens, during which time he and his team discovered the well-known Bronze Age site at Flag Fen, Peterborough. Since 1995, when he started working for Channel 4's Time Team, *he began a second career as a writer. His books include* Seahenge, Britain BC, Britain AD, Britain in the Middle Ages *and* The Birth of Modern Britain *(all for HarperCollins). In 2010 he completed* The Making of the British Landscape, *followed in 2014 by* Home: a Time Traveller's Tales From Britain's Prehistory *(both for Penguin Books). In 2014 he published his first crime thriller,* The Lifers' Club *(for Unbound). You can follow his blog at https://pryorfrancis.wordpress.com*

ALAN GARNER: CRAFTSMANSHIP

Philip Pullman

The Voice that Thunders came out in 1997, and I read it voraciously. There was so much craft in it: so much that was shaped by the craft of the writer, so much about craft and craftsmanship. Reading it again recently I also saw much that was crafty, and I mean that as a high compliment. There's an area of human activity where wiliness and cunning share a border with magic and the ability to call spirits from the vasty deep, and to call a storyteller crafty is not to disparage his craft, but to acknowledge the borderland between conscious skill and inspiration from somewhere unreachable by logic and reason. Devotees of logic and reason are uneasy with art of all kinds, because they can't see how it works, and they suspect its practitioners of dishonesty or at least disingenuousness. They would be simply baffled by what Garner has said on the subject of inspiration: 'Here I must say, and can't explain, that in writing there are moments when things are brought, given and imposed.'[1] Logic has its place, but as an equal, not as a master: 'The disciplines of heart and head, emotion and intellect, must run together: the heart, to remain open to the potential of our humanity; the head to control, select, focus and give form to the expression of that potential.'[2]

There's much that I've stolen from Garner, but this interest in craft, and the craft of storytelling in particular, has been one of

1 Alan Garner, 'The Valley of the Demon', text of an illustrated lecture first delivered at Knutsford Literary Festival, October 4, 2003

2 Garner, 'Achilles in Altjira', in *The Voice that Thunders* (1997)

the most rewarding. I once saw Garner's craft on display in the unforgettable lecture from which the first sentence I quote above is taken. He gave it at Magdalen College, Oxford, and it concerned a particular Pennine valley and landscape that had provided the setting for his novel *Thursbitch* (2003). It was a fine shivery tale about a valley where the local doctor dreaded having to make night calls, and where the vicar had been told it wouldn't be safe for a man of the cloth to go; and where a local farmer told him, 'There isn't a farmer in all these hills around as will open his door after dark, not even to cross the yard.'

There were other intriguing nuggets of story-gold: a stone commemorating the death of a packman called John Turner 'in or about the year 1755', who had been beset in a snowstorm, and whose body was found with the print of a woman's shoe in the snow beside him; and a mysterious chapel dedicated to John the Baptist; and hints of bull-baiting. There was also a great rock with an iron ring set in it, which Garner and his wife saw and photographed; when they then came back three weeks later, the ring was gone, the surface of the stone unmarked – and here were the photographs to prove it.

I call it a tale, but it wasn't exactly a tale so much as the elements of a tale laid out in an enigmatic pattern. That evening, in that lecture theatre, we had to make the connections ourselves. We were invited to share in the craft.

What I took from that lecture, and what I've subsequently replenished from reading *Thursbitch* and rereading *The Voice that Thunders*, and what resonates through *The Stone Book Quartet*, was a sense of the depth of Garner's craftsmanship. His ancestors were craftsmen, and he writes of them with pride. Craftsmanship involves a number of things, one of them being an engagement with the material one's working with. A worker in wood, for instance, will develop a feeling for the weight and the heft and the quality of a piece of timber, and will tell by eye and hand and nose what kind of wood it is, and what it will do when under strain, and how finely it can be worked, and what it will do to the sharp edge of a chisel or the teeth of a saw, and how it will respond to planing and sanding and polishing: all that, and much more, and at once.

Garner's material is language, which he knows in many forms. Reading what he says about Welsh, for example, which he learned in order to write *The Owl Service*, a book in English, we can see the sort of acute sensitivity to the material that doesn't by itself make a craftsman, but without which no craftsman can become an artist. For Garner, words are not just units of meaning whose form and sound are irrelevant, as they might be for a bureaucrat or a politician (a Secretary of State for Education, for example). Words have weight and shape and music and taste. Hence the power of a sentence like this, from *Thursbitch*. Jack the jagger, or packman, says of himself and his beasts: 'There's not a brow nor a clough nor a slade nor a slack, nor a cop nor a crag, nor a frith nor a rake, nor a moss nor a moor, as we don't know it, by day or by night, for as far as you can see and further.'[3]

Another thing that craftsmanship implies is the presence of the past. There are traditions in every craft, by which the knowledge gained by our forebears is passed on – knowledge not just of how to hold a plane or sharpen a saw, but of how to evaluate the work and give it the attention it deserves. Garner's grandfather, for example, a whitesmith, passed on that kind of wisdom to the young Alan.

> He uttered two precepts. They are absolutes. The first was: 'Always take as long as the job tells you, because it'll be here when you're not, and you don't want folk saying, "What fool made this codge?"'.
>
> The second was worse: 'If the other feller can do it, let him.' That is: seek until you find that within you that is your unique quality, and, having found it, pursue it to the exclusion of all else and without thought of cost.[4]

Deeply implicated in the notion of craft is a moral relationship. In an essay about letters from readers in *The Voice that Thunders*, Garner says: 'In working the language, as a farmer works the land, we seek to strengthen it against abuse, to protect it against decay, to encourage it towards growth. We hope to leave the language the

3 Garner, Thursbitch, p.34
4 Garner, 'Aback of Beyond', in *The Voice that Thunders* (1997)

better for our writing . . .'[5] A craftsman in stone or wood might say exactly the same: this piece of limestone or quarter-sawn oak deserves the best work you can do with it; don't leave it the worse for your handling. These things, the stuff the world is made of, language as well as stone and metal and wood, are valuable. We owe them the duty of everything our talent and training and experience can bring.

All these elements of craftsmanship are things I'm conscious of in my relation to my own work. To find them stated so firmly and manifested with such power by Alan Garner is, to say the least, reassuring.

But craftsmanship can't exist in a vacuum, and I want to end by considering two elements of the background against which stories are told. One of these is landscape. It's well known that Garner lives in the same part of the world where he was born, and that much of his work is directly inspired by Cheshire and Alderley Edge in particular. He says of that experience, 'It was imperative that I should know my place. That can be achieved only by inheriting one's childhood landscape, and by growing in it to maturity.'[6]

This intense identification with one region of Britain is not peculiar to him among writers, of course: Thomas Hardy's Wessex is only one of many other examples. The reason I notice this with a mixture of envy and curiosity is that my own childhood was spent all over the world, my father and then my stepfather having been posted by the RAF to various parts of the soon-to-be-gone British Empire. By the time I entered secondary school in Harlech in North Wales at the age of 11, I had lived in Norwich, Harrow, Southern Rhodesia, Norwich again, South Australia, and Battersea. Every 18 months we were uprooted, and I had to go to a new school, make new friends, learn new ways of speaking and playing. A substantial part of the time in between was spent on board ship. Consequently I have no memory of a lifelong inhabitation in one place, no native soil, no childhood landscape to inherit. As for a native dialect, mine came from no region in particular; it was the

5 Garner, 'Hard Cases', in *The Voice that Thunders* (1997)
6 Garner, 'The Edge of the Ceiling', in *The Voice that Thunders* (1997)

commonplace workaday social language of the upper edge of the lower middle class, military division.

There were advantages in all that, and I don't regret any of it. But I do wonder what it must be like to live all your life in the landscape where you were born, where your ancestors lived for hundreds of years before you, where every fold of the landscape was known intimately by men and women bearing your own name – at least, I would wonder, but Garner has made it so clear that I don't have to. I can read it in his work, which shows what 'knowing your place' means in every sense. Not having that experience, I have instead the experience of being a perpetual stranger, not quite belonging anywhere, a newcomer, a passer-through. I never feel that I know the world around me well enough to write about it without making large and grievous mistakes, which is one reason I found it such a liberating experience to write fantasy. If I make it up, no one can contradict me.

The second aspect of the background against which Garner's craftsmanship thrives is myth. He has said of his own work 'Each novel has at its heart a myth, which should not be recognised by the reader, but provides the aetiology for the book.'[7] It's the word 'aetiology' that I find so helpful here. I wouldn't want a myth to figure so closely in a book I was writing that it thrusts its bony shoulders into the matter of the story: 'Further back,' I'd say. 'Conceal yourself. Have a little modesty.' Aetiology is to do with earlier, deeper things. In my case, the myth that lies behind *His Dark Materials* is the one we can read in Chapter Three of the Book of Genesis: the story of how Eve was tempted by the serpent into eating the fruit of the knowledge of good and evil, which she and Adam had been forbidden to touch; and how Adam ate it too, and how they lost their home in Paradise as a result. The traditional interpretation of that myth involves Original Sin, and seems to lead inexorably to Redemption, and the Virgin Birth, and the Resurrection, and all the dusty apparatus of theology. But it doesn't have to go that way, I realised; there might be a more optimistic and liberating

7 Garner, 'The Voice in the Shadow', in *The Voice that Thunders* (1997)

outcome. At the heart of the story is a psychological observation about self-consciousness, and it didn't only happen once, in an imaginary garden, it happens in the adolescence of every human being.

But we can't choose a myth to work on as we might choose a new shirt. For a myth to inform the craft in the first place, I'd say that it needs to be absorbed so fully into the storyteller's mind that it has become part of the unconscious. Deployed consciously it can be precious and superficial. It might be best not to think about it at all, once we've finished with the long process of reflection and consideration and discovery and quiet secretive obsession that's needed to lay the material down. What's more, if that process didn't begin many years ago, in our increasingly distant childhood, it's probably too late to start now. 'Mine was a glorious childhood,' says Garner, after an account of nightmarish ill health and near-death from meningitis, adding 'I would not wish it on anyone, nor on me again.'[8] It was glorious because of what it enabled him to absorb and transform and work on, myth and landscape inextricably mixed, craftsmanship bringing the best out of both.

Philip Pullman was born in Norwich in 1946, and educated in various parts of the world before studying English at Oxford. He was a schoolteacher for 13 years, during which time he began to write for children. His most well-known work is His Dark Materials, *comprising* Northern Lights, The Subtle Knife, *and* The Amber Spyglass, *the first of which won the Carnegie Medal in 1996, and the last of which was the first children's book to win the Whitbread (now the Costa) Book of the Year Award, which it did in 2001. Philip Pullman lives near Oxford.*

8 Garner, 'The Edge of the Ceiling', in *The Voice that Thunders* (1997)

RIGHTEOUS GARNER

Ali Smith

I will have been seven, eight at the most. I was looking at the word and wondering how on earth did you say it? Brising, with the 'i' as in brimming, or since there was only one 's', was the 'i' like the 'i' in brine, and what was Brisingamen? Was it a place or a person or was it maybe an entity or a concept like honesty or loyalty? Did it have the word 'amen' at the end of it because it was a kind of prayer? I knew what 'weird' meant, and what 'stone' meant, but what did they mean together and how was it that putting those two words together like that made something somehow bigger than just the sum of what the two words meant separately?

I'd taken it off the school library shelves because one of my older sisters had started reading over and over again another book by this writer, about some kind of church service involving owls, and I'd noticed two other books by the same name on the library shelves. Both the titles of these other books were strange, though I had flicked to the end of the book with the unicorn on the cover and discovered a word I knew really well, Findhorn, the name of a place just up the coast from where we lived, where there was a very good golden beach; the hippies had a commune there where they talked to their vegetables and flowers to get them to grow bigger.

But in this book Findhorn was the name of the unicorn on the front cover and there was a particularly fascinating bit quite far into the book where a scribble of what looked like a word – in someone's handwriting rather than in the same print as the rest of the words in the book – actually turned, before your eyes, into the shape of a horse, or a unicorn; several classmates, knowing how much I loved horses, had shown me the pages where this happened.

This word-drawing was definitely different from an ordinary book illustration. It suggested that written words could change into something else, something that could have the properties, say, of both real horse and legend. Words could be more than themselves. Words, even words you thought you knew, could shift out of recognition into a different recognition.

At home my sister was on the couch, reading over and over that other book, which wasn't about a church service, I discovered when I filched it when she went up town with friends and took it upstairs and flicked through it, it was about a mysterious dinner service. Ah, okay – like in fairy tales, like in all sorts of tales. Such strangeness we were quite used to, from stories of all kinds, like *Gulliver's Travels,* like lots of the books on those school library shelves.

But the strangeness in the language in this writer's books was another thing altogether and the compulsion I sensed in my much older sister's revisiting of that dinner plate story in the owl book signalled a magnetism that was different from the usual.

Then *The Owl Service* came on TV. Our whole family watched it, week to week, and what I remember of the atmosphere of those afternoons – and it's interesting that I remember it quite so clearly – was that we were, as a family, part of a story that tapped deep into some kind of unease, had a mystery that wasn't easily answered, unmasked, reduced or dismissed, that it all had something to do with things that couldn't be said easily, things that were pent-up – and that the release of such things involved a powerful kind of anger, the kind we didn't much hear in stories or see much on TV.

I was growing up in a family where our father had nightmares about his time in a bombed ship in the war. He'd come down to breakfast dark round the eyes, his forehead heavy and hunted-looking. Our mother would tell us to leave him alone, he'd had another bad dream. He'd seen a doctor after the war who'd helped him with his temper. We knew about pent-up angers and things that weren't to be said.

There was also a girl in the story called both Ali and Alison. I got called both too, except I liked being called it and she didn't. I read the book. I didn't understand it. Owls, flowers, a girl, a hole in a stone, through which time melts. It was like a poem. Could a novel be a poem?

I read it again. I went back to his other books, the ones in the school library.

More than 40 years on, I've just read them again. The opening of *The Weirdstone of Brisingamen* (I'm still asking myself how you say it) is a consciously double-structured thing. First, as a kind of preface, there's an old, old story, the kind you'd expect, about a farmer, a market, a white horse, a disguised wizard, an offer of sale, a refusal, a denouement, an underground cavern full of knights and white steeds. It has a glorious opening phrase: 'At dawn one still October day in the long ago of the world.' Then in a clash of legend and litter, a parallel and much more literal and contemporary story opens. A couple of children on a train, surrounded by their own very modern travellers' mess ('apple cores, orange peel, food wrappings, magazines') are in a state of almost-arrival, 'caught, like every traveller before or since, in that limbo of journey's end . . . those last miles were the longest of all'. They're on the way to the Edge, where land that seems flat suddenly drops away from itself into steep cliff-fall.

The edge of things is the natural habitat of the story. Garner famously grew up on an edge, Alderley Edge, 'a Beauty Spot in summer and at weekends, but its long history and prehistory make it unsafe at all times. It is physically and emotionally dangerous,' he said in a talk he gave in 1983. I remember what to me was the most terrifying moment of edge-crossing in *The Weirdstone*, set in the Edge: quite early in the story a strange woman tries to persuade the children to get into her car. They almost do – they wake from a trance just in time to foil her from driving away with them to God knows where. For the child me and still for the adult me the true moments of thrilling danger in Garner's work weren't the gallivantings in caves with dwarves or miniature Vikings, or the encounters and adventures with the lords of good or evil, but those crossover moments, the boundary moments, crossing places between the 'real' and the 'imagined' worlds, times and stories, the places where the very ordinary and the very unordinary coexist, leach into each other: the strangeness in the known, the familiar in the strange.

Elidor was by far my preferred read and I remember vividly in particular the opening, four children playing with the Manchester street map, choosing where they'll go at random by spinning its wheel, sending all the possible real streets spinning in potential. I loved and still love its revelation of what was below or behind the surface – the slum at the back of the smart shopping streets, then the mythical world couched behind the slum, through the old church in mid-demolition. I can see now that what I loved was the way that it demolished realism without ever losing sight of what we call reality.

The children in *Elidor* move out of surburbia into a semi-rural village. But in their new take on map-reading, they've stumbled on a power which has made them much more meaningful than they are in everyday 'reality'. This power follows them, electric. It interferes with their electricity, so much so that the family can't watch TV, the car in the garage ignites its own engine, the mixer and the washing machine turn themselves on when all the power's switched off and an unplugged razor in its cover vibrates on a table by itself, turning on its own 'like the head of a tortoise'. The scene in which the electrical items go mad was another of my favourites, perhaps because my own father was an electrician, and I wonder if there's something equally personally attributable for every reader somewhere in a Garner work – his worlds are peculiarly personally alive.

This isn't really surprising when you consider he is a writer keen to involve his readers at a very direct level, the lowest facet of which is maybe a hooking detail like that last one, ringing coincidentally and truly with the trappings of a single child's life, done by touching on the contemporary with adeptness, and the highest of which is the way he leaves story ambiguous, open to interpretation as part of its nature, so that some involvement on the reader's part in interpreting and constructing its shifts of meaning becomes the core of its common truth.

'Man is an animal that tests boundaries,' he wrote in 1975, '. . . a *mearcstapa*, "boundary-strider", and the nature of myth is to help him understand the boundaries, to cross them and to comprehend the new; so that whenever Man reaches out, it is myth that supports him with a truth that is constant, although names and shapes may change.' Unforgettable, to me anyway, the children in *Elidor* carrying from old house to new house salvaged bits of junk which are really mythically-charged symbols and 'Treasures' – or are they carrying 'Treasures' which are really just a pile of junk? Electrical charge and potency play back and forth, ever-adjusting along not just every realism we take for granted, but also every unexpected imaginative leap of faith. That's truly thrilling and terrifying. 'Wasteland and boundaries: places that are neither one thing nor the other, neither here nor there – these are the gates of *Elidor*.' They're the gates of the imagination, and the cue for a physical shift of focus. 'You know how at the pictures,' a character in *The Owl Service* says on his first brush with a pile of old plates in a loft which are charged with an unexpected energy, 'it sometimes goes out of focus on the screen and then comes back? It was like that: only when I could see straight again, it was different somehow. Something had changed.'

For the child reader I was, all sorts of things changed because of Garner. Language could be powered and strange – and could also be found in all sorts of unexpected places, places where there was, strictly speaking, no language. Stones had a language – of stone. Dogs had a language in the bark. Owls could understand English. In any case, English itself was much more interesting and spiky than everyone pretended.

His 1960s books, I can see now, are always in dialogue with dialogue itself, in an argument between received pronunciation, dialect and idiolect, and also between English as the dominant language of the United Kingdom and the different languages of the different countries held in that bordered whole. This was almost never said out loud back then, and it went deep, made dimensional sense to me. In Inverness, where I grew up, there was always an invisible question as an undercurrent to the English we all spoke – an unarticulated question about the so-called gone language, Gaelic.

We knew without knowing that this question was there beneath everything we said. *The Owl Service*, I see on reading it more than 40 years later, is furious about the relegating of Welsh, and adept at making English richer and stranger by influence of otherness.

It's also pretty clear on an adult reread how angry the book is about the historical and, you might say, very realist relegation of people via the power-hierarchies we call class. Class hostility through history is one of its taproot themes. It asks: in whose service, exactly, are we? What a piece of fury it is, aimed at all the post-war and pre-war realisms. How it understands hurt, the self-hurt history causes in its people when abuses are repressed, and the violence too in the surfacing of what's been repressed.

In the 1980s Garner talked about how daily life, when he was growing up through the Second World War, 'was lived on a mythic plane of absolute Good against absolute Evil', and of the 'need . . . to be tempered in whatever furnace was required'. His memory of sneaking into the cinema as a boy and seeing the footage from Belsen concentration camp, not once but four times, 'the bulldozer ploughing its graceful hideous choreography into the mass grave,' put the world in very real perspective and made him 'violently wise'.

I know that sewn into in the lining of my own post-war-lucky imagination there are the following things: watching my sister, 17, ten years older than me, unable to stop reading a book; a run of dark winter Sunday afternoons with the whole family, my brothers, my sisters, my parents and me, at all our ages, all round the screen watching a story whose strangeness was both relief and taboo; an image of three children so mesmerised by the artifice of a dangling apple blossom branch made of silver and mercury that they lose their personalities and are lucky to be saved.

That's one of the creepiest of Garner's images, one of the toughest of his questions about the relationship between artifice and beauty. His revelations, inevitably, are always tough-tempered.

In there too, properly shining, is the strangeness and starkness I've just refound in a reread of the very end of *Elidor*, with its four children, after everything fades, standing in the post-war rubble. 'The children were alone with the broken windows of a slum.'

But even though the story had faded, now we knew. We'd seen. Nothing and nobody and nowhere was dismissible.

What powerful vision his fiction gave us all.

Ali Smith was born in Inverness in 1962 and lives in Cambridge. Her latest books are How to Be Both *(Hamish Hamilton 2014) and* Public Library and other stories *(Hamish Hamilton 2015).*

FEEDING THE SPARK

Ian Thorpe

In 1946 Alan Garner entered Manchester Grammar School from Alderley Edge Primary School, winning a scholarship and therefore a place with full remission of fees under the Direct Grant Scheme. MGS provided Alan with an academic education culminating in the Classical Sixth Form and entry to Magdalen College, Oxford, acting opportunities with the Dramatic Society and physical training which established him as an international standard junior sprinter.

Fortunately the school magazine, *Ulula*, provides a unique insight into this remarkable individual both as a pupil and as an Old Mancunian. As a sixth-former Alan caught the editor's eye, and as an adult he has generously contributed pieces to the magazine.

The editions of 1951–52, Alan's second sixth form year, carry in their original writing sections three short pieces by him.

Beneath a Silver Birch in August

> Through the lace-like branches of the lady of the forest, the sky is clear save for a solitary speck poised in the blue; the faint song rests gently on the ear; the lattice-work of leaves is a delicate gateway to a serene heaven of blue and billowing white. At the foot of the tree a lawn of green satin rolls in small undulations towards the cool fronds of bracken nodding in the distance. The air is full of sweetness and caresses the wood with the gentlest of breezes, presenting a selection of nature's perfumes to the senses. Perhaps there is such a thing as Peace after all.

The Obelisk

> The obelisk rose into the deep blue-black of the cloudless night, majestic, mellowed by the light of a full moon which cut a path of silver across the waters, momentarily picking out the boats of the natives in black relief as they lazily plied their way, each to his respective haven. Under the caress of the moon the time-worn characters cut in the weathered sandstone sang the praises of their lord as they did three thousand years ago. 'King of the North and South, Nefer-Ka-Ra Triumphant, giver of health, strength, and life, beloved of Amen, living forever.' Thus ran the eulogy until the voices were lost high up on that soaring column. 'Praised be the Son of the Sun' echoed faintly from above, and another tram rattled by on its way to Charing Cross.

Alan has described the third piece, published in the same edition of the magazine – which on other pages described him 'fire-dancing and fire-eating in Aristophanes' *The Birds* and, in the athletics report, as 'of course, a brilliant runner' – as a cynical response to Eliot's *The Waste Land*, which he had just read and thought was tripe. 'Mauldeth Road Station' was written to unmask T.S. Eliot:

> Rain sliding stickily down the sky. Drizzle. Train in half-an-hour. Perhaps. Who cares? Nobody here, staff died years ago, all dead, dust to dust, ashes to ashes, corpses scratching behind dirty windows. Drip, drip, drip. Roof leaks. Walk along the platform. Planks rotten; worms and fungus. Mind your step. Count one, two, three, four. Every day count the planks. Five, six, seven, eight. How many nails? Seven hundred and eighty-four planks, not counting level-crossing. Always the same, year in year out. Six nails for each plank. Rust. Everything rust, everything dead. Decayed. Ten past four says the clock. Always the same time. No spring. Perfect clock. Right twice a day. Lewis Carroll. Rain, rain go to Spain. Ten minutes left! Oh God, let me live! Look up the line. Mist.

> Cold, damp. Souls of the departed dwell in mist. Odysseus dug a trench in Hell. Sheep's blood. Mist. The dead drinking. For the blood is the life. Scarlet mist! Wires quiver, the signal creaks. Life! All clear. Green eye of the little yellow god. Who said that? The train is here; black hearse. Nunc dimittis.

In 1990, joining in the celebrations to mark the 475th anniversary of the founding of MGS, Alan wrote about his experience of the school, comparing his athletic endeavours to his development as a writer:

> It is hard to impart the delight of the execution of an intellectual pursuit, allied to emotional communication, which is the reward of a writer. True excellence can never be achieved, but to know that it exists, and to be equipped to seek it out, is the legacy of MGS. Fortunately I developed a physical analogue, which I may be able to describe. Along with academic growth, I became an athlete.
>
> A born athlete has certain physiological differences from the average. The development and co-ordination of those differences is called training. Training is unpleasant, tedious, time-consuming (two to three hours a day, the year round, and try fitting that into an MGS routine!) and so requires dedication, single-mindedness and a high threshold of pain. The season is short, and the whole activity centres more around press-ups in January than sprinting in June. Training is repetitive. Each action and movement has to be developed until it is instinctive, and the physique must be brought to a pitch where the body does not recognise stress. And all, in my case, in order to run faster than anybody else. But, without that stage being reached, there can be no beginning.
>
> When the reaction to the pistol becomes a reflex, when the head and torso are at the precise, efficient angle; when lungs, limbs, heart are synchronised, worked to their full limits, yet not hurting, then we can start.
>
> To run at that degree of fitness is to enter a new world.

I have just described the physical equivalent of the Lower and Middle Schools at MGS. The Upper School is the new world, where the training first pays off.

Running, when fully prepared in mind and body, is not racing. It is relaxation, in perfect balance, with no sense of strain. It is not floating. It is not flying. It is freedom. And to accelerate out of the final bend, as a slingshot, towards the finishing tape is the ultimate high. One is alone in a glorious and silent dimension, oblivious of crowds or competitors, aware only of the numinous wonder of pure movement. The winning was never in question: work had seen to that. What the athlete had to do was to bring the year of preparation into focus, and all would be well. For those timeless seconds, no preparation is too much, no distance too great to travel. Winning follows, as unavoidable, and as meaningless in itself, as exams. They are not what it is about.

I got the identical buzz that I got from athletics in the Sixth Form when reading Aeschylus' *Agamemnon*. The future writer in me recognised the line: 'A great bull has stepped upon my tongue' and Thucydides' 'My work is not designed to meet the taste of an immediate public, but was done as a possession for ever,' has never let go of me. The frisson caused by such insights made the hours of wrestling with particles and irregular verbs as trivial as the press-ups in the snow.

Yes, I am pleading for an elite; but not for a master rat race. The confusion is usually made, by boys as often as by parents. I made it, too, but [High Master] Eric James put me right.

It was in Room 23 on a day in October, 1950. I can remember the window, the desk, the swirl of his gown as he turned and said to me (only because I was the boy in his line of sight!) that, for each generation, the *Iliad* must be told anew.

The moment is so sharp because it was the first realisation that privilege is service before it is power; that humility is the requirement of pride. Without that realisation, I should not have found the temerity proper to the will to write. And, without MGS, I should not have been taught to think with the degree of clarity to find that truth.

In 1968, having had four novels published, Alan wrote about his writing in an article submitted to *Ulula*:

> The first draft is in longhand, revised to the point of illegibility, and the resulting mess is typed, some revision taking place on the typewriter. This first typescript is corrected, and when it is as good as it can be made, a clean, second typescript is prepared, corrected and sent to the publisher, who sends back a long editorial comment. Any second thoughts engendered by this are put into the typescript, and the book is finished. Proof corrections are almost entirely of compositor's errors.
>
> The internal activities, however, are nearly impossible to describe. Each book is the first – or ought to be. By this I mean that any facility gained through experience should be outweighed by one's own critical development. The author should become harder and harder to please. And not only is every book the first by that definition, but no two books ever 'arrive' through the same door. Yet, as a rough generalisation, there does seem to be a flexible pattern common to them all.
>
> It is this. An isolated idea presents itself. It can come from anywhere. Something happens: something seen: something said. It can be an attitude, a colour, a sound in a particular context. I react to it, perhaps forget it; but it is filed away by the subconscious.
>
> Later, and there is no saying how long that is, another idea happens involuntarily, and a spark flies. The two ideas stand out clearly, and I know that they will be a book. This moment is always involuntary and instantaneous, a moment of very clear vision.
>
> But the spark must be fed, and I start to define the areas of research needed to arrive at the shape of what the story

is going to say. It is a pure hallucination, but there is always the feeling that the book exists already, and the job is not so much invention as clarification: I must give colour to the invisible object so that other people can see it. The period of research varies in length. It has never been less than a year, and the most was three years.

As well as writing for his old school's magazine, Alan visited over the years to give talks to groups of English students and to the Philosophical Society. In 1985 his son, Joseph, applied for entry to MGS. I was at that time in charge of a quite demanding entrance procedure but felt, when I met Joseph's parents, that the grilling they gave me about the sort of place MGS had by then become, was every bit the equal of our tests. Joseph duly became an MGS pupil and went on to New College, Oxford where he gained a first-class degree in Biological Sciences. He is now a professor at Stanford University.

In 1997 the newly elected Labour government brought the Assisted Places Scheme to an end. MGS responded by starting a Bursary Appeal to raise funds to support its own means-tested bursaries in order to continue its long tradition of admitting bright boys who happen to come from poor homes. Alan Garner generously gave the school the performance rights to his play *Holly from the Bongs*, and its production at the Library Theatre in Manchester with a cast drawn from MGS and local girls' schools created a wonderfully successful launch event for the campaign. The production went on to success at the Edinburgh Festival.

Alan's links to MGS remain strong to this day. The Junior section of the J.L. Paton [High Master 1903-24] Library is named in his honour. Alan recently enjoyed returning to the school a Sanskrit Grammar that once belonged to Paton which in 1952 he rescued from a skip where it had been dumped during a book cull.

The Blackden Trust has the school's energetic support. All Year 8 pupils visit Blackden each year and a member of staff is on the Board of Trustees.

MGS is very proud of this working-class pupil who, knowing

his destiny and following the school's motto *Sapere Aude* (Dare to be Wise), endured 'four years of dole queues and National Assistance' while his first novel was written and published.

Alan Garner as the Ghost of Hamlet's father in the 1953 Dramatic Society production at Manchester Grammar School.

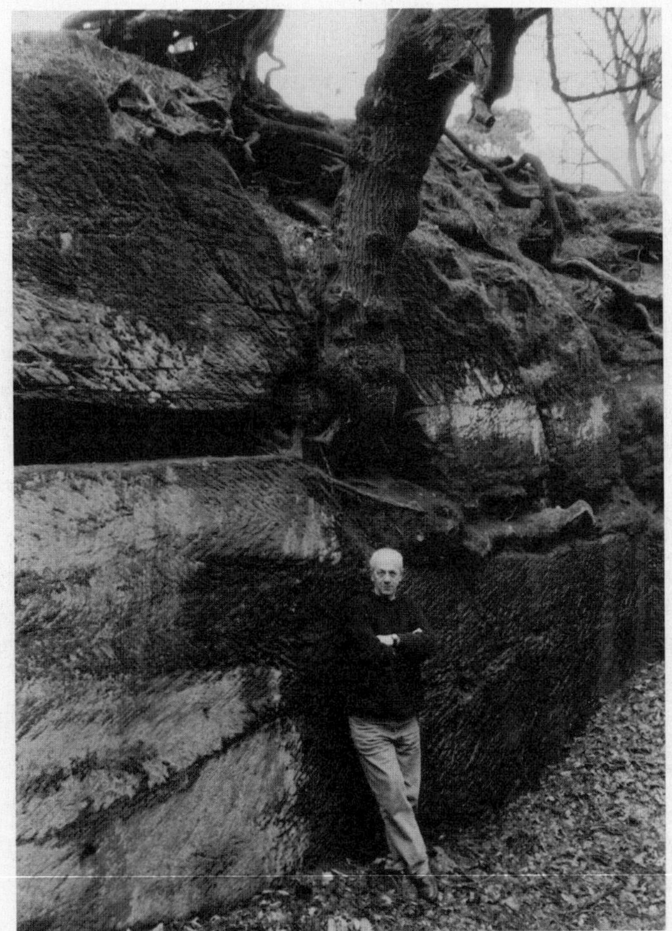

Alan Garner on Alderley Edge, 1999.
(Photo © Sefton Samuels / National Portrait Gallery, London)

Ian Thorpe was a pupil at Manchester Grammar School in the 1960s, benefiting from a place under the Direct Grant Scheme. He read English at St John's College, Cambridge and began his teaching career at Bromsgrove School. He joined the staff at MGS in 1977, serving for 10 years from 1980 as Head of Lower School and then becoming a Surmaster (deputy head). In 1997 he was appointed Director of the Bursary Appeal launched in response to the demise of the Assisted Places Scheme. Subsequently he became the school's first Director of Development. He is now semi-retired and serves as Development Adviser.

QUIET IN DISQUIET: THE OWL SERVICE

Salley Vickers

In October 1967 I went up to Newnham College, Cambridge. I had won an exhibition there the previous year. I had also won a scholarship to Oxford but the perverseness which attended me at that time had led me to go for the less illustrious option.

I had come from a school celebrated for its academic achievement. I had gone there on a state scholarship from a state primary school, which made me a comparative rarity among the other pupils. My father, a convinced socialist, was opposed to my attending this school. He argued, quite sensibly, that I would do as well at the nearby direct grant school (less famous but of undeniable excellence). My mother, also a socialist, was more ambitious. My father came from a moneyed upper-class background which had given him a less than reverential attitude to aspiration. My mother, who came from lowlier origins, and was more worldly, was having none of it. So off I went with a fair bit of ambivalence. That is to say I was proud of my achievement in getting a coveted place at the school – but apprehensive.

The apprehension was justified when in my first term of my new school a fellow pupil asked if I maybe lived in a 'council flat'. My report of this back home made my father guffaw and much to my mother's annoyance he thereafter brought it up as the greatest joke. (We did in fact live in rented accommodation, in a flat in the same road where the pupil in question lived in a grand house.) A more telling occasion was when, after handing in an essay on the civilisation of the Egyptians – in which, after a visit to the British

Museum I was currently taking a keen interest – my history teacher suggested that it was too sophisticated for me to have written and it must be the work of one of my parents. (My father, she suggested, pressing me further – it was a puzzlement to me then that she would suppose he was more literate than my mother.) To my lasting shame (I had grasped the unspoken assumption, which was that a state school girl could not have written to this standard) I conceded to this falsehood, wrongly supposing it was better to own up to being the cheat that I wasn't than to seem to stick to a lie and earn a lasting mistrust. To her credit, years later, when she taught me for A-level History, the same teacher obliquely apologised, saying that she believed she had once done me 'an injustice'. She was a fair-minded woman, if prejudiced, and I didn't hold it against her.

The relevance of all this is that by the time I went up to Cambridge I was a well-concealed emotional mess. I had held my own at the school. I was considered clever. I was popular. I was good at games and I had been, in their terms, successful. All this together with my mother's expectations was a colossal strain. Looking back I can see that I arrived in Cambridge on the precipice of a breakdown.

All my life I have been a reader. I read early, and I had read often. By this time I had read most of the books which were counted classics, and had never thought of going to sleep without reading a book first. Quite suddenly out of the blue – so it seemed – I could no longer read.

I knew what the words said, of course. But I had no ability to welcome them into my mind, let alone enjoy them. Books had suddenly and frighteningly, turned against me. And this of course posed a huge problem. I had come to read English Literature and reading books was not optional.

What happened then is a longer story but part of that story is *The Owl Service.* I found that for all my aversion to my required reading I could still read children's books. I have never lost my love of children's books. As I wrote recently to another author I admire, children's writers are the most vital, for they lay the foundations of imagination.

Other dimensions, magical worlds, spirits, angels, elves – these are the common materials of children's fiction. In that regard, in my own writing, I have taken my key from children's writers, but it's harder, writing fiction for adults, to have such subjects accepted. I am always liable to be dismissed as fey or (worse) whimsical.

There is nothing inherently fey or whimsical about the use of other dimensions. Indeed, they convey better than anything the richness and strangeness of the human psyche. In 1968, feeling particularly at sea, stupid, scared and hopeless, I picked up a book in Heffers' children's department.

I'm not sure know what led me to it. Not the cover, which, in that first edition, was not especially enticing being, so far as I can recall, dark green with an image of flowing blue lines (it flew off, somewhere along the way of my later life, and I am sad that I haven't that copy still). But the title from the first resonated. I've always been attracted by owls.

How can I describe what reading that book did for me? There is currently a movement of reading as therapy and I can report from personal example that it works. The intense, compelling story of the three adolescent children, trapped in relationships that they can neither see nor free themselves from, that evocation of the misty Welsh valley and the legend that lived on there, acted as what T.S. Eliot famously called an 'objective correlative' to my troubled spirit. The very disquiet that the book brilliantly evoked quieted me. It gave substance to the miasma of incomprehensible melancholy to which I had succumbed.

I have written elsewhere that a great book is not so much something that we understand, but rather which understands us. *The Owl Service* understood me, when I was far from being understood or understanding myself. As I read it, it read me.

I had found myself at school in an environment that had left me guilty about leaving my less affluent primary school friends. My very presence there was against my father's principles. I had been seen as inferior and had had to rise above this perception. And I had since been laden with expectations, which I was far from certain I could justify. There were many good and valuable things too about my education. But this became apparent to me much later. In 1968 I was adrift, a lost and unhappy soul.

It was not that I could see or put my difficulties any more clearly after reading *The Owl Service*. That isn't how the therapy of reading works. Something was reflected back to me that had a shape I recognised. Children lost in a mist of emotions they can't understand. A class unease which has a dimension in a much older story. A girl suffering a breakdown. Some sort of meaningful pattern behind the everyday – pattern is important in this story. Moreover, a pattern capable of being interpreted in more than one way. Is it owls or is it flowers? It depends which way you look, or take it. A meeting of diverse elements to which someone, somewhere (Alan Garner in this instance) had given a reality; not the quotidian reality, that seemed to me then no reality at all, but one that my conflicted unconscious self recognised.

Years later, I gave Alan Garner's book to my son, who shares my continued love of children's books – as Rupert Kingfisher he has became a writer of children's books himself. I have never described to him how I first encountered *The Owl Service*. But he too has a special relationship to it and it has affected his writing in turn.

In our woefully materialistic age it is essential that we have stories like this, weird but truthful – truthful because weird, for as Wilde says, truth is rarely plain and never simple – wise but inexplicitly so, cruel sometimes, because that too is part of our nature but showing us too how cruelty is close to love and how breakdown, though painful, may presage recreation.

Salley Vickers is the author of eight novels – including the word-of-mouth bestseller Miss Garnet's Angel, The Cleaner of Chartres *and, most recently,* Cousins *– and two short story collections, of which the most recent is* The Boy Who Could See Death. *A former university teacher of literature and psychoanalyst, her fiction is noted for its interest in place and its effects on the psyche and the sometimes strange reaches of the human spirit.*

HERE OR THERE OR ELSEWHERE

Elizabeth Wein

My first map – the map I first remember being aware of, the earliest I can remember understanding that there is a connection between the lines on paper and the features of a landscape – was an untinted Ordnance Survey chart about half a metre square, Sheet SJ 87 NE, copyright 1954, which, at six inches to one mile, shows in great detail the two civil parishes of Mottram St Andrew and Over Alderley in Cheshire, England. We lived in Mottram at the time – about a mile, as the crow flies, from the geological feature which gives Alderley Edge its name.

My parents spent many evenings over this map, shading it with coloured pencils. I'm not sure what their system was and I can't ask – they have both been dead for over a quarter of a century. I remember watching them at work as they filled the black and white chart with colour. I was five years old, fascinated and envious; they would not let me help because they didn't trust me to do the work evenly. Now, over 45 years later, when I look at this map my eye is drawn immediately not to our own village, but to Alderley Edge, in the lower left hand quadrant of the sheet, because that is where the greatest concentration of colour lies. All the wooded areas are dark green, but the Holy Well, Castle Rock, the Beacon and the Goldenstone are highlighted in red.

Alan Garner was my father's contemporary, though not his like. In 1968 my American father, Norman Wein, was funded by the Bernard van Leer Foundation to help set up the Head Start program in Manchester, England, training educators at what was then Didsbury Teachers' College. Our young family embraced our two-year stay in England. We were all in love with the place and the people. My first full school year was spent in the village school in Mottram St Andrew – my beautiful young teacher wore miniskirts, but our classroom was heated by a roaring open fire. My American mother, at the advanced age of 26, learned to drive in a 1959 Ford Anglia. My father, a voracious reader and inventor of stories with a taste for the occult (in later years he gave Tarot card readings in exchange for haircuts), discovered and read aloud to me and my brother, aged five and two, the recently published children's novels *The Weirdstone of Brisingamen*, *The Moon of Gomrath*, and *Elidor.*

Norman Wein was born, raised and educated in New York City. My father earned an MA from Columbia University in Upper Manhattan; his own father had been a grocer in Brooklyn. My parents met and married in New York and had begun to raise their family there. The rolling fields of Cheshire, the green Pennines hemming the horizon, and the local deep roots of history and folklore were intoxicating to my uprooted immigrant city-bred father. He was a tourist in Cheshire, an avid and thirsty alien, and he used Alan Garner's fiction as his travel guides. Why not? There were clear maps printed on the endpapers.

Every weekend we took family outings, picnics and hikes, as my father sought out the settings for Garner's books. Soon, the landmarks of the Edge, the old mine entrances and the Scots pines of Stormy Point, were as familiar to me as my village school classroom. My brother and I drank from the Wizard's Well and thumped on the overhanging rock yelling Cadellin's name, hopeful the wizard might actually appear. We had hiding places in the ruins of Errwood Hall and fed ducks on the banks of Redesmere. We were exactly the kind of Sunday visitors Susan and Colin scorned.

If this sounds like a rollicking literary romp, let me remind you: I was five years old. I lived in terror, sheer terror, of being taken to Alderley Edge. I fully expected svarts to come swarming out of the Devil's Grave at any moment and only felt safe on the Elf Road. We once suffered a flat tyre on a visit to Errwood Hall, stranding us at twilight on the long driveway out of the grounds, and the story goes that I kept my spirits up by singing 'Onward Christian Soldiers' at the top of my voice while my father changed the tyre. In Wilmslow I dreaded passing by the eerie Lindow Common with its Black Lake, from which Grimnir emanates in fog in *The Weirdstone of Brisingamen*. In 1984, when I was 20, the body of a 2,000 year old human sacrifice preserved in peat was discovered there. My first reaction to the news was: I was right all along about Lindow.

Here's the thing: when I was five, I didn't really know the difference between the 'setting' of the stories I loved and their real world counterparts. I knew that the stories were stories; I don't ever remember naively believing that Susan and Colin existed or that this set of adventures had ever happened to anyone. But the physical stones and water and the invisible paths Garner described were there and were real. And that suggested that the rules and inhabitants of this world, the supernatural underpinnings of the story, might be real too. I felt, at the time, and in some sense I still feel, that there is a connection between the physical world and the imaginary world that gives a nebulous reality to fiction.

Alan Garner's fiction is so deeply and densely connected to its setting that it is impossible not to imbue the real world counterparts with the magic he assigns to them: and of course, the emotional magic was there originally or he would not have drawn upon its power. The Legend of Alderley is older than Garner. The folly at Mow Cop really does sit on a county boundary. The unexplained stones stand in the valley at Thursbitch. Lindow Man was there all along, preserved in peat with a rope around his neck, without any of us knowing it.

I left England at six and did not go back until I was 20. When I graduated from college in 1986 I headed straight to Cheshire, where I spent half a year living and working in and around Stockport. I bicycled to Alderley Edge, seeing it through fresh eyes as I now used *The Stone Book Quartet* for my guide book. And . . . what possessed me? I went looking for the actual mechanical street map described in the first chapter of Alan Garner's *Elidor*. What did I think I was going to find? The book was over twenty years old by then, the bomb site waste of post-war Manchester long since reclaimed. What made me think Roland's fictional street map would still be standing in Piccadilly?

I found it.

Here's what I recorded in my journal at the time:

> There are two panels; one contains, under plastic, half a scrunched-up street map, and numbered references to key places (stations, town hall, important roads, etc.). The other panel is empty except for bunches of tangled, torn, meaningless wire. The shell of Roland's map. But unquestionably the right one. And the funny thing is, I think I feel better about finding it like that than I would feel if it were working and intact, but without Thursday Street [marked on it] . . . the fact that it's a useless wreck connects it to the ruined churches and towers of Elidor far more distinctly, secretly and eerily, than a replacement or an updated version possibly could. That's what *Elidor* is about – waste places, boundaries, out of date wreckage that connects and links directly to something else . . . Somehow a part of both worlds.

In *Elidor*, Roland turns an ordinary door into a portal between two worlds, using the front door of his own house as an imaginary template to open the portal. A writer's imagination has a similar, real effect on the palpable objects included in the story. Plates, axe, book carved from stone, ruined hall, memorial marker, folly, church window – for each of these, Garner's gift of story imbues its subject with life and meaning and emotional import, with sentience, that might never otherwise have existed in such a random object.

The concept of 'sympathetic magic' is a nineteenth century scholarly attempt to theorise about the supernatural and its meaning in society. In the eye of the believer, objects exert action 'on each other at a distance through a secret sympathy'[1]. The magician believes there is some kind of sympathetic connection between the act of invocation and the object on which the magic acts. The

1 J. G. Frazer, in *The Golden Bough*, 1922

need to see and touch the things that our fictional heroes and heroines see and touch, and to walk the paths where they fictionally set foot, is a need to turn figurative speech into something physical. It doesn't just bring us closer to our favourite books: it brings us closer to being part of their world. And the connection brings sense to the senselessness and order to the disorder of our own world.

Alan Garner is not the only literary mentor whose craft has influenced my own writing, but I have no doubt that he is the reason I have never written a single work of fiction, of any length, without referring to a map. The physical journeys of my characters and the landscapes they inhabit are as central to my stories as the characters themselves – a few of them are map-makers. The narrator of my own novel *Black Dove, White Raven*, herself a writer and storyteller, observes: 'I'm not going to stop making up stories. But I'm thinking they are not always just a maze to get lost in so you can run away from real life. They can just as well be maps to help you navigate.'

The mechanical map from *Elidor*, when I found it, was decades out of date and derelict. But it was there. It was real. And that made it feel as if *Elidor*, too, could be real. That is the writer's magical power, what Alan Garner taught me: both can be true.

Elizabeth Wein is the author of young adult fiction including the Arthurian/Ethiopian series of historical fantasy known as The Lion Hunters, *and the award-winning World War II thrillers* Code Name Verity *and* Rose Under Fire. *Her most recent novel for young people is* Black Dove, White Raven. *Elizabeth lives in Scotland with her husband. They share an unusual passion for aeroplanes and church bells, and have two children.*

The title of this essay is from T.S. Eliot, *Four Quartets*, 'East Coker' l:49–50.

Some of the ideas developed here are also explored in my essays 'Unreal City: A Visit to the Oxford of *His Dark Materials*' (in *The World of the Golden Compass*. Ed. Scott Westerfeld. Dallas, Texas: Benbella Books, Inc., for Borders, Inc., 2007) and 'Sympathetic Magic' (Guest author post for Smugglivus 2013 at http://thebooksmugglers.com/2013/12/smugglivus-2013-guest-author-elizabeth-wein.html)

Other references outside the works of Alan Garner:

Alderley Edge and its Neighbourhood. E.J. Morten, Didsbury: 1969 (facsimile of edition printed at Macclesfield by J. Swinnerton, 1843).

Sir James George Frazer, *The Golden Bough*. New York: Macmillan, 1922.

ALDERLEY: FOR ALAN GARNER

Rowan Williams

Edges: where we stop, guessing
the drop, the angle and the impact;
where a blade has driven down
with God knows what weight
of anger, longing or blind loss,
to carve letters too large to read.

Edges: where owls and snow drift
down, spill quietly and stifle
the long clefts where something once
was said (the little words
and their big letters), some hurt never
to be read, never to be levelled.

Edges: the clean, trimmed frame
where the blade flew through
the granite, where the longing
or the anger made a door
in the world's wall, in the hard
screens of time, of forgetfulness.

Edges: the single black walker
between snow and pregnant sky,
Between the caves here and the hollow
nightfall there, between the bone
and the star, a bladed foot falling
to cut the unlevelled path,

A story voiced from the long
letters in a stone book, here
but not now or then; the one
who sits down by the well's lip,
watching for it to open, for the memory
forcing edge from edge.

Rowan Williams was born and grew up in South Wales, later studying and teaching theology in Cambridge. After some years as Professor of Divinity in Oxford, he returned to Wales as Bishop of Monmouth in 1992, and served as Archbishop of Canterbury from 2002 to 2012. He is now Master of Magdalene College, Cambridge. He has published a number of books on religious, ethical and literary subjects, and five volumes of poetry, most recently The Other Mountain *(Carcanet 2014).*

THE CAVE OF WONDERS AND THE PEOPLE OF THE WEST

Michael Wood

The discovery of the Staffordshire treasure not long ago, with its twisted gold, garnets and amethysts, its prayers and curses which seemed to reach mysteriously over the pagan–Christian divide in English history, set me thinking, not just about history, but about stories and poems from the West Midlands: from Gawain to *Mercian Hymns*, and of course the magical landscapes of the *Weirdstone* trilogy. There's a story Alan tells that takes us back to the very beginning of his career as a writer; indeed even before it. The tale comes from his thirties childhood at Alderley Edge, and was told by his paternal grandfather. Described in a lecture given in 1977, it is printed in *The Voice that Thunders*. I have often wondered – though he does not say so directly – whether the effect of that story on a young mind aged about four acted as an inciting incident in his life as a writer, sparking the curiosity of the storyteller, unravelling hidden meanings, conjuring magic and enchantment from the creative imagination of the ancestors and the lived life of the past.

The story goes back to Tudor times, though as we shall see it is surely much older. It centres in the region between Mobberley and Macclesfield. At first sight it might seem a bit of a stretch to see Congleton as a fount of myths of Albion, but south-east Cheshire is the land of *Sir Gawain and the Green Knight*, which, with the other poems of the *Pearl* manuscript, was composed in the mid- to late-fourteenth century near Congleton in an old dialect come down from the days of the Mercians. This brief note is really just a 'gloss', as the medieval scribes would call it, a marginal note attached to Alan's tale. In it I want to speculate that the tales which came down to Alan go back long before even the fourteenth century, to a time when the British language was still spoken in the Cheshire plain, and when the old Celtic mythic universe was transmitted by the storytellers – including perhaps the one Alan's grandad told him in the 1930s:

A farmer goes from Mobberley to Macclesfield to sell his horse, a milk-white mare. At Alderley Edge – which as all know who have been there, is a place of beauty, mystery and danger – he meets an old man who asks to buy the horse. He refuses and goes on to market, where he finds no buyer. In the evening, making his way home, the old man awaits him and the farmer agrees to sell. Whereupon he is taken to a chasm in the Edge where a door opens into a magic cave. There a sleeping king lies with 149 knights and 148 horses: the farmer's white mare will make up the numbers for the enchanted sleepers. He returns to the real world of Mobberley with treasure to amaze his family. But of course fairylands cannot be revisited, and he can never find his way again to the cave of wonders.

The tale is a variant of a famous myth, the tale of the Sleeping Hero, which in many versions is associated with King Arthur and the Knights of the Round Table, but is no doubt much older. But here my concern is not so much the tale itself, but its local setting, which Alan explored in his schooldays and later, after the war; trying as it were to look deep into the ground, staring 'slitty-eyed' as my kids used to say when they were little.

The Cheshire Plain carries the imprint of its archaic past in its landscape and place names. The plain is framed to the north by the Mersey – the name is Anglo-Saxon for 'boundary stream' but its original Welsh name is still carried in upper reaches beyond Manchester where one of its headstreams is still the Tame ('The Dark One'). To the west the Dee is another boundary stream whose name comes from Deva, the Great Goddess of the Celts; to the east Goyt, Dean and Dove flow down from the Pennine foothills whose ancient name in Old Welsh was the Lyme, 'wild desolate land': this survives today in a dozen place names along the South Pennines from the Forest of Lyme to Ashton and Newcastle, which are still 'under-Lyne/Lyme'.

People have lived in this landscape for thousands of years. And following our theme of buried treasure, one crucial part of life at Alderley Edge has always been mining. From the Bronze Age to the Victorians, the place is scarred by old mine tunnels; an ancient wooden shovel found by Victorian miners was thought to be from the eighteenth century until a few years ago – when incredibly, it was carbon-dated to 1800 BC – a story in which Alan himself played a key role, as John Prag tells in this volume. Only recently, a hoard of Roman coins from the fourth century shows the mines were still worked then. So tales of buried treasure, one might guess, are very old in these parts.

Let's remember here too that the DNA of the core population of Britain – that is, of most of us whose ancestors go back before the mid-twentieth century – is largely pre-Roman. We may call ourselves English, but hidden in our genes is our Celtic ancestry: a wonderful metaphor for this story. From the fifth century, Anglo-Saxon migrants speaking dialects of Old English came to Britain and gradually changed the culture and language of the majority. By the ninth century most people in England, with the exception of Cornwall and the far West, spoke dialects of Anglo-Saxon. But until then the lands bordering Wales in a great belt from the Severn estuary to the Dee remained a mixed Anglo-Welsh culture whose tribal groupings in Anglo-Saxon times still corresponded to ancient British kingdoms. It was this borderland which gave the Anglian-speaking Mercians their name – Mierce: 'The Border People' – that is, the dwellers on the frontier with Britons.

So where does the Cheshire Plain fit into this story? The region is one of the least known areas of England after the Fall of Rome. Virtually no documents have survived. We don't even know what its people called themselves. But there are clues. A mysterious list of peoples known as the Tribal Hidage, is preserved in BL MS Harley 3271. Of seventh or eighth century origin, this gives the names of

34 kingdoms and tribes, many of which still cannot be placed on the map. The list starts with the heartland of the Mercians in the upper Trent valley, what the list calls the 'Original Mercia'. Then comes a medium-sized tribe or kingdom called the 'Wrekin Dwellers' who lived in North Shropshire up to the Dee. Then third comes a similar sized people called Westerna, the 'People of the West'; after them come the 'Peak Dwellers', then over the Peak to Elmet, a British speaking kingdom in South Yorkshire which survived as an independent entity until the seventh century. The list makes a clockwise journey from the heartland of the Mercians to the British-speaking peoples to their west, north and east.

So who were the enigmatic 'People of the West'? Though virtually totally ignored by historians, the strong likelihood is that as they lived between the 'Wrekin People' and the Derbyshire Peak, they occupied the Cheshire Plain: and in the late seventh or eighth century they were a sizeable province with their own sub-kings or governors. Moreover, as the Hidage clearly distinguishes the people of the Cheshire Plain from the Anglian speakers of the 'Original Mercia', they must have been a British people, presumably descended from the late Iron Age and Romano-British tribe called the Cornovii.

The 'People of the West' remain a complete mystery, largely because of the loss of the pre-Conquest local archives, but many of the other peoples in that great arc between the Severn and the Dee kept long links with the Welsh. They had Britons in their royal pedigrees; in later times they spoke Old English, but they were still ethnically British. As late as the early eleventh century these once important districts in Herefordshire, Shropshire and even parts of Staffordshire kept their old Celtic tribal names and regional identity.

A good guess, then, would be that in Cheshire too, in a largely rural society, Welsh survived among the peasantry till the eighth century. We have little pre-Conquest archaeological evidence in the Cheshire Plain, but the Welsh place names in the valley of the Goyt, for example, might suggest that even the odd Welsh speaking community might have survived up to that time. As for Alderley itself, there are no Anglo-Saxon remains, but with the recent late

Roman coin hoard, might one speculate the place had once been an important place to the 'People of the West'?

That is as far as the historical facts can take us . . . But if, as Alan encourages us to do, we enter the realm of sympathetic imagination, then we might guess that through the Dark Ages the 'People of the West' like their neighbours in Powys and Gwynedd, carried down an older imaginative sensibility which still permeated their poetry in the fourteenth century. Could this be why in Cheshire the core area bounded by the rivers Goyt, Weaver and Bollin gave birth to tales like *Sir Gawain and the Green Knight*, with their deep affinity with the old Welsh tales of the *Mabinogion*?

Perhaps this encourages us to see the Alderley legend in a longer perspective. Stand on the Edge on a summer evening – with that amazing view across to the Pennines and the headwaters of the Dove and Dean – the place-names are still resonant: 'the demon-haunted wood'; 'the Holy Well' and 'the Holy Well stream', for all Alderley itself is now a place of footballers' and millionaires' mansions. Before the modern age this was a landscape of scattered manors and farms. Nether and Over Alderley are both in Domesday Book, owned before the Conquest by thegns of the Earls of Mercia. One of these men, Godwin, also held Eddisbury, an Iron Age hill fort refortified as a royal borough in the year 914 in the Viking wars. So very likely these lands at Alderley had been owned by the Mercian kings: perhaps taken over at some point in the seventh century when the 'People of the West' came under Mercian rule. As for those older layers, all we know is that in the eleventh century Nether Alderley itself is recorded as 'Athryth's clearing': a woman's name, Aelfthryth or Aethelthryth. Who was she? When did she live? If only we knew!

There's a last clue, which may mean anything, or nothing. The Edge itself (from the Anglo-Saxon 'ecg') is part of Nether Alderley, an ancient chapelry of Prestbury parish which had an unusual independent status at least as far back as 1300. Prestbury, 'the Priest's manor farm', had a church in Anglo-Saxon times. Had it perhaps been necessary to create a chapelry at the Edge to exorcise its pre-Christian ghosts at the pagan Holy Well? Nether Alderley itself has a circular churchyard, which is usually seen as sign of an ancient sacred site – and in such places, the spirits can be unusually tenacious.

So there we are. Myths, names, and landscapes. Faint seamarks on the surface of history. The story remains tantalisingly suggestive yet frustratingly opaque. The legend of the Sleeping Hero; the mines, the wooden shovel, the Roman hoard, even the woman Aelfthryth. The eagle-eyed reader will note my argument is just a chain of speculations. But the story one would guess was deep in the culture here in the North Cheshire Plain: a land of storytellers where magic and mystery come naturally out of the landscape and the lives lived in it. Alan knew it all along, of course. He had heard it from the ancestors.

Michael Wood was born in Manchester and, like Alan Garner, educated at Manchester Grammar School. For over 30 years now, as an historian and broadcaster, he has brought history alive for viewers and readers in Britain, the US and further afield. The Independent *called his* Story of England, *which told the tale of one village, Kibworth in Leicestershire, through British history, 'the most innovative history series ever on TV'. His study of the first king of England,* The Lost Life of King Athelstan, *is to be published by Oxford University Press in 2017. He was recently awarded the Historical Association's Medlicott Medal for 'outstanding services and current contributions to history' and in autumn 2015 the British Academy President's Medal for services to history and outreach.*

Alan Garner: A Selected Bibliography

The Weirdstone of Brisingamen (1960)
The Moon of Gomrath (1963)
Elidor, with illustrations by Charles Keeping (1965)
Holly from the Bongs: A Nativity Play, with photographs by Roger Hill (1966)
The Old Man of Mow, with photographs by Roger Hill (1967)
The Owl Service, decorations from the original plates by Griselda Greaves (1967)
The Hamish Hamilton Book of Goblins, with illustrations by Krystyna Turska (1969)
Red Shift (1973)
The Breadhorse, with illustrations by Albin Trowski (1975)
The Guizer (1975)
The Stone Book, with illustrations by by Michael Foreman (1976)
Granny Reardun, with illustrations by Michael Foreman (1977)
Tom Fobble's Day, with illustrations by Michael Foreman (1977)
Potter Thompson: a Music Drama in One Act, music by Gordon Crosse; libretto by Alan Garner (1977)
The Aimer Gate, with illustrations by Michael Foreman (1978)
The Stone Book Quartet: all four titles published without illustrations (1983)
The Lad of the Gad (1980)
Fairytales of Gold, with illustrations by Michael Foreman (1980)
Alan Garner's Book of British Fairytales, with illustrations by Derek Collard (1984)
A Bag of Moonshine, with illustrations by Patrick Lynch (1986)
Once Upon a Time, with illustrations by Norman Messenger (1993)
Jack and the Beanstalk, with illustrations by Julek Heller (1993)

Strandloper, glyphs drawn from nineteenth-century sources by Griselda Greaves (1996)
The Little Red Hen, with illustrations by Norman Messenger (1997)
The Voice that Thunders: Essays (1997)
Grey Wolf, Prince Jack and the Firebird, with illustrations by James Mayhew (1998)
The Well of the Wind, with illustrations by Hervé Blondon (1998)
Thursbitch, with chapter heads drawn by Griselda Greaves (2003)
Collected Folk Tales (2011)
Boneland (2012)
The Beauty Things, with Mark Edmonds (2016)

Acknowledgements

This has been an extraordinary project to work on. As I indicated in my introduction, it has been a privilege to act as a conduit for the strength of feeling Alan Garner's work provokes across so many disciplines; I couldn't have assembled this book without the help of many others.

First, Elizabeth Garner and The Blackden Trust, who proposed this idea to me; I think Elizabeth wondered whether I'd say yes, which is, frankly, astonishing. *First Light* was always conceived as a project to be done with Unbound – so a huge thanks to Rachael Kerr and John Mitchinson, my boon companions at Quo Vadis; and not forgetting Isobel Frankish, Lauren Fulbright, Caitlin Harvey, Mathew Clayton – and everyone else in that wonderful and innovative company. Thanks to my agent Ant Harwood who made everything run smoothly, as ever. And to Ben Haggarty, who told me, once upon a time, that he *did* know who Alan Garner was.

I'm grateful to Angie Colls, Jo Crocker, Christine diCrocco, Merrilee Heifetz, Jo Hornsby, Vivienne Schuster, Karolina Sutton and Jessica Woollard for author liaison; to Nicholas Lake at HarperCollins, Michal Shavit, Mikaela Pedlow and Tom Atkins at Penguin Random House for help with permissions, and to Tom Gatti for some early reading. Thanks to Paul Laity, Alison Flood and Bob Fischer who helped publicize the project in its early days and gave me great encouragement – and of course to every wonderful tweeter, blogger and Unbounder who helped spread the word.

My husband Francis and son Theodore are patient and inspiring fellows both: without them nothing happens at all.

And thanks (more than thanks, more than I could ever say) to Alan and Griselda Garner, who know Trouble when they see it.

Do visit the website of The Blackden Trust: www.theblackdentrust.org.uk

All quotations reprinted with permission.

From *Strandloper* by Alan Garner, published by Harvill Press. Reproduced by permission of The Random House Group Ltd.

From *Thursbitch* by Alan Garner, published by Harvill Press. Reproduced by permission of The Random House Group Ltd.

Quotations from *The Weirdstone of Brisingamen* reprinted by permission of HarperCollins Publishers Ltd.
© Alan Garner, 1960

Quotations from *The Moon of Gomrath* reprinted by permission of HarperCollins Publishers Ltd.
© Alan Garner, 1963

Quotations from *Elidor* reprinted by permission of HarperCollins Publishers Ltd.
© Alan Garner, 1965

Quotations from *The Owl Service* reprinted by permission of HarperCollins Publishers Ltd.
© Alan Garner, 1967

Quotations from *Red Shift* reprinted by permission of HarperCollins Publishers Ltd.
© Alan Garner, 1973

Quotations from *The Stone Book Quartet* reprinted by permission of HarperCollins Publishers Ltd.
© Alan Garner, 1983

Quotations from *The Voice that Thunders* reprinted by permission of HarperCollins Publishers Ltd.
© Alan Garner, 1997

Quotations from *Collected Folk Tales* reprinted by permission of HarperCollins Publishers Ltd.
© Alan Garner, 2011

Quotations from *Boneland* reprinted by permission of HarperCollins Publishers Ltd.
© Alan Garner, 2012

List of Supporters

Unbound is a new kind of publishing house. Our books are funded directly by readers. This was a very popular idea during the late eighteenth and early nineteenth centuries. Now we have revived it for the internet age. It allows authors to write the books they really want to write and readers to support the writing they would most like to see published.

The names listed below are of readers who have pledged their support and made this book happen. If you'd like to join them, visit: www.unbound.co.uk.

Tom Abba
Patrix Abbi
Tamsin Abbott
Sarah Acton
John Adams
David Adger
Robert Alcock
David Aldridge
Karen Alexander
Jen Allan
Angela Allen
Sue Allen
L Allen-Jones
Joanne Allison
Glenda Allister
Sally Alsford
Kerry Aluf
David Ambrose
Teresa Anderson
Will Anderson
Catherine Annabel
Sylvia Antonsen
C Appleby
Helen Armfield
Richard Ashcroft
Jean Atkin
Michael Atkins
James Aylett

Angela Bachini
Megan Baddeley
Duncan Bailey
Nadia Bailey
Simon Baines-Norton
Sharon Bakar
Brian Baker
Sarah Baker
Mel Bale

Jane Ball
Josephine Balmer & Paul Dunn
Roger Barberis
Oliver Barker
Carrie Barlow
Barry Barnes
Jill Barnes
Perdita Barran
Chris Barron
Cara Bartels-Bland
Chris Bartlett
Belinda Bauer
Elizabeth Sawyer Bayliss
Rachael Beale
Bob Beaupre
Maureen Beirne
David Belbin
Catharine Benson
Janet Bentley
Alan Berry
Tristram Besterman
Christopher Bissell
Quentin Blake
Mark Bold
Richard Bollard
Alison Bond
Helena Bond
James Boocock
Jack Bootle
Stephen Boucher
Richard Boulter
Ruth Bourne
Adam Bowie
Philip Boyde
Daniel Bradley
Marianne Bradnock
Richard W H Bray
Nigel J Brewis
Christopher Brewster
Janice Bridger
Bill Bridges
Lucy Brooke
Laura Brough
Chris Broughton
Janice Brown
Malcolm Brown
Matthew Brown
Nicholas Brown
Sara Brown
Virginia Buckley, CultureCrowd
Susan Bugler
Julie Elizabeth Bull
Mark Burgess
John Burnham
Mary Burns
Geoff Burton
Catherine Butler
Clare Butler
Eamon Byers
Jamie Byng

Alan Calder
Christopher Calnan
Roger Calvert
Heather Cameron
Lorna Campbell
Tim Campbell-Green
Clare Carlin
John Carr
Jim Carroll
Sally Carter
Katy Cawkwell

David Lars Chamberlain
Richard Chapman
Kate Charles
Monique Charlesworth
Children's Publishing, Oxford Brookes University
Jenny Chittenden
Andrew Chitty
Rebecca Christopher
Penny Church
Karen Claber
John Clark
Tim Clark
David Clarke
Elanor Clarke
Freyalyn Close-Hainsworth
Ann Coburn
Philippa Cochrane
Daniel Cohen
Pamela Collett
Fiona Collins
Dom Conlon
Kirsteen Connor
Wendy Constance
Amanda Cooke
Cheryl Cooper
Marc Cooper
Jane Corlett
Neil Coupland
Jack Coutts
Chris Cowan
Marian Cowler
Gordon Cowtan
John Crawford
June and John Crebbin
Nancy Bauman Cristiano
Ben Critchley
Suzi Crockford
Corbyn Crow
Alexander Cunliffe
Deborah Curtis

Andrew Dale
Elizabeth Darracott
Catherine Davidson
Rhiannon Davies
Jennifer Davies-Reazor
Laura Davis
Andrew Davison
Heather Dawe
Philip de Jersey
Richard de Souza
Gail de Vos
deadmanjones
Roz DeKett
John Dexter
Nigel Dibben
Peter Dicken
Miranda Dickinson
Paul Dixon
Stuart Dixon
Emma Jane Dobell
Richard Dobell
Brighid Ó Dochartaigh
Maura Dooley
Warren Draper
Rebecca Dridan
Graeme Drumm
Annie Drynan
Jackie Duckworth
Katharine Dufton
Peter Dunn

Vivienne Dunstan
Kit Dyer
Pamela Dyson

Joanna Eden
Kathryn Edwards
Anna Eisler
Ngiare Elliot
Patricia Elliott
Victoria Elliott
David Elworthy
Iain Emsley
Cath Evans
Christine Evans
David Evans
Emrys Evans
Lissa Evans
Joyce Evers

Terry Fahy
Ciara Farrell
Virginia Fassnidge
Doug Faunt
Daria Fedorova
Madeleine Fenner
Marilyn Ferguson
Jacky Findlater
John Mark Findlater
Bob Fischer
Flora Fisher
Ruth Fitzgerald
Frank Fitzpatrick
Kim Fitzpatrick
Fiona Fitzsimons
Lotta Fjelkegård
Dane Flannery
Tony Flavell
Sheila Fletcher
Ruth Follan
Elizabeth Ford
Colin Forrest-Charde
Charles Foster
Bob Fox
Richard Fox
Robert Francis
Isobel Frankish
D Franklin
Matt Freake
Steven French
Cheryl Fretz
Allan Frewin
Geoff Fuller

Jacqueline Gabbitas
Mary Galbraith
Alex Gallacher
Mark Gamble
Saffron Gardenchild
Maria Gardiner
Owen Garling
Alison Garner
Dan & Barbara Garner
John Garth
Annabel Gaskell
Will Gatti
Amro Gebreel
Francis Gilbert
Matthew Gilbert
Adrian Gilmour
Peter Ginna
Helen Gittos
Anna Glazier

Lis Golding
David Gooda and family
Victoria Goodbody
Scott Goodfellow
Norman Goodman
Martin Gough
Vanessa Gould
Jill Gover
Neile Graham
Nick Grainger
Christina Grande
Ann Gray
Muriel Gray
Gilbert Greaves
Malcolm Green
Robert Green
Bedene Greenspan
Jenny Gregory
Chris Gribble
Charlotte Grimshaw
Michael Grindrod
Steve Grocott
Nicola and Bob Grove
Laura Gustine
Lucy Gwynn

Stephen J Hackett
Daniel Hahn
Carole Hailey
Mandy Halsall
Ann Hamblen
Elizabeth Hammett
Stephen Hampshire
Lucie Hankey
Nick Hanlon-Brooks
Jane Harland
Candy Harman
Adrian Harper
Linda Harradine
John Harries
David Harris
Jane Harris
Samantha Harrison
Donna Harvey
Graham Harvey
Neil Harvey
Susanne Haselgrove
Guy Haslam
Paul Hassett
Anthea Hawdon
George Hawthorne
Pamela Hay
Jake Hayes
Kate Haywood
Hedgespoken
Angela Hegarty
David Heke
Steve Hemmings
Joan Henderson
John Henderson
Julie Henderson
Sarah Henson
Jacqueline Henzell
Linda Hepburn
Jon Herring & Nick Campbell
Ros Hewes
Mark Hewlett
John Heywood
Phil Hickes
Clive Hicks-Jenkins
Matthew H. Hill
Laurence Hills

Ann & Robin Hine
Dougald Hine
Richard Hing
Susan Hirschman
John Hoad
Sheila Hockin
Daniel Hodgkin
James Edward Hodkinson
Stark Holborn
Geraldine Holden
Andrea Holland
Neil Holland
Ley Holloway
Derek Holmes
Sophie Hood
Andrea Horbinski
Rachel Hore
Brett Hornby
Ann Horne
Ruth Hough
Karen House
Paul Howard
Alan Howe
John Hudson
Bethan Hughes
Tom Hughes
Mick Hulme
Andrew Humphreys
Laurie Hussain
Kim Hutson

Johari Ismail
Martin Izat

Paul Jabore
Diana Jackson
Martin Jackson
Ceri James
Ken and Christine James
Laura James
Ian Jamison
Toby Jeffries
Gregory Jennings
Paul Jeorrett
Ric Jerrom
Michelle Jervis
Alex Johnson
Zebee Johnstone
Antony Jones
Dave "Jock" Jones
Freddie Jones
Heather Jones
Ilys Joy Jones
Nicolette Jones
Peredur Jones
Steven & Patricia Jones
Justine Jordan

Judith Kahn
Caroline Kail
Henry Kaiser
Georgiana Keable
Matthew Keeley
Aidan Kendrick
Nidge Kendrick
Mike Kennedy
Ros Kennedy
John V. Keogh
Dan Kieran
Sue Kilcoyne
Steve Killick
Gerri Kimber

Linda Kingsnorth
Debbie Kirsch
Paul Kitching
Richard Knowling
Reka Komoli

Cassandra L
Gregory Lake
Anne Lane
Alison Langley
Katherine Langrish
Phyllis Larkin
Sienna Latham
Karen Lawrence
Alison Layland
James Layland
Kim Le Patourel
Caroline Lee
Marion Leeper
Sarah Lees
Kathy Lemaire OBE
Rich Lennon
Phil Lenthall
M.G. Leonard
Alick Leslie
Andy Letcher
Anne Lever
Roger Levy
Bernadette Lewis
Matt Leys
Robert Light
Sylvia Linsteadt
Steve Linton
Bob Lister
Mia Litherland
Earl Livings
Rene Llowarch
Amy Lloyd
Jonathan Lloyd
Peter B. Lloyd
Michael Lloyd-Jones
K. M. Lockwood
Adam Long
Stephen Longstaffe
Mark Loudon
M B Loughlin
Matt Loughney
Paul Love
Bryan and Carol Lovell
Graham Lowell
Trish Lowndes
David Luke
Judy Lund
Chris Lynch
Mike Lynd
William Robert Lyne

Dr Marianne M & Norman Alan Gilchrist
Janet MacDonald
Kate Macdonald
Liz MacKinnon
Honor Mackley-Ward
Gordon MacLellan
Steven Maher
Daniel Malin
Tony Malone
Clare Manifold
Rob Mansfield
Robert Mapson
Sarah K. Marr
Susannah Marriott

Janette Martin
Paul Mason
Phil Mason
Sue Mason
Sophie Masson
Kate Louise Mathis
Brian Matthews
John Matthews
Paul May
Walter Mayes
Jan Mayor
Niki McCann
Darryl McCarthy
Hazel McDowell
Stephen Mckay
Stephen Mckay & Janet Fishwick
Janet McKnight
Sheila McQueen
Vanella Mead
Susan Memmott
Kai Meyer
Miranda Midlane
Viorel Mihalcea
Fiona Mill
Ian Miller
Jeremy Milln
Owen Minns
Miromurr
David Mitchell
Laurence Mitchell
Sarah Mitchell
John Mitchinson
Ronald Mitchinson
Lucy Moffatt
C Montell
Bel Mooney
Matt Morden
Ellen Morgan
Dr Moriarty
Eva Morris
Henry Morris
Jane Morris
Joanna Morris
Mercy Morris
Richard Morris
David Mosley
Luisetta Mudie
Victoria Muir
Alison Murphy
Jenni Murphy
Melissa Murray
Elizabeth Musgrave
Maureen Musson
Benjamin Myers

Sally Nash
Stu Nathan
Carlo Navato
Francis Needham
Sha Nevin
Debbie Newell
Catriona Nicholson
Jon Nicoll
Naomi Nile
Garth Nix
James Norcliffe
Martin Norfield
Gregory Norminton
Poppy North
Bryony & Peter Nowell
Su & Philip O'Brien

Rodney O'Connor
Mark O'Neill
Kai Okada-Thomas
Kaylene ONeill
Michele Osborne
Charlotte Owen

Sarah Paddock
Anthony Page
Julia Parker
Alan Parkinson
Mark Passera
Sarah Patmore
Barry Patterson
Ian Patterson
James Patterson
Katrina Patterson
Laline Paull
Ben Peace
Paul Pearson (Greenmantle)
Bernard Peek
Janet Pegg
John Pendlebury
Nicholas Perkins
Mike Perry
Stuart Petch
David Phelps
Gillian Philip
Philippa Philippa
Debbie Phillips
Karon Phoenix-Hollis
Mick Phythian
Oliver Pickles
Robert Pickles
Piggott's Daughter
Andrew Plant
Caroline Platt
Karen Plummer
Stephen Pochin
Justin Pollard
Ann-Marie Pond
Stuart Pond
Robert Poole
Max Porter
Christine Poulson
Rachel Powell
Kate Power
Sarah Poynting
Paul Probert
Malcolm Prue
Rosy Prue
Francis Pryor
Helen Purcell
Lesley Purcell
Tam Purkess

David Quantick

Michael Sholto Radford
Gita Ralleigh
Robert Ratcliffe
Jalpa Ratna
Jane Rawson
Andrea L T Rayner
Becca Read
Colette Reap
Jenny Reddish
Dahl Redman
Mike Reed
Barbara Evans Rees
Alexander Reip
Dan Rendell

Sandra Rennie
Paul Rhodes
Sioned-Mair Richards
Carole Richmond
Ruth Rigby
Andy Roberts
Judy Roberts
Imogen Robertson
Wendy Robertson
Jodie Robson
Diane A. Rodgers
Susan Roe
David Rogers
Jean Rogers
Anne Rooney
Gregory Rose
Claire Rowe
Patsy Roynon
Katherine Rundell

Lydia Sage
SF Said
Ben Sansum
Linda Sargent
Alex Sarll
Michael Scaife
Danny Scheinmann
Sandra Schramm
Vivienne Schuster
Jenny Schwartzberg
David Scoffield
Bridget Scott
Elspeth Scott
Rosemary Scott
Adam Scovell
Carol Seed
Judy Selfe
Dick Selwood
Tracy Sexton
Tom Shakespeare
Julian Sharpe
Simon Shaw
Ben Sheldon
Laura Shepperson-Smith
Dearbhla Sheridan
Emily Shipp
Jenny Shippen
Joe Shrewsbury
Eileen Silcocks
Denise Skea
John Skelton
Mark Slater
Sadie Slater
Paul & Emma Slavin, on our first wedding anniversary
David & Karen Smith
Harold Weaver Smith
Kieron Smith
Kirsty Smith
Nic Smith
Nigel Smith
Peter Smith
Colin Smythe
Hills Snyder
Paul Sorensen
Carole Souter
Jeremy Sowden
Maureen Kincaid Speller
Ben Spencer
Diana Spencer
Martin Spencer-Whitton
Jose Spinks

Annette Stansfield
Mary Steele
Gabriela Steinke
George Stirling
Gillian Stokes
Amanda Stone
Tim Stone
Ian Storey
William Streek
David Suff
Sylvia Sumira
Dan Sumption
Nigel Sustins
Richard Sutherland
Karolina Sutton
Penelope Swan
K Swire
Jamilah Syal
Ian Sykes
Richard Sylvester
Susie Symes
Catherine Syson

Felix Taylor
Helen Taylor
Ian Taylor
Liz Taylor
Lucy Taylor
Marjorie Taylor
Nansi Taylor
Paul Taylor
Sean Taylor
Andrew Thomas
Gareth Thomas
Jo Thomas
Wayne Dilwyn Thomas
Bill Thompson
Paul Thompson
Pete Thurlow
Amanda Thurman
Mike and Liz Thurman
Mat Tobin
Howard Toghill
Amy Tompkins
Amanda Towers
Emma Townshend
Simon Trafford
Christopher Trent
Lindsay Trevarthen
Ben Tye

Paula Urwin

Charles Vane
Annie Vickerstaff
Elizabeth Vooght

Richard Wadge
Jenny Walford
Paul Walker
George Walkley
Craig Wallace
Jane Walmsley
Michael Walters
Carole-Ann Warburton
Annabel Wardrop
Marina Warner
Paul Warren
Stuart Watt
S Way
Cat Weatherill
Andrew Weatherston

Andrew Weaver
Graham Weaver
Sarah Weaving
Emily Webb
Elizabeth Wein
Steve Weiner
Jane Weir
Christina Welch
Rob Welch
Peter Wells
Helen Wendholt
Lars Werdelin
Samuel West
Richard Whitaker
Sandra White
Christine Whittemore
Melanie Wilde
Susie Wilde
Naomi Wildey
David Wildgoose
Nick Willder
Liz Williams
Nathan Williams
Thomas Williams
Damaris Wilson
Donna Enticknap Wilson
Stephanie Wilson
Clive Winchester
Margaret Windelinckx-Buckley
David Windsor
David Murakami Wood
James K Wood
Ken Wood
Robert Woodshaw
Steve Woodward
Elli Woollard
Brian Woolley
Richard Worth
Nick Wray
Anne Wright

Nobuko Yanai
Jon Young
Philippa Young

Susan Zasikowski
Charlotte Zeepvat
Clare Zinkin